FITZROY RAW

Other work by the author

Fiction

Raising the Shadow

The French Mathematician

The Twelfth Dialogue

The Death of Pan

Quaternia

Poetry

The Blossom Vendor

Offerings: Sonnets from Mount Athos

Inheritance

Naming the Number

Four Quarters

My Father's Tools

Breadth for a Dying Word

Steles

Plays

The Drought

The Picnic

Elena and the Nightingale

Salonika Bound

Hypatia's Circle

Euler's Vision

FITZROY RAW

TOM PETSINIS

TANTANOOLA

First published 2020 by TANTANOOLA
a literary imprint of Australian Scholarly Publishing Pty Ltd
7 Lt Lothian St Nth, North Melbourne, Vic 3051
Tel: 03 9329 6963 / Fax: 03 9329 5452
enquiry@scholarly.info / www.scholarly.info

ISBN 978-1-925984-82-8

Cover design: David Thomas and Alexia Petsinis

Acknowledgements

The author is most grateful to the following institutions for supporting the development of the novel:

1. The State Library of Victoria for a Fellowship which provided access to a writing space and research material.
2. The Château de Lavigny in Switzerland for a writer's residency.

1

Kolche has no memory of the man everyone refers to as *tatko ti*. His father has been away three years, half the boy's age, an eternity in childhood. His mother often sighs that his father's working in Australia, a country on the other side of the world, thirty days and nights by ship. Not long ago Kolche's teacher pointed to Australia on the map hanging from the classroom wall: pink, jagged on top, a waveless sea all around. It seemed a lonely place, friendless, shunned by other countries. He wouldn't live there for anything. He's happy in the village, in their two-storey house, together with his mother, and his grandparents *Dedo* Risto and *Baba* Lena. The house was built by his great-grandfather with stones carted down from the surrounding hills. Outdoor stairs lead up to the bedroom he shares with his mother. It's the biggest room in the house. Her bed has metal ends and stands against a wall hung with a *kilim*. His is smaller, on the opposite side, beneath the window set in the thick wall. Some nights as she sits reading again the letter from Australia and the lamp's soft glow holds her shadow still on the wall, he lies on his side and stares at the girl in the *kilim*. He likes her white shirt and colourful vest hung with gold coins. She's been at the fountain ever since he can remember, her cheeks red with sunset, filling the same pitcher, and still it's not full. Ah, if he could only step into the *kilim*! He'd make that tap run faster, wet his handkerchief to cool the girl's cheeks, help her carry the pitcher home. Other nights, lying on his left side, he looks out the window and over the barn's steep roof at the outline of the distant mountain range and the wide spread of stars like wheat on a dark threshing floor. When *Dedo* taught him to count to ten on his fingers, he went on to say he could now count all the stars in the sky. At the time Kolche looked at his hands, then up at the sky, unable to make sense of what he'd been told. But not so long ago he counted a hundred stars before sleep got the better of him. His mother looks sad most days and sometimes cries at night reading the letter from Australia. When he asks why, she calls him to her bed and hugs him, her tears warm on his cheek.

A sprawling quince tree shadows the corner of the yard. The fruit hangs big and heavy, reminding Kolche of the bell in the church tower. On windy days he listens for the thud of quinces falling. *Dedo* peels and slices them with a pocketknife and toasts the pieces on the stove, filling the kitchen with a sharp, mouth-watering smell. A loom stands at the back of the kitchen. It clatters as his mother weaves coloured *chergi* from strips of whatever she can find. She spreads them on the floor at Easter, when lots of visitors come for *Dedo*'s nameday and click glasses of *rakija* to his health. But there seems to be no end to the *cherga* she's been weaving for months. Each night her quick hands clatter the loom, feeding it strip after strip, adding to the layered pile on the floor.

'Why are you weaving more *chergi*?' Kolche asks.

'We'll need them in Australia.'

'Are we really going there?'

'Yes, when your father has saved enough for our fare.'

Her large brown eyes light up whenever she talks about going to Australia, but something in Kolche darkens, like when the shadow of a cloud passes over the yard on a sunny day. He wishes that mysterious person never saves enough for their fare, so they never have to leave the village.

'But why's this *cherga* so long?'

'If your father can't save enough, we'll spread it over the sea and walk to Australia.'

He's suddenly alarmed by a vision of his mother fixing one end of the coloured rug on their doorstep and unrolling the rest over fields, mountains, endless seas, all the way to distant Australia. And the pleasant sound of the loom, especially in accompanying his mother's melodious humming, now takes on a mocking note, each clatter reminding him of Australia.

Kolche speaks Macedonian at home and Greek at school and in church, but they're one language to him. He is Kolche to his mother and Nikolaki to his teacher. He asks his mother for a glass of *voda*, his teacher for *nero*, and though the words shape his lips and tongue differently, the taste of water is the same. *Dedo* Risto says just as they have a right hand and a left, so there's an advantage in things having two names. If one's lost, there's always the other. And he points to the name of their village: Vevi when approached from the south, Banitsa from the north.

Baba Lena can't write but she can read the weather from the clouds. She can't count past the last knuckle of her little finger, but she can knead a heap of dough, pull out thirty balls, and bake a month of full moons in the oven. She knows the religious significance of each day of the year, starting with the first of January, when Saint Basil comes from Caesarea to bless their celebrations. Her mincemeat pie contains the lucky coin. She cuts it in wedges and gives everyone a piece. Kolche eats his carefully, hoping to bite the silver, hole-in-the-middle *dekara*. If his slice has the coin, *Dedo* will offer to buy it from him for a whole drachma, worth ten *dekari*. More often than not *Baba* is tight to the point of stinginess, and when sometimes he complains of this, she has a way of slapping and pinching his legs at the same time. Yet when the cuckoo first sounds in spring she doesn't hesitate in unlocking the cupboard and offering him a sugared almond.

Toy watches are popular with the boys in the neighbourhood. His friend Telli, who's forever marching up and down the lane, drumming on a tin can strapped over his neck, has been showing his watch off all morning. Kolche wants one, but his mother has gone to help *Dedo* harvest the corn. *Baba* makes a threatening gesture with her hand at the very mention of a watch. Determined to have one, he goes down to the shop in the village square and gets one on credit, telling the owner *Dedo* Risto will pay for it later in the day. When *Baba* sees it on his wrist, she takes it from him, slaps and pinches his bare thighs, and reduces him to tears. *Dedo* arrives home with his mule and finds him sobbing in the yard. Kolche's choking, unable to find the words for his distress. *Dedo* takes his hand and leads him inside. He could hear the boy crying from the village square, he scolds *Baba*. When she explains what he has done, he snatches the watch from her and straps it around Kolche's wrist.

'A boy needs to tell the time,' he says.

'But it's not real,' she snaps.

'Still, it's right twice a day,' he smiles.

Dedo takes Kolche down the narrow lane to the elm tree overlooking the village. They sit on a bench next to the trunk. *Dedo* holds his hand and, in an affectionate voice, begins teaching him how to tell the time. He explains the numbers, the divisions, the minutes and hours, the quarter-before and quarter-after and half-past. He turns the watch's dial and positions the hands at different times, saying each aloud, instructing the boy to repeat it. Kolche learns quickly. *Dedo* tests him and he replies with the correct time. *Dedo*'s blue eyes moisten with tears. His stubbled cheek prickles Kolche's as he hugs and sits him on his knee.

'Promise you won't forget me,' says *Dedo*. 'Promise you'll come back.'

'I'm not going anywhere,' says Kolche.

'One day you'll leave to join your father in Australia.'

'No,' Kolche protests. 'I'll never leave you, *Dedo*.'

'Yes, you will,' he says, eyes glistening.

Kolche holds him tightly, against the pull of a terrible stranger whose letters from Australia make everyone cry. At first, when those letters arrived, his mother would sit him on her lap and read them aloud in a voice broken by sadness. He'd stand beside her when she wrote back, her pale hand struggling with each word, tears smudging the ink. She'd place his outspread hand on the sheet and trace the outline of his fingers over the words. But Kolche's interest in his father soon faded, until he was nothing more than the flimsy letter they received every few months, though his presence did become somewhat stronger whenever the letter contained a crispy Australian five-pound note. In time, though, even this failed to bring him to mind.

When not at school, Kolche joins *Dedo* on various jobs around the village. He's always whistling softly in whatever he does. Kolche recognises some of the tunes from when the band plays in the village square, others from when the priest sings in church. They go to fields bristling with barley and wheat. As he cuts them down with a sickle grinning at each bite, Kolche amuses himself drawing with a stick in the dust, building pyramids from stones, following lines of ants. Other times he watches as *Dedo* beats branches with a long stick, until the punished trees surrender and rain almonds on his head. One day, they return from the vineyard with a cart full of black grapes. *Dedo* empties them into a wooden tub and gets Kolche to dance on them as he whistles a lively melody. Kolche likes the nights when his mother embroiders on a hoop and *Baba*'s knitting needles are kissing at each stitch. *Dedo* sits him on his lap and tells him stories from the Bible. When he asks how five loaves could feed thousands of people, or how a few words could bring a young girl back to life, *Dedo* smiles that miracles were more common in those days because faith was real as golden bread straight out of the oven.

It's the middle of August, the morning's hot and the church bell's clanging from the other side of the village, reminding all that tomorrow's an important occasion – the day Christ's mother died and went to heaven. His mother and *Baba* have been fasting and preparing for the Assumption all week. Kolche's sitting on the steps of the house, turning the hands of his watch, thinking about winding it back to the beginning of time, before numbers were invented. The bell becomes louder, as if trying to tell him something, its tongue swinging from side to side. He tries to pick out a word from the clangs spreading over the village like ripples on a pond. Yesterday his mother explained the Assumption by pointing to the glass-covered icon above the cupboard in the entryway. It shows Christ's mother asleep on a bed, surrounded by people looking down at her. It happened ages ago, before *Dedo* was born, before the elm tree was planted, when people told the time by the length of a shadow. On the side, an angel has cut off a man's hands with a bloodstained sword. The poor man reaches out to the sleeping woman with his bleeding stumps, while his hands hover in the air like a pair of wings.

'Why were they cut off?' he asked, angry at the angel.

'He wanted to believe with his hands instead of his heart,' she said.

Christ's there above the heads of the people – he knows him from his beard and dark eyes. He's holding a baby wrapped in white, whose face is the same as the sleeping woman's.

Is the bell's tongue sounding *Bogoroditsa,* as his mother calls Christ's mother, or *Panaghia*, as the priest says? He listens even harder: his mother's voice sounds in one clang, the priest's in the next, and a sweet blend of both in every third.

Seeing Kolche moping around the women busy in the kitchen, *Dedo* seats him on the mule loaded with tools and they set off in the direction of the hills above their house. Cicadas clash as they climb the stony path. *Dedo* whistles, the mule snorts, and Kolche gazes up at what looks like a large house.

'Who lives there, *Dedo*?'

'It used to be a monastery.'

'What's that?'

'Monks used to live there in the old days.'

His mother once pointed out a monk walking across the village square. His black robes were like shadows, a beard covered his chest, and his hands were wrapped in a knotted cord. He frightened Kolche so much he dreamt of him that night. The monk was chasing him around the schoolyard, calling out his name, robes flapping like the wings of a crow.

'What do monks do?'

'They pray day and night, even in their sleep.'

'Why?'

'So the world won't come to an end.'

The boy thinks about this for a moment, intrigued by the idea that everything around him – the sun, the hills, his love for *Dedo* – depends on a prayer, a few words whispered by bearded old men.

'They also pray for Christ's Second Coming.'

'When will that be?'

'The world's been waiting almost two thousand years, so it can't be far off.'

'Will they crucify him again?'

The picture hanging above the blackboard in the classroom has always unsettled Kolche. It shows Christ wearing a wreath made of thorny branches like those in the abandoned house where he scratched himself looking for their cat. The whites of his eyes are frightening. It seems like he's looking up for help, but nobody's there to remove the wreath. The drops of blood on his forehead are bright as the berries on a rosehip bush.

As *Dedo* hoes between rows of vines, Kolche sits in the dusty shade of a fig tree, striking sparks from white pebbles, sniffing the thunderstorm in each flash, thinking about the Second Coming. Suddenly, drawn by curiosity, he sets off without a word and soon finds himself a stone's throw from the monastery. Scrambling up the hill, ears drilled by cicadas, he trips, grazing his knees. Where the trickle of blood would have concerned him on any other occasion, he now wipes it with a leaf and continues as though on a mission. Climbing on hands, the sun-baked stones almost too hot for his palms, he finally reaches the monastery. The surrounding wall has crumbled in several places. The cicadas are deafening. A crow eyes him from the broken spine of a roof and swoops over his head. The courtyard is covered in weeds. A small church stands in the centre, guarded by two sharp cypress trees, its front door partly open. Drawn by the cool coming from inside, he stops at the entrance, recalling *Baba*'s stories of vampires and wolves. What if a monk grabs him and ties his hands with a knotted cord? But the coolness is inviting, his curiosity aroused. He braces himself and enters. The inside has been stripped back almost bare to stone. Here and there the remains of painted figures cling to the walls. Sunlight streams in from the dome's arched windows. Christ is up there, tight-lipped, sharp-eyed, with a crack passing through his halo and cutting across his left cheek. He holds an open book from which the words have faded. *Dedo*'s story echoes in the coolness. Will the Second Coming take place in here? Suddenly he's tired from the climb and the heat. He needs to rest before the journey down. Lying on the stone floor, hands under his head, he gazes at the light-filled dome, at Christ's face, the deep crack. A pleasant feeling runs through his body, pulling at his eyelids. And then Christ drifts down from the dome and holds the book flat for him to read.

'The pages are blank,' Kolche says.

Christ brings the book closer.

'There's nothing there,' he protests, eyes filling with tears.

Christ's glowing index finger taps the page just like the teacher's ruler taps the blackboard.

'I can't read yet,' he cries, wanting to run away, yet caught by the crimson of Christ's fingernail.

He concentrates on the blankness, hoping something will appear, a picture or a letter, to save him from this situation. His tears are now flowing, blurring everything, until through them he recognises the sharpness of Alpha, the roundness of Omega.

2

The neighbourhood boys are playing soldiers in an abandoned house when Kolche spots the postman, leather bag strapped over his shoulder, limping up the road in their direction. In recent months there's been talk of tickets and medical examinations, and now something tells him the postman is delivering the dreaded letter from Australia. His first reaction is to marshal his friends, fill their pockets with stones, and bombard the postman from the upstairs windows, preventing him from delivering the letter. But he quickly realises this is only a short-term solution, for he's certain to be back later, with the police. Another idea suddenly takes hold of him. Setting off alone, he marches down to the postman struggling with his limp, cursing this high part of the village and its steep paths. Kolche greets him politely and offers to help him by delivering the letters meant for their neighbourhood.

'Only one today, for your mother,' he says, extending a familiar envelope. 'You'll earn yourself a nice *dekara* for bringing good news.'

Kolche races off with the letter, but stops in the lane a short distance from home. What should he do? Tear it up and bury it under a rock where it will never be found? He recognises the uneven writing and the stamp with the woman's profile. But what will this achieve? Another letter will arrive next month. And what if the postman meets *Dedo* in the café this evening? No, he can't change the course of things. People are leaving the village for overseas. Not long ago his best friend Telli the drummer left to join his father in Canada. Besides, his mother will be pleased: she won't have to spread the long *cherga* after all.

Menka, his mother, has been packing for weeks, not knowing what to take and what to leave behind, putting in something today only to take it out tomorrow. Her bright flush of excitement about leaving has started to pale with apprehension. Having accepted what can't be changed, Kolche's now looking forward to travelling by train to Athens and then the month-long journey by ship. In helping his mother pack she asks whether they'll need this or that, whether the winters in Australia are as cold as those here, whether that place has looms and embroidery hoops and crochet needles. Sometimes she sighs in frustration and wishes she could fit the entire village into her brown dowry chest. Struck by her words, Kolche imagines the house, the village, the mountains, the whole country fitting into a kind of magic chest and emerging intact in Australia. If miracles happened in *Dedo*'s Bible stories why can't they happen now? But then he wonders: if the village could somehow fit in this chest, would the chest also be inside itself, and how would that be possible?

In the days before they leave, the word Australia settles on the house like a cloud. Kolche doesn't like the sound of the word, it's harsh and frightening, especially the 'stra' part. He's not the only one who feels this way. Whenever people in the village say that word, they follow it with a curse, or breathe out a sigh, or wipe away a few tears.

He's sitting on the steps of the house, playing with their ginger cat, when it leaps from his knees and springs across the sunny courtyard. *Dedo*'s moving the pile of coal delivered this morning, storing the large clumps in the shed in readiness for winter. Kolche offers to help, thinking how he won't be here to roast chestnuts and quince with him on the heater. He says he doesn't want his little white dove blackened before it flies off to Australia. Brown coal-dust streaks *Dedo*'s face as he brushes his blue eyes. That word, thinks Kolche, and spits on the pile shining in the sun.

Down the lane the cat slips into a house with rusty bars on the windows and a gaping entrance. Kolche looks for it among the stones and nettles and broken beams. This house has always made him uneasy, especially walking past it at dusk. *Baba*'s warned him not go inside, saying a bad thing happened there years ago, and it's now home to vampires and evil winds. Spooked by a creak from a broken staircase leading nowhere, he dashes out and continues running to the big elm tree overlooking the village. From here he can see the square, the school, the church, the cemetery, and further away the patchwork of fields. He squats in the shade and begins drawing in the dust with a twig, when a pair of large boots with laces undone trudges over his figures. It's Mimi, the dwarf, whose face is already that of a grown man. He's singing what sounds like a church hymn, the words mashed by a thick tongue that doesn't like the darkness of a closed mouth. He's wearing a coat even though it's hot, with a white oleander flower in the lapel. Without stopping he calls on Kolche to go with him.

'Where are you going?'

Mimi's narrow forehead creases. When Kolche repeats the question, he grins, chewing on his thick tongue. Having nothing better to do, Kolche sets off after him. His head swaying from side to side, he begins whistling, clear as the *bilbil* bird that sounds in the hills at night. As they walk along a dusty path away from the village, Mimi says he recently caught a bus to Salonika all by himself.

'Big sea, big sea,' he says, making a swimming action with his arms.

Kolche's never seen the sea, but he's heard its whisper in the large shell next to the clock on the kitchen shelf which *Dedo* brought back from Salonika.

'Is it bigger than the village?' Kolche asks, thinking of their coming voyage.

His words garbled, Mimi relates how the waves shuffled after him and tried to catch him by the ankle, how he managed to run away, how, after learning its secrets, he caressed it and drank a mouthful, only to spit it out because it was saltier than water used for sore gums.

'Who put the salt in there?'

Mimi chews his tongue harder, as if a piece of tough meat.

They climb over a stone wall into a field of clover, where Mimi instructs Kolche to pick purple and yellow flowers. When they have each gathered a bunch Mimi raises his to the sun and calls on Kolche to follow. He's never ventured this far from home, but another gruff call draws him along, and they're soon on the side of a grassy hill. As the slope starts to level off, Mimi points to a small white house with a cross above the door. They stop at a wall of big rocks overgrown by a blackberry bush. Mimi picks a handful of berries and stuffs them in his mouth, grunting with joy, urging Kolche to do the same. The dark juice stains his shirt. What will his mother say? For a moment he sees the outline of Australia in the stain, just like in the map at school.

Mimi rattles the latch on the front gate of the white house. He tells Kolche not to be afraid, chewing his purple tongue in frustration, as though his words would be clearer without it. His boots crunch the loose pebbles on the path. He peers through a window in the door and pulls a cord. Kolche follows him inside. It's just like the village church, with the same oily smell, only smaller. The walls and ceiling are painted with similar scenes and figures. The still flames stir as they walk past the candle-stand. A wooden crate rests on two trestles in front of the altar screen. Mimi turns and whispers for Kolche to do exactly as he does. First he places his bunch of flowers among the others on the floor. He then takes a candle from a tray, lights it, and stands before the crate, looking inside, his head swaying from side to side, the way *Baba*'s head sways when she's upset. Kolche follows his lead and stands next to him, only to be taken aback by a small girl sleeping inside the crate, dressed in white, her arms folded on her chest. Mimi crosses himself – touching his left side then his right. Kolche knows it should be right then left, but does the same, thinking maybe that's how it's done in this small church. But why is she sleeping in there? Why is that icon under her arms – the one with the baby Christ on his mother's lap? And who put those coins on the icon?

Mimi plants his candle in the stand and signals for Kolche to do the same. He then leans into the crate, kisses the girl on the forehead, and kisses the icon.

'We'll wake her,' Kolche whispers.

'Dead, dead,' he says, the word coming from the back of his throat.

Kolche's stunned, suddenly afraid, like when passing that house at dusk. Mimi takes him by the hand to the edge of the crate. It contains neatly folded clothes, embroideries, socks, shoes, slippers, a comb and a mirror. He recognises the girl from school: she's a year or two older. What happened to her? How did she die? Mimi nudges him, but he can't bring himself to kiss her forehead. Bowing to the icon, he notices a *dekara* in one of her slippers. Mimi's standing with head bowed, eyes closed, chewing his tongue in what sounds like a prayer. Kolche picks up the coin intending to place it on the icon, but his fingers tighten to a fist.

He follows Mimi down to a creek, where they wash their faces and cool their feet. They return to the village square hot and tired, just as a bus pulls up in front of the café, on its way to town. Without a word Mimi runs off and jumps aboard. The bus toots and roars off in a burst of blue smoke. Mimi waves from the back, his face squashed in pressing hard against the window.

The *dekara* is sweating in Kolche's fist as he passes the corner shop. He thinks of buying a bag of sweets or a bottle of fizzy *gazoza*. But reaching for the handle he sees the girl's face in the glass door instead of his own. A shudder goes through him at the thought of vampires and evil winds. He hurries home, clutching the coin as though for dear life.

Only a spread of coal-dust remains where the pile stood. The cat lies curled on the steps. The house is empty. Where have they gone? A bowl of cold lentil soup has been left for him on the table. He eats and goes up to his room. His mother has been packing, sorting out piles on the floor, deciding what to take and what to leave behind. He lies on his bed and examines the coin, turning it this way and that, noting the year is the same as when he was born, looking at the ceiling through the hole, looking until the room dissolves in his drowsiness. A bell begins tolling slowly, faintly, as though from another world.

He wakes to the cries of jackdaws. Someone has come in and drawn the curtains as he slept. Was it all a dream? Mimi, the small church, the girl? No – the coin is still in his fist. He goes to the kitchen, where *Baba*'s scraping ash from the coal-fired stove.

'Ah, finally decided to get up,' she says, wiping her brow with the corner of her black shawl. 'And where were you? I was worried a vampire had carried you off.'

Through the small kitchen window Kolche's struck by twilight's unusual crimson hue above the distant mountains.

'*Babo*?' he says, unsure of how to begin.

'What is it, child?'

'When people die ...'

'Yes, separations are like death,' she says, as though speaking to herself.

'Why are things put inside with them?'

'Who told you about that?'

'Mimi told me.'

'Ah, that Mimi, always doing and saying things he shouldn't.'

'Why are things put inside?'

'For the same reason people fill their suitcase going overseas.'

'And what are the coins for?'

'He told you about the coins, too? Ah, that Mimi's bad company.'

'What are they for?'

'To pay for the dead person's fare, just like your fare to Australia,' she sighs.

'Where does the dead person go?'

'Up to *Dedo* God in heaven.'

A knot tightens in his stomach.

'And if they haven't got enough for the fare?' he asks, clutching the coin.

'Their poor soul's stranded between heaven and earth.'

As she clatters the sooty poker in the stove, everything goes dark for a moment, and then he dashes out of the kitchen, desperate to make it to the small church on the hill. He races down the lane as *Dedo* rounds the corner returning from the café. He catches Kolche in his arms in front of the haunted house.

'What's your hurry?'

'The little girl,' he says, trying to break free.

'Yes, Kolche, it's very sad,' he says.

'She needs this *dekara* for her fare to heaven.'

'You're a good boy to think of her.'

'Let me go, *Dedo*, please. She's in the church on the hill.'

'No, they buried her this afternoon.'

Kolche's body goes limp. A flock of jackdaws cries overhead. As *Dedo* carries him away he looks into the abandoned house, at the dark nettles stirred by the evening breeze.

They leave on a hot September morning. In the end Menka filled the chest with *chergi*, *flokati* rugs, blankets, an icon of Saint George, and other things for setting up a house in Australia. A few days ago *Dedo* and some neighbours carried it down to a truck waiting in the village square, from where it would be taken to Athens and the port of Piraeus. The green suitcase now standing on the doorstep with its long shadow contains all they'll need for the journey. The potted oleanders on the stairs have started dropping their bright flowers. Strings of peppers are drying on the wall. A solemn crowd has gathered in the courtyard. *Baba* Lena breaks off three pieces of bread and hands them to Menka, who crosses herself slowly before throwing each over her left shoulder. *Baba* Tonka, his other grandmother, places a glass of red wine on the doorstep and instructs Menka to tip it over with her right foot. Menka's twenty-five, with thick chestnut coloured hair swept off her forehead and tied at the back. Her movements are usually quick, whether with needle and thread, or in the kitchen, or carrying tins of water from the tap near the village square. This morning, though, she seems dazed, unsure of herself, asking relatives whether anything else needs to be done.

The church bell strikes against the clear sky as they leave the house. Tears mingle with sweat, sobs are muffled in handkerchiefs, shadows turn to dust on the path leading down to the station on the outskirts of the village. Kolche sits on *Dedo*'s shoulders, thin legs straddling his head, holding his breath against the methylated spirits he uses after shaving. As they pass a sheep-pen a few new-born lambs falter toward them, fleece still stained with blood. Menka gives a start and reaches into her handbag – the passport's golden letters flash in the light.

The train's smoking at the station. More embraces and tears. The two *Babas* smother Kolche with their sobbing. At the sound of a whistle they climb aboard, along with another family leaving for Australia. *Baba* Lena falls to her knees on the grey stones beside the tracks and wails *le-le* in a high-pitched voice, pleading with them not to go. When the station officer gives the all clear, she lunges forward and throws her arms across the track as a way of keeping the train from moving. Women drag her away, her small body limp and shaking. Menka's also crying, promising *Baba* Tonka they'll return in a few years. Silver tears roll off her cheeks and spot the lap of her floral dress. Kolche feels he should be crying too, but the tears won't come, maybe because this is his first time on a train. A whistle sounds again, followed by a jolt, and the surroundings move. *Dedo* raises a hand with the amber worry beads Kolche would click when learning to count. He waves back, but *Dedo* and his two *Babas* are already moving away, becoming smaller, even though they're standing still.

3

The cabin's small, with a bunk bed, and down lots of steep stairs from the windy deck. A month of ocean, says Menka, her lips dry and cracked. Kolche asks about Australia, though not about his father, whose presence in a few weeks fills him with apprehension. Her answers are vague, sometimes trailing off to silence, failing to satisfy his growing curiosity. Sometimes she just sits there on the edge of the bed, caressing the passport, gazing from the port-hole at the green swell rising and falling. He traces the trail of a tear down her cheek and licks his fingertip: it is saltier than the sea-water he tasted in Piraeus, where they boarded the *Marcus Aurelius*.

'We mustn't lose our passport,' she says. 'It's our key to the new world.'

Suddenly the little book becomes like *Dedo*'s Bible. It fires Kolche's imagination and he begins to believe in its magic power. During a rough part of the voyage when seasickness keeps his mother in her bunk for days, he weaves daydreams around its dark-blue cover, gold letters, coat-of-arms with two figures club in hand, standing guard on either side of a gold cross topped with a crown. The pin pricks across the top of the cover intrigue him. Why do they pierce only half the pages? Are they a secret code? Holding the passport to the porthole, he makes out the letter K, followed by the number 484076. He closes his eyes and runs a finger over the dots, hoping for something, maybe a vision of the new world. Nothing, but that's not to say the numbers aren't magical, it means his fingers aren't sensitive enough to their secret. He opens the passport to the small black and white photograph taken in the village square by a photographer who croaked like a frog in getting their attention. His mother's hair is loose, features sharp, cheekbones round, eyes set deep, afraid, straining to grasp something in the distance. And he's beside her, six and fair, a scab on his forehead from a recent fall, eyes open, startled by the camera's flash.

The ship's cruising through a narrow strip of water people call the Suez Canal. The decks are crowed: women in bright dresses, men in white shirts and sunglasses, children in singlets, running around barefooted. The heat stings Kolche's bare arms and legs. He glances up and wonders if a different sun shines on this part of the world and a different God, because *Dedo* would say God lives on the dark side of the sun, where shadows came from. The sand on either side of the Canal spreads as far as the horizon. From a distance it must appear the ship's ploughing through a field of gold. Some of the bigger boys are saying the Canal was dug out by men and machines to connect the Mediterranean Sea and the Red Sea. After a while the ship stops and passengers trade with dark-skinned people waving and shouting from below. Baskets tied to ropes fly up and down with money and colourful objects. Feeling better on this part of the journey, his mother is also on deck and asks what he'd like from the vendors down below. The offer surprises him: she's never bought him a toy before. Is this a present for the long journey ahead? He points to the camels lined on a green blanket. One of the ship's attendants helps them with the exchange and in a flash he's holding a camel stitched from white leather with a red saddle and small wheels on the soles of its feet. For days he rolls it on the floor of the cabin, along the corridor, on deck. He even takes it to bed and falls asleep imagining he's the young Alexander in *Dedo*'s story about the conqueror's horse. He faces the wild animal toward the sun, so not to be spooked by its own shadow, and leaps onto its saddled hump. In an instant he's flying across Macedonia with his Bucephalus, over sand and sea, conquering everything, even distant Australia.

One morning, as the ship ploughs through the restless Indian Ocean, Kolche's rolling Bucephalus on the deck when a push sends it flying off the edge. He runs to the rail only to see it somersault in the air and fall into the water. He looks around for help, yet knowing the helplessness of the situation. Gripping the rail, he watches Bucephalus bobbing up and down on the swell until swept up and swallowed in the ship's frothy back wash. The sorrow at his loss is mingled with fear of being scolded by his mother. But she's in her bunk, feeling seasick again, and when he tells her about the camel, tears spring to her eyes and she calls him to her side.

'Your *Dedo* Petro died not far from here,' she says, embracing him.

Kolche can still see Bucephalus tossed about by the green waves.

'He was buried at sea, near the port of Colombo.'

He tries to imagine people underwater with shovels in hand.

'He's been down there more than ten years.'

'But how did they dig his grave?' he asks.

'He was wrapped up and dropped in the sea,' she says, caressing his head.

Her words send a shiver through him and he grips her hand.

'Where others have graves to look after and bones to dig up and wash in wine after seven years, your poor *Baba* Tonka has nothing to ease her sorrow.'

His *Dedo* Petro is a shadowy figure, nothing more than a name sighed in conversations between his mother and *Baba* Tonka, who always wears a black dress and scarf. They'd visit her on Fridays when she'd cook his favourite meal: fish and chopped onions baked in the woodfired oven. After cleaning up, she'd take down the silver cup from the icon case, fill it with oil, and light the floating wick in memory of *Dedo* Petro. She'd then hold out the match for him to blow out, saying his breath would take the flame to his lost *Dedo* and bring a little joy to his darkness.

'Don't be upset at losing your little camel,' his mother says. '*Dedo* Petro will find it and make his way back to Macedonia on it.'

Moved by her sad words, Kolche sees *Dedo* Petro's skeleton rising from the depths, mounted on the red-saddled camel, and as it rises the sun fleshes it in light and the sea dresses it in foam. Whole again he rides over the ocean's hills and valleys, across the sand, through the village square, into *Baba* Tonka's yard. He plucks a bright flower from the oleander beside the front steps, holds it up like a flame, and knocks on the door. The scene lifts Kolche's spirits and he feels better about losing Bucephalus.

Menka's seasickness becomes worse after the brief stop in Colombo. It's two weeks across the Indian Ocean to Fremantle. The rough sea lurches the ship from side to side, covers the decks in spray, sweeps plates and cutlery off the tables in the dining room. Her face is pale as the bed sheets, eyes dark with purple circles, lips badly cracked, bleeding. She has lost her appetite and is too weak to leave the cabin. The woman from the village looks after Kolche and brings Menka dry biscuits and peeled apples. When Menka moans she'll never make it to Australia, the woman scolds her, sits her up, cuts some apple and forces her to eat. Kolche's a helpless onlooker when the woman's around, but when she leaves, he dashes off and fills a glass with cold water from a tap in the corridor. He holds her head as she sips with parched lips. Other times he presses a moist towel on her forehead. But he avoids looking into her eyes, afraid of being drawn into their darkness, of breaking down in tears.

'I can't go on,' she sighs. 'I won't make it to Australia, just like my father.'

Kolche swallows back a swell of emotion and promises not to leave her side until they reach the new world together.

He has made friends with a few boys his age. They play hide-and-seek on the decks and in the maze of corridors. Sometimes he feels uneasy having fun when his mother's so sick. It's windy on deck and wet from the spray. He's running to find a hiding place beneath a boat raised in the air, when he slips and falls. The ship suddenly sways in the same direction and he finds himself sliding toward the rail. He tries to scramble the other way, but the drift's too strong, the boards too smooth. It's like being in one of those dreams when his legs won't move even though he's trying to run away from someone chasing him. At the sight of the ocean opening to swallow him, he thinks of what his drowning will do to his mother. *Dedo* Petro flashes to mind and Bucephalus. He doesn't want to be down there with them. His mother needs him to get to Australia. With his legs now over the edge, he closes his eyes for the fall, when a hand grips him by the arm and pulls him back. A man in a grey overcoat and black and white shoes helps him up and takes him to the safety of a nearby corridor. His heart's still running away from the heaving ocean, his ears sounding with the surge of the ship. The man leans forward and says something in a foreign language. Kolche wants to thank him, but his throat clots with words. As the man walks off down the shining corridor, his attention is caught by the click of his step and the silver half-moons smiling on each heel.

The ship berths in Fremantle on a warm, windy morning. It's stopping here most of the day and passengers are allowed off until later in the afternoon. Menka's exhausted, struggles to walk, so Kolche holds her hand in crossing the narrow bridge between the ship and stairs leading down. A man salutes a flag beating in the wind, saying in Greek this is what they must now salute. Kolche feels a little homesick recalling the striped flag at school, and how he'd march behind it on important days, and how the teacher would get him to stand beside it and recite poems because he had the best memory in the grade. This flag's dark, with big white stars and something like a smaller flag in the corner. He tries counting the number of stars – five or six or seven – but it's flapping around too much. Is its dark colour a sign of what awaits him in this country? His teacher would tell the class to love their flag as much as they loved their mother. She'd point to the striped cross in the corner whenever they said the Our Father prayer. She'd tell stories of heroes who gave their lives so they could raise the flag free as the wind. Her clear voice now echoes against what the man has just said. What did he mean they'd have to salute this flag? Is he supposed to forget all he's been taught? Turn from the heroes who died for his freedom? Throw overboard all those stories that fired his imagination? Honour the heroes of this foreign country? Develop feelings for this dark colour, these white stars, this piece of cloth beating in the wind? No, he'll never forget his flag. It will always stay in his heart, so when the time comes, he'll follow it back to *Dedo* Risto and his ancestors.

Relatives greet them on the dock and drive them to their place for lunch. Kolche has been in buses and on the back of noisy trucks, but this is his first time in a car. It's fast and smooth, and the road is wide and straight, nothing like the winding dirt lanes in the village. On the way, as the grown-ups talk about conditions on the ship and relatives back home and the journey to Melbourne, he gazes out the window at Australia. Where the village is ringed by hills and distant mountains, this place is flat and spacious and surrounded by horizon. The light here has a different shine and slant, the shadows seem quicker, the sky's spread with a paler blue, and the clouds carry shapes unlike anything he's seen before. Strange, white and pink-skinned trees line the road, with leaves like knives and crows bigger than those at home. Learning of Menka's ordeal, the relatives suggest they travel the last leg of the journey by train, as the ocean in this part of the world is very rough. They offer to arrange everything, including paying the fares, but Menka refuses, saying they've made it this far and will endure whatever lies ahead.

It's dark and Kolche's lying on the upper bunk, too excited to sleep, when the endless drone of the ship's engines suddenly subsides. A long, deep hoot sounds from above. Menka rustles in the bunk below and calls his name. He's heartened by the fact that she's found strength to speak. The past four days have been the roughest of the entire voyage: huge waves washing against the porthole, strong wind lashing the decks, the roll making it difficult to walk a straight line in the corridors. Menka turned pale the moment they boarded again in Fremantle, and from there she turned yellow, green, and deathly grey. She moaned and heaved and retched, unable to keep down a sip of water, as though something was tearing out her life. Now and then she called on God to end her suffering. He cried with her and cooled her lips with ice and placed a moist towel on her forehead. Anger rose from his despair, not at God who made the ocean so wild, but at the man who insisted they leave the village to join him in Australia.

'Kolche,' she calls. 'Look – there's Melbourne.'

Through the porthole he sees a wide band of lights glittering in the distance, as many as in the night sky above the village. Yes, we've reached paradise, he thinks, recalling his *Dedo*'s words about it being somewhere among the stars.

'Come and give me a hug.'

He climbs down the ladder and snuggles up next to her, his head under her chin, both on their side, facing the porthole. As she holds him tightly, he stares at the lights, until his attention catches on a red one which seems closer and bigger than the others. It goes on and off, as though winking at him, drawing him toward it. Suddenly there's something unsettling about this light, reminding him of the eyes of the black bear which a gypsy recently brought into the village. They gathered around it in the square, afraid and excited, as it rose on its back legs and danced to the sound of a tambourine, shaking and turning and trembling all over. Sometimes the gypsy would pull on the chain attached to a ring through its moist nose, when the creature would let out a growl that sent the children scrambling for cover. But as the winking light draws closer, the bear gives way to the face of a red-eyed man. He snuggles closer into his mother, more afraid of him than the bear. He knows his intention: he wants to throw Kolche overboard and take his place in the warmth of the bunk. His mother must also sense this: she holds him tighter and whispers it's time to sleep because they mustn't appear tired for tomorrow's long-awaited reunion.

A small boat tows the ship to the crowded dock, where it's secured by the thickest ropes Kolche has ever seen. His mother's looking much better this morning: she's wearing a bright dress, her hair's tied back, and glossy lipstick covers the cracks in her lips. They lean over the railing as people below throw coloured streamers up to fingers grasping for a first connection before hugs and handshakes. Kolche's complaining of a stomach pains, but his mother takes little notice. She's concentrating on the crowd below, trying to spot the person responsible for her month-long sickness.

Menka holds Kolche in one hand and the heavy green suitcase in the other as they file past several men in uniform. His heart contracts as she extends the passport to a grim-faced official. He opens it, folds back the covers in a careless manner, and looks hard first at her, then down at him. Here and there orders are shouted, suitcases opened, belongings strewn on tables. Suddenly he's afraid the man might keep the passport in exchange for allowing them into Melbourne. It's ours, he thinks, with rising anger. We'll need it for the journey home when we've had enough of this place. Saying something Kolche doesn't understand, he stamps the passport with a thud that sends a shudder through his body. He breathes easier when the man reaches over the counter and returns the passport, together with a faint Australian smile.

Kolche offers to help with the suitcase, but his mother struggles on in silence, face set with the determination that carried those heavy tins of water uphill from the village tap, without spilling a drop, even over ice and snow. Stepping out onto the wooden boards of Melbourne's Station Pier, they're caught up in a storm of excitement: people are waving handkerchiefs, shouting names, crying in joy, rushing to embrace. Kolche recalls *Baba* Lena's reply to his question: where do people go when they die? To heaven, she said, crossing herself, where they're welcomed with happiness by those who've gone there before. And it occurs to him that all these passengers, including himself and his mother who almost died, have been buried in this ship for a month, and that they're now being greeted by family and friends who've been here years, just as *Baba* Lena said.

'There he is,' says Menka, pointing over the boy's head.

Kolche starts, his grip on her hand tightens. His first reaction is to pull her away, back to the ship. But two men are pushing through the crowd toward them. Which of these strangers is his father? The taller one wearing sunglasses? Or the other, wearing a straw hat with a green band? For some reason he expected the taller, but the other embraces his mother and kisses her on the mouth. Kolche's heart pounds, his ears ring. Kneeling, the man hugs him, saying how much he's grown in three years. He pushes back his hat and extends a block of chocolate wrapped in purple. Kolche thanks him in Greek, surprised at the weight of the chocolate. The other man sounds a loud clap and laughs.

'Hear that, Vangel? Your son's a little Greek.'

Stung by the man's words, Vangel holds the boy by the shoulders and studies him a moment.

'Kolche,' he says, 'Australia's a free country – speak Macedonian.'

Reacting to the edge in his voice, Kolche turns to his mother, who nods. No, he'd rather throw the chocolate in the sea than thank a stranger who has just scolded him. Suddenly, he wants to go home to *Dedo* Risto and his friends in the village. His mother prods him with a sharp look. After what they've been through in the past month is she now turning against him? He manages to hold back a swell of tears. No, he wants to remain close to her, even if it means thanking a stranger and calling him father.

'*Spolayti*,' he says, the word catching in his throat.

'Bravo,' shouts the tall man, 'said like a true Macedonian.'

He takes the suitcase and pushes open a path through the crowd. The family follows: the father arm-in-arm with his wife on one side, holding his son's hand on the other. As they make their way to a line of waiting taxis, Kolche pulls back from a big seagull lunging for his chocolate. Vangel curses the bird and draws his son closer.

4

On their third day in Melbourne, Friday, still feeling the sway of the ocean under his feet, Kolche goes with his father to be enrolled at the local school. George Street Primary is a short distance down the street: a two-storey, red-brick building surrounded by a wire fence woven in diamonds. The Principal invites them into his office and shakes even Kolche's hand, which would never have happened in the village. As the two men go over the formalities, the boy's attention is caught by a large photograph on the wall behind the Principal: a portrait of an attractive woman wearing a sparkling crown and necklace. He recalls the picture of Christ above the blackboard in the village classroom. Is this woman the God of Australia? Do people here pray to her as he was taught to pray to Christ? Her features are gentle, peaceful, so different from Christ's, whose forehead was scratched and bleeding from the thorny crown. The Principal presses his notes with a sheet of blotting paper, closes the fountain pen, and welcomes the boy to the school.

'Right,' says the Principal, beaming. 'What should we call your son?'

'Him name Kolche in Macedonia,' says Vangel.

'Can't think of anything close,' says the Principal, shaking his head.

'Him Nikolaos in Greek passport.'

'Too long – we need something shorter.'

'What you tink good name?'

'Nick – we'll call him Nick.'

On the way home Kolche repeats the name to himself, trying to come to terms not only with the sound, but with the fact that he has gone from four syllables in Greek, two in Macedonian, down to one short sound: Nick. That night, alone in the bedroom, he cries because something has been taken from him. He's afraid to face tomorrow with such a cropped name. Nick, he whimpers, thinking of the Macedonian word *nikoi*, nobody, *nishto*, nothing, and *nikde*, nowhere. And that's exactly how he feels: a nameless nobody. Hearing his muffled sobs, his mother comes in, wipes his tears, and whispers he'll always be her Kolche.

The following Monday, at seven-thirty in the morning, Menka and Nick leave the house together. A relative has arranged a job in a shoe-factory off Smith Street and she's anxious to be there before starting time at eight. She walks him into the empty yard, to a sheltered doorway, and tells him to wait there until the teacher calls everyone inside. She does the top button of his shirt, adjusts the brown bag strapped over his shoulder, and hugs him tightly, saying they'll be together again this afternoon. Nick swallows hard to keep from crying out he hates Australia. He watches as she walks up George Street, but not with the strong step with which she brought home tins of water from the village taps. Alone in the doorway, he observes a few shining crows squabbling over scraps of bread. And then a truck drives into the yard, stopping in front of a shed. Two men in shorts jump out and start unloading crates rattling with small bottles of milk. Nick closes his eyes, imagining being back in the village classroom, the teacher's favourite, reciting the Our Father to the class. As other children begin arriving, he retreats further into the doorway. A few bigger boys approach him, say something, tug at his bag and run off. Soon a crowd gathers, laughing and prodding. He presses against the brick wall, wishing it would swallow him. Why has his mother left him here all alone? Why have they come to this unfriendly country? He wants to go home to the village, his grandparents, his school, the language he knows. Not having a word with which to defend himself, he begins to cry, hoping his tears will stop their taunts, but this only increases their laughter. Everything suddenly blurs and he runs from the doorway across the yard. The others follow, shouting and screaming. His first instinct is to run home, but he doesn't have a key, so he stops at the front gate and begins swinging the bag to drive them away. A boy with glasses and squinty eyes comes to his rescue, shouting away the troublemakers. He speaks Macedonian to Nick and stays with him until the bell rings and the doors open. They aren't in the same grade, but the boy seeks him out at recess and lunch time and walks him home after school. Les becomes his first friend in Australia.

A week, two weeks, and Kolche's feeling more comfortable with Nick. But he's still resentful at having been forced to leave the fenceless village for a tin-clad backyard. They live in a rented room on Chapel Street: a narrow, back-lane-of-a-street with small houses pressed together and red-brick factories at both ends. Their house has no front garden or even a veranda. A worn bluestone step rises from the narrow footpath to a door that opens straight into the hallway. And on the glass above the door, the year of construction: AD 1867. Two other men from the same village board with them, sharing the kitchen and bathroom and toilet in the back corner of the yard. Nick hates the smell of the house and the glossy paint on the walls. He sees scary faces in the floor-covering's yellow flowers, which look like the *vampiri Baba* Lena said would catch him if he didn't come home before sunset. Their room's the largest in the house, but even so, it's stifling on these hot November days because the window's right on the street and can't be left open from fear of crooks. There were no locks and latches in the village, Nick thinks. Maybe they were too poor to afford them, or maybe there were no crooks.

But he's even more resentful at how a stranger has come between his mother and him. He now looks back with fondness on the month aboard ship. Yes, his mother suffered on the journey, but there was a kind of sweetness in being together, in caring for her the whole time, in looking into her suffering face with a love that will never come again. They sleep in a double bed, while Nick's is no bigger than a cot, behind a white sheet hanging from a cord stretched across the room. Vangel put it up so he wouldn't disturb the boy when getting up early for work. But Nick knows better: it's his way of separating him from his mother. His father isn't a bit like *Dedo* Risto who's kind and gentle, even with fierce sheepdogs. Where others would pick up sticks and stones at the sight of those red-furred creatures, *Dedo* Risto had a way with them: he'd squat and make a sucking sound with his lips and before long they'd come to him with jaws closed and a sorry look in their eyes. No, the man trying to win his affection with blocks of chocolate can't be trusted. He's quick-tempered, loud at times, and likes his beer and *rakija*. He drinks the clear, homebrewed stuff from a small glass, tossing it back in one gulp, and wiping his smile with the back of his hand. When in a playful mood he holds the glass under Nick's nose and sings as the boy pulls away from the sharp smell.

There was no beer in the village, at least not in their house, but men here drink lots of it, filling their glasses from bottles and jugs and even barrels at weddings and parties. Those brown beer bottles are all over the place: backyards, lanes, gutters. The rougher kids in the neighbourhood smash them for fun, sometimes on the street, to flatten the tyres of passing cars. A house up the lane has pieces of broken bottles cemented along the top of the back wall. Nick likes the way the sun shines and sparkles on them, but he can also imagine the pain of a crook trying to climb into the house. He enjoys stacking the empty bottles along the fence, arranging them neatly in rows one on top of the other, and counting as the pile grows. One afternoon, having nothing better to do, he counts one hundred and twenty bottles. And then he wants to see if he can rearrange the rows in the shape of a triangle. He tries different numbers of bottles along the bottom row until he's delighted to find that building up from fifteen and finishing with one on top makes a perfect triangle from all the bottles.

Nick learns the new alphabet quickly because some letters are the same as the Greek. The English letters are single sounds, easy enough for a baby to say: Ay, Bee, See, Dee. The Greek have two or more sounds and seem more grown-up: Alpha, Vitta, Gamma, even Omicron and Omega. He soon begins putting letters together to read simple words. The first three he read were the ones on the front of his exercise book. He didn't understand their English meaning, but each one made perfect sense in Macedonian. Name, he read as *neme*, Grade as *grede*, School as *skoolye*. Put together these three Macedonian words expressed perfectly his feelings: I don't want to come to school.

He begins speaking English while playing on the street with Les. At first, they speak only Macedonian, until Nick gradually starts slipping in a few English words, replacing *billi* with marbles, *doma* with house, *den* with day, *stol* with chair, *nos* with nose. In six months, he thinks, he'll be able to speak three languages: Macedonian at home, Greek with some cousins (though it's already fading) and English elsewhere. His attachment to the village will probably weaken as his English improves. Drawn into the new language, he'll feel more at home in Australia. Not only this, his memory of things that happened in the village will begin to blur and take on a dreamlike quality. And then he'll need his mother's help to determine whether a vision in his mind is a memory or a dream or just his playful imagination.

In time Nick's resentment gives way to acceptance. It happens as naturally as a boy grows taller when measured against his father, as effortlessly as he now finds himself stringing together English words. Vangel likes his beer, especially after work, so Nick's quick to have the bottle and opener on the table before he sits down. He has to live with this man for a long time, so he may as well make things more comfortable for everyone, especially his mother who's finding adjusting difficult. He's a lively man, especially after a bottle of beer, when he'll sometimes dance around the table, drawing Menka and Nick after him. He never leaves the house without a hat, and has several for different occasions, some with a small coloured feather in the band. Nick's learnt to judge his moods from which hat he wears and how it's angled. When he's had too much *rakija* he breaks out in Macedonian songs. It seems to Nick he becomes a different person singing these songs. His eyes close, head sways from side-to-side, the thick veins in his neck swell, and emotions flit across his face. The old words rise from him as though from a deep well, old words made new by his blood and breath, bringing to the present the feelings and experiences of his ancestors. His favourite songs are slow, sad, with long notes and lots of *le-le*s. Nick doesn't know what the word means, or if it's even a word, but *Baba* Lena used it when an accident happened or when bad news arrived. The song pours from him, fills the kitchen, flows from the small house and spreads over Fitzroy, rich, earthy, like the smell of roasted malt coming from the breweries on Victoria Parade.

Vangel's playing cards with the other men in the house, hat pushed back, swearing at what he's been dealt. Nick's keeping score, adding each player's points with a small pencil. When one of the players scoops up the pile of cards with a red jack, Vangel thumps the table at his bad luck. Startled, Nick swallows the pencil, whose end he's been biting. It goes down just like a lolly. He gags, Menka panics, Vangel looks under the table. Menka insists they take the boy to a doctor, but Vangel silences her with a sharp look, saying the pencil's small and will come out the other end. Nick sits on the seat of the backyard toilet for what seems hours, but nothing comes out. Menka harangues her husband, saying he's endangering the boy's life. He counters by saying the boy's in no pain which means the pencil's making its way out. To help matters he goes to the local milk bar on Smith Street and returns with a bottle of castor oil, which he forces into the boy with several cups of warm milk. Nothing happens. Menka curses Australia, curses the fact they left the village, curses Vangel for being so stubborn.

That night Nick sleeps between his parents, whimpering during the night, though more because of his mother's tears than from pain or discomfort. He tosses and turns and finally drifts off in a dream. The pencil's growing out of his stomach, growing and growing, until the size of a light pole. He wants to climb to the top of it, certain of seeing *Dedo* and

Baba and his friends counting one-two in playing soldiers along the lane. In the morning, Sunday, Vangel sits the boy on a bucket and crosses his arms. Menka strokes his head, urging him to push with all his might. Nick takes a deep breath and strains to bursting, until everything comes out in a rush. Menka pokes around in the bucket with a stick and cries out in joy. Vangel pushes back his hat and nods, saying anyone who likes pencils so much is destined to become a writer. Menka washes the little pencil and gives it to Nick as a keepsake.

Saturday night, the middle of January, heat radiates from red-brick walls, corrugated fences, bitumen, the bluestone lane beside the house. Too hot to stay indoors, Vangel's taking his wife and son to see the film *Alexander the Great* at the cinema on Johnston Street. He's wearing a light-coloured hat with a green feather that appears to have a watchful eye. It's tilted in a way that tells Nick his father's in a good mood. Menka and Nick are excited by the thought of an indoor cinema. An army jeep would come to the village on summer evenings with a projector on the back. The villagers would set up their chairs and stools in front of a white sheet covering the wall of the barber's shop. When it got dark the projector would light up and people came alive on the sheet. Hearing this, Vangel pulls a face and inserts his toothpick in the band of his hat.

'Never trust Greeks bearing gifts.'

'It was fun,' says Nick.

'Propaganda,' he says, sharply.

Nick doesn't know what the word means. Vangel explains that those pictures are a cunning way of forcing the Greek language into our people's heads. *Baba* Lena knows three Greek words, if those pictures can teach her ten, they'll have succeeded in their propaganda. Nick can't see how those pictures are forcing *Baba* Lena to do anything, but maybe his father knows more about these matters.

They walk down Johnston Street and wait at the Post Office to cross Brunswick Street. As there aren't many cars Nick wants his parents to run across so they don't miss the start, but Vangel stands firm and points to the traffic signal sweeping through red. Nick frowns, wondering why the arm takes longer to travel through red than green, even though both arcs are the same distance.

A crowd's milling about in front of the cinema. The windows are covered in posters showing a blond Alexander on horseback. Nick can hear Greek and Macedonian spoken among the crowd. Vangel knows people wherever they go. He introduces his wife and son to a few families. A man with slicked-back hair pushes through and points to the poster.

'There,' he says in Greek, 'even the English call him Alexander the Greek.'

One of Vangel's friends, a broad-shouldered man with biceps straining a short-sleeve shirt, taps the poster.

'That says Great, not Greek,' he says.

'Great, Greek – it's the same thing.'

'He was Macedonian, you *vlaka*.'

Stung at being called a fool the man throws back *malaka*. Nick knows it's a bad swear word, but not why it always seems to upset men so much. He grips his mother's hand in fear. Vangel and a few others push through to support their friend. Menka calls on him not to get involved. Others rush out from the foyer to assist the Greek. Shouting escalates to pushing and shoving, until a punch is thrown, when the two sides leap at each other. Women scream, some of the bigger boys try to restrain their fathers, ushers in white shirts and red bow ties call on them to stop. Nick's terrified by this explosion of Greek and Macedonian: the two languages seemed like one in the village, while here they're worst enemies. At the sound of a siren the fighting stops and the men, flushed and still seething, act as though nothing has happened. A tall policeman with hands the size of shovels threatens to cancel the picture and send them all home.

'You're in Australia now,' he says. 'Forget the past, look to the future.'

Nick's wide-eyed at the enormous screen and the fact that the film's in colour – the ones in the village square were always black and white. The audience is restless, with people asking one another what this or that means in English. The policeman has stayed behind and stands with arms crossed beside a side door. The audience becomes livelier with each of Alexander's victories. Whenever he refers to his army as Macedonian and his birthplace as Macedon, a cheer erupts from one section of the audience. When he calls himself commander of the Greek forces against the Persians, a different section whistles and applauds. The opposing sections taunt each other, shout abuse, swear in Greek and Macedonian. As tempers rise again, Nick fears another fight, but the policeman quells the unrest by standing in full view of the audience. As the film continues, Nick's absorbed, despite understanding little of what's said. His heart races at the thunderous battle scenes, his fists clench as though gripping the reins of Bucephalus, his eyes fill with tears as soldiers file past the dying king. And on the way home, Alexander's final words – to the best – echo in his ears.

That night Nick's restless in bed, unable to sleep due to a combination of over excitement from the film's images still vivid in his mind and a longing to become like Alexander. Hearing him tossing and turning, Menka whispers to Vangel that he must have a temperature. Nick's forehead is burning with a fever, like Alexander's in Babylon. What if he dies like him? Alexander was in far off Persia, he's in far off Australia. Suddenly he's Alexander, propped up on his deathbed. People are filing past: his parents, *Dedo*, *Baba*, his friends, the whole school. He acknowledges them all with a slight nod. Then Mimi appears and bows over him.

'Alexander,' he whispers, chewing his tongue, 'are you Macedonian or Greek?'

'I'm big enough to be all things.'

Mimi reaches into his pocket, takes out a handful of coins, and selects two, not shillings, but *dekari*, which he places over Nick's eyes. But Nick can see him through the holes as Mimi shambles off toward the cemetery.

Vangel sits Menka and Nick at the kitchen table for a lesson on this country's currency. He spreads the different coins before them and begins naming each, starting with the almost worthless half-penny or ha'penny, followed by the big dark penny, then the tiny thruppence or tray with the three stalks of wheat like that in the village, the sixpence or zac, the shilling or bob, and the two shillings or two bob. They should respect the kings and queens on the faces of the coins, he says, because they allowed foreigners to come to Australia. Nick's favourite is the penny – it's the biggest of the coins, yet worth so little. He likes the kangaroo leaping to the left, toward a seven-pointed star, its back and tail curved, small ears swept back in flight. The penny has a smooth rim and makes a dull sound when dropped on concrete. One almost fills his palm. Vangel points to the year under the kangaroo.

'Always note the year of every penny,' he says.

'1953,' Nick exclaims. 'The year I was born.'

'But the year I was born is even better,' he says. 'A 1930 penny is worth a thousand pounds.'

He doesn't know why, something to do with the fact that not many were made that year. A thousand pounds for a penny! Nick imagines coming across one. It's like finding a magic coin – one that reproduces itself over and over again without any human effort. How many pennies in a thousand pounds? Twelve pennies make a shilling, Vangel explains, and twenty shillings to a pound. Nick's quick to see that 240 pennies make a pound, so there must be 240 thousand in that magic amount. He thinks of his secret *dekara* – the one he took from the girl. He's kept it hidden from everyone, even God, since that strange day just before they left for Australia. It's so light compared to this penny, and yet it weighs on his heart like a gravestone. He thought about burying it in the village cemetery, but those last days were busy and he couldn't sneak away. In the end he slipped it under the lining of his new shoe, where it's remained ever since. Who knows, it might turn out to be a magic coin, too, with the power to take him back to that girl lying in her coffin.

On Saturday mornings he goes shopping with his father on Smith Street. They start from the Johnston Street end and make their way along the Collingwood side. A lot of shops have Greek writing on their windows, but Nick's already confusing the Greek P, which has an 'r' sound, with the English P. What should be a short outing takes a couple of hours because Vangel stops every few minutes to chat with a relative or friend. Nick pulls him by the hand when the conversation lengthens, impatient for his weekly horse ride. Approaching the chemist on the corner, he breaks from his father's grip and runs to the horse at the front door. It's white with black spots, a thick ginger mane and tail, legs flung forward and back as though in flight. He sits on the saddle (far more comfortable than *Dedo*'s mule), grips the leather reins, and waits for his father to slip a few pennies in the slot. As it rocks back and forth, back and forth, he imagines he's Alexander mounted on Bucephalus, leading an army to the end of the world. Vangel waits on the side, hat pushed back, chewing on a toothpick, smiling at his boy's happiness.

Thursday's payday and Nick waits for his mother in front of the large grey building at the corner of Gore and Greeves Streets. She appears from the Smith Street end, walking briskly, her brown handbag in the crook of her arm. The evening meal has to be prepared before his father gets home, so he trots beside her in keeping up. At home she opens a small golden envelope and spills money on the table. They count it together: four pound, seven shillings and eight pence. He unfolds the white ribbon of paper with her pay details. She can't read a word of English, so Nick does his best to make out the handwritten information and confirm what lies on the table. It doesn't seem much for a whole week's work. At the factory Menka's job is to glue the soles of women's shoes. The glue's smell is horrible, she says, especially in hot weather. Standing at the bench, she glues hundreds of pairs a day. Nick recalls her hands working happily at the loom. No wonder she comes home exhausted. She complains of a man she calles *bosso.* They add a short 'o' to certain English words when using them in Macedonian. Street become *streeto,* light is *lighto,* sink *sinko.* By a quirk of language, some of these new words have their own meaning in Macedonian: *bosso* means barefooted, *sinko* is son. Other English words sound the same as some Macedonian words and sayings: l*ook* means garlic, *top* means cannon, *pet* is five, while *ne-ce-ssary* translates to don't shit yourself.

This *bosso* walks up and down the factory floor in heavy boots, pushing the women to work faster, shouting at Menka if she uses a drop too much glue. Nick's never seen his mother look so tired, not even on those long, hot days in the village when she'd get up early to fetch water, spend all day harvesting, then come home to bake bread and weave on the loom. He reaches across the table for her hands and looks into her green-brown eyes. Does she regret leaving the village? Does she miss *Baba* Tonka? She promised *Baba* Lena they'd return in a few years, together with her husband. Will that happen? Somehow Nick doesn't think so. They're already talking of having almost enough for a deposit on a house. Maybe this is what his mother needs – a place of their own, where she won't have to share the kitchen and bathroom with others. A place where she can proudly spread the *chergi* woven on the loom, dress the furniture with her spider-webbed crochet, decorate the walls with her colourful embroidery. Nick feels sorry for her. While his father seems happy enough, and he has settled into school, she's still pining for the village. Nick encourages her, saying they'll all be happier in a place of their own. She pushes a sixpence toward him for his moneybox. He races off and returns rattling a green tin in the shape of a building: State Savings Bank of Victoria.

'Use it to buy a scooter,' she says, as he slips the coin in the slot.

Les has been racing up and down the footpath on a new scooter with brakes controlled from the handlebars rather than a pedal on the back wheel. He charges the boys a penny for a ride around the block.

'No,' says Nick, 'I'm saving for our house.'

She sits him on her lap and hugs him. Her palms have become hard from all those shoes and her clothes smell of glue.

On payday Vangel comes home from work later than usual, smelling of beer, having met with friends at the Birmingham Hotel at the corner of Smith and Johnston Street. He works for the Railways, cleaning and maintaining trains at the Spencer Street yard. He's thankful not to be in a noisy factory, keeping up to a machine, with no time to scratch himself.

Working for the government, he's able to set his own pace, and when things are quiet, as they tend to be after lunch, especially in the warmer months, there's even the opportunity to stretch out for a nap in one of the carriages. Nick opens his brown workbag with its metal clasps at either end and takes out his empty lunch box. Vangel pulls out his pay-packet and gives him a shilling. The other men also come home at about the same time. They've become fond of Nick because they have families in the village, and he reminds them of their sons. They also give him a shilling each. Vangel rattles the moneybox.

'Sounds almost full,' he says.

'Vangel, your Kolche's a good saver,' says Uncle Simo, a man with a big red face.

Nick calls both men uncle even though they're not related.

'What are you saving for?' asks Uncle Milo

'For our house,' he says.

The men laugh and congratulate Vangel on having such a smart son.

'How much is a house?' he asks his father.

'About three thousand pounds.'

'You must have at least three pounds in there,' says Uncle Simo.

'You need to fill a thousand of those,' laughs Uncle Milo.

Nick begins calculating: it's taken about six months to fill one tin, so it will take a whole year to fill two, and five hundred years to fill a thousand. His heart sinks at the thought. Vangel opens a bottle of beer and Menka brings three glasses. Nick likes sitting at the table with the grown-ups, listening to stories of village-life, the Greek Civil War, conditions under the Ottomans, and a topic that always surfaces and arouses strong feelings: are they Macedonian, Greek or, what's new to him, Bulgarian? He first came across the third possibility from his mother's uncle, *Dedo* Naum, whose red hair and freckled hands could pass him for an Australian. He came to Australia in the twenties and, along with others from that period, started a Bulgarian-Macedonian church in Northcote.

This evening the men aren't discussing events in the Balkans a hundred years ago, but something that happened in Fitzroy yesterday. A young friend of theirs from the Macedonian Club on Gertrude Street was arrested for killing his father with a butcher's knife. Nick listens to the details with horror and fascination, remembering how Uncle Milo, who works at the abattoirs, slaughtered a lamb in their backyard and held it over the gully trap, pressing down on it with one knee, until its thick blood drained away. From what he can pick up, it seems the man had wanted to marry an Australian woman, but the father objected, saying he'd disown him if he brought her home. The father stormed through the house, shouting that Australian women couldn't cook or sew or look after a family. They grew their finger nails and painted them red like the women of the street. It was impossible to make *maznik* with long nails. The dough could not be kneaded and rolled and stretched paper-thin with red nails. He'd never accept a daughter-in-law who couldn't make his favourite *maznik*. They argued, tempers flared, and the father let fly at the son with the back of his hand. Blinded by anger, the son grabbed the knife and turned on his father.

'Ah, the poor father,' says Uncle Simo, his face like a watermelon sliced in half. 'He survived Asia Minor, the Civil War, the journey to Australia – only to be killed by his own son. Is there anything more tragic than that?'

'It ended for him in a second,' says Uncle Milo, wiping froth from his mouth. 'I pity the poor son. He'll live with his father's death through years of prison and for the rest of his life. That moment will haunt him for ever.'

'It's this country's fault,' says Vangel. 'No traditions, no respect, sons turn on fathers like hungry wolves.'

The story grips Nick's imagination. Why did the father object to his son marrying an Australian woman? His teacher's Australian – she's blonde and pretty and tall and wears a different dress each day. Yes, her nails are long and painted, but she can draw lifelike figures on the blackboard. And suddenly he's struck by the thought: what if he marries someone like his teacher? Will his father object? Will they fight? And then it occurs to him that by raising the knife against his father that son has in a way saved all other sons from doing the same. He's committed a terrible crime to spare other sons from committing a similar crime. In this, he's a both a criminal and a kind of hero.

After a few more bottles of beer and three glasses of *rakija* Vangel releases a Macedonian song. The two men listen thoughtfully, staring into their glasses. Menka wipes her eyes with the corner of her apron in bringing to the table a plate of fried liver cut in pieces. The men congratulate him on his singing. Nick doesn't understand why people enjoy listening to sad songs.

'Ah, Vangel,' says Uncle Milo, 'you took me back to the village.'

'We feel right at home in your songs,' says Uncle Simo.

'Enjoy them while we can,' says Vangel, raising his glass. 'They'll mean nothing to my boy when he's our age. He'll be singing and dancing rock and roll.'

5

Their first Easter in Australia, Menka and Nick have fasted all week. As the food here is so different from the village Nick doesn't know what's allowed and what's not. He's constantly asking his mother about this or that. Are chocolates allowed? No. Twisties? No. Potato chips? No. Bananas? Yes. At school kids turn pale if they unintentionally eat something forbidden. Others, a bit older, eat regardless, saying their parents will never find out, and that a different God rules Australia. Vangel says food has nothing to do with the soul and the afterlife. He asks Menka if she's ever seen a thin priest. He fasted in the village all year round from necessity and has vowed never to fast again. Menka sees the look in his eyes and doesn't push the point further. The question of which church to attend arises next. As Vangel worked overtime last night they didn't attend the Good Friday service. He's avoided going to church in his time here, but when compelled it's been to St George, the Macedonian Church on Young Street.

'That's where we're going tonight,' he says, tapping the laminated table with his toothpick.

Menka bites the inside of her mouth and glances at the icon resting on top of the kitchen cabinet. A small flame in a cup of oil stares fiercely at them, like the single eye of God that looked down on Nick from the triangle above the altar in the village church. He helped his mother set up the icon when the wooden chest was delivered just after their arrival. It shows a young man in armour mounted on a white horse, killing a dragon by driving a spear into its fiery mouth. At first, he thought it was Alexander on Bucephalus, but his mother said it was Saint George and pointed out the Greek letters of his name. Nick's now confused: is Saint George Greek or Macedonian? Visiting the Macedonian church for a wedding not long ago, he couldn't understand much, the language used by the priest sounding different from what they speak.

'Is that the right church for us?' Menka says softly.

'We're Macedonian,' he says, throwing her a dark look.

'We were born in Greece, not Tito's Yugoslavia.'

'We'll go where I say.'

'And when word gets back to the village you're anti-Greek?'

'And what if it does? We've been silent long enough.'

'There are spies here, Vangel, you've said it yourself. Our own people who report back to the police in the village. A Greek pencil's worse than a gun – they're your words. A black mark beside your name and you'll never be allowed back to the village. Do you want that? We're guests in this country, Vangel. What if tomorrow they don't want us in the factories? What if they tell us to go back to where we came from? Where will we go back? Yugoslavia! We've got parents in the village, brothers and sisters, property and fields. Are you going to turn your back on all that for your precious Macedonia? We've just come out of a Civil War, Vangel. People sang and cheered the Communist promise, but what did that promise bring? Hatred and bloodshed and death in numbers worse than anything we saw under the Germans. Families torn apart, your own uncles fled over the border, forbidden ever to return. Communism was defeated in Greece, Vangel. Don't make the same mistake for the promise of Macedonia.'

Nick's never heard his mother say so much, with such feeling, her bony cheeks red as the pomegranates. He hasn't understood everything, but for some reason his heart's racing, as if to get away from the bloodshed and death. Vangel sits with a grim look, jabbing the back of his hand with the toothpick.

It's dark when they leave the house and set off up George Street. The night's cool, the street lights covered in misty colours. They meet others walking in the same direction. Nick feels safe between his parents, holding their hands tightly, buttoned in his new grey gabardine coat. They turn right into Gertrude Street and pass the Macedonian Club where his father plays cards on most Saturday afternoons. The owner has promised Vangel a job on weekends. What seems like a pile of rags stirs in a dark doorway that stinks of the toilet-can in the village. Vangel says he's a homeless drunk and the street is full of them. The pile groans as they walk past. Nick's unable to comprehend the word homeless. Everyone in the village had a home, even Tanas who lived up the lane and would often stagger drunk up from the village square, cursing the boys for teasing him.

'Isn't he cold?' Nick asks.

'He's got his bottle of methylated spirits.'

'Does he keep warm by rubbing it onto his cheeks?'

'By drinking it,' Vangel laughs. 'It fires his body just like *rakija*.'

Nick doesn't understand: Australia's supposed to be a rich country, richer than the village, and yet people are sleeping in doorways and drinking what *Dedo* called poison. Further on his grip on their hands tightens as two men approach, swaying as they walk. They're long-haired and black skinned, much blacker than the gypsies that came to the village. *Baba* Lena would often warn him about coming home after dark, saying the gypsies would grab him and carry him off to their wagons and eat him. The thought terrified him because he once saw some gypsies kill a snake and boil it in a pot for their dinner.

'How 'bout a bob, mate?' says one, putting out a big flat hand.

'Sorry, no hev money,' says Vangel.

'Get stuffed then,' he says, pointing upward with his thumb.

'Are they gypsies?' Nick asks, remembering how they went around the village begging.

'Aborigines,' says Vangel. 'Lots of them live in Fitzroy.'

'Why are they so black?'

'It's the way God made them, just like he made you white.'

'Where are they from?'

'They've always lived in Australia.'

Nick's confused: he thought Australians were white, with names like Timmy Conway and Julie Reed, and all the others here have come from somewhere else.

'They're the true Australians,' he continues. 'They were here even before Alexander's time. This is their land.'

'If it's their land why are they begging?'

'Let's cross,' says Vangel.

A tram rattling up from the Smith Street end rings several times and grinds to a stop in front of them. A lot of people get off, all dressed for church, some speaking Macedonian, others Greek. The conductor's arguing with a man about paying his fare.

'Money, money, I want your money,' says the conductor, shaking the coins in the leather bag strapped over one shoulder.

'Moo-ni, moo-ni, I not have a moo-ni,' says the man.

Laughter burst from all sides.

'Don't swear at me in your lingo,' says the conductor.

The older boys in the village school made the girls blush by saying this Greek word. Nick thinks it's like when the boys here tease the girls with: I'll give you a zac if you open your crack. Kitse, Vangel's friend, jumps off and comes over to them.

'There'll be a good turnout tonight,' he says.

'We're not going to St George's,' says Vangel, lowering the brim of his hat.

Kitse lights a cigarette and gives Nick the lighted match. He's taught him to hold it this way and that until the stick's completely black. Fire needs to be fed, he told Nick some time ago, and it's wasteful to throw away a partly burnt match.

'The wife wants to go to *Evangelismos*,' says Vangel.

'It's what I know from the village,' says Menka.

'But you're Macedonian, your boy's Macedonian.'

'And his boy will be Australian,' says Menka.

Kitse shakes his head and walks off toward narrow Young Street. They continue with a group of other Macedonian-speakers down Napier Street, toward Victoria Parade, and the small, red-brick Greek Church on the corner.

The midnight service ends with firecrackers: penny bungers explode in the background, while packs of tiny tom-thumbs stutter and crackle cheekily around people's feet. A bell rings. People shake hands, greeting each other with 'Christ has arisen' and replying 'He's truly arisen'. Within minutes a firework display bursts from the Macedonian church on the other side of Victoria Parade. A bell also rings, deeper in tone than the one here. For an instant it's like both bells are in a contest, each trying to out-sound the other, to convince the world that it has the true sound, the rhythm that best expresses Christ's resurrection. But then, maybe because of his drowsiness, the competing bells begin to sound friendlier toward each other, to resonate with each other, like two instruments playing the same melody, so there's no more right or wrong, Greek or Macedonian, just the happiness of two bells each ringing a different tone, but uniting to produce a common melody, one that quivers in the air above Melbourne. The flame spreads quickly from the priest's thick candle to hundreds of smaller candles straining for light. A man standing next to Nick lowers his candle with a smile. He's unshaven, wearing a dark overcoat, with a gleam in his light-blue eyes. For an instant Nick feels he's been in this situation before, receiving the holy flame from this very stranger, even though it's his first Easter in Australia.

As they set off, Nick holds the candle close to his chest, guarding the flame from a light breeze by cupping it with a crimson hand. He's determined to keep his alight all the way home. In the village last Easter, he was the only one in the family whose flame didn't go out. His mother took it from him and made a black, smoky cross on the lintel of the front door. She then walked with the candle through the dark house, making the sign of the cross in each room. She kissed him on the forehead for being so protective of the flame and said his efforts would be rewarded with good health and good fortune. Her words now echo in his ears. They have good health but need good fortune to buy their own home and settle in this country. No, he can't save much in his moneybox to help toward the house, but he can protect the flame. He can guard it with his hand despite the heat.

They stop under the leafy elm trees in the middle of Victoria Parade as two groups of youths hurl abuse at each other from either side of the street.

'We should be on the other side,' says Vangel, blowing out his candle.

A red-tailed rocket from the Macedonian side whizzes over the Greeks. They respond with a volley of penny-bungers. Soon both groups cross the street and throw crackers at each other from behind the hedges running along the tram tracks. Caught in the cross-fire, Vangel shepherds them to the shelter of a tree trunk. The sudden movement extinguishes Menka's candle. Nick now guards his so closely the pain's unbearable. They huddle at the foot of the tree, waiting for a chance to slip away. The exchange of crackers intensifies, the shouting and swearing increases, threats to kill each other fly back and forth. The anger's worse than at the cinema.

'I thought we left this madness in the Balkans,' says Menka.

'Our boys will teach them a lesson,' says Vangel, a glint in his eyes.

'No respect for Christ,' she sighs.

There's an explosion nearby and a Greek youth covers his face and screams he's been blinded. In an instant both groups jump over the hedges and charge at each other in a terrible scramble on the tram tracks.

'Let's go,' says Vangel.

He leads them away from the fighting, to a break in the hedges, through which they hurry to the other side. The sudden rush stirs Nick's flame. For a moment it appears it might flutter off in the night, never to be seen again, but he manages to calm its fears and restore its stillness. Making their way to George Street, Nick glances over his shoulder at the scramble of bodies: there's no telling Greek from Macedonian, and even their voices mix to a meaningless babble.

6

Vangel bought the two-storey house on McKean Street against the advice of relatives who said he'd never get his money back when time came to sell. The house has five bedrooms, fireplaces with marble surrounds, a steep flight of stairs, and a balcony trimmed with lacework that looks over rooftops to the elms of the nearby Edinburgh Gardens. There are more rooms than they need, but Vangel bought it knowing he could rent them to new arrivals from Greece. He also laughs they'll need the extra rooms when other children come along. This kind of talk disturbs Nick. He doesn't want a brother or sister. It's been hard enough accepting a father into his life, and now they want him to accept brothers and sisters. No, he's happy being an only child. They'll need his approval if that's what they're planning. After all, he's the one who'll be most put out by an addition to the family.

A month after moving in Vangel rents one of the upstairs rooms to two sisters from Kalamata. Too poor to provide dowries, yet not wanting his daughters to be spinsters, their father sold a plot or two for their fare to Australia, seeing this as less draining than a dowry. Once settled and working the girls are expected to help pay the way for other family members to join them. At first Nick resents their presence as an intrusion to their quiet life. His Greek fading, he struggles to understand them. But the women are affectionate toward him, never failing to give him sixpence on payday, which endears him to them. They remind him of his teacher in the village when they recite the alphabet and the numbers and the Our Father, which he's almost forgotten. They've also got him to do his cross before going to bed each night, saying it will keep bad dreams away. Bristling at his son being subjected to Greek, Vangel holds back, not wanting to offend two clean, hard-working boarders who pay their rent on time. Yes, he thinks, better his boy learns a Greek prayer than carry a mortgage around his neck for longer than necessary.

Nick's happy in North Fitzroy: it's sunny and spacious, unlike Fitzroy, with its tiny rundown houses, smelly back lanes, and those pubs along Gertrude Street whose homeless drinkers end up in doorways and lanes. Something about the light and sky here reminds him of the village, even though his memories of that time and place are becoming less clear. The streets are much wider, the backyards bigger, and then there's the freedom of the Edinburgh Gardens. The park, as the neighbourhood boys call the Gardens, is bounded on one side by the wide arc of Alfred Crescent – a street with large double-fronted homes, a two-storey residence with a tower, and a mysterious place called The Haven.

Within days of arriving Nick makes friends with the neighbourhood kids. They're from different backgrounds – Italians, Greeks, Australians, Macedonians, Serbs, Maltese – yet they're all alike in having a sense of adventure, a street-cunning sharpened by want, and a nose for making a penny, if not a quid. Most go to Fitzroy North Primary on Alfred Crescent. The Italian boys are either at St John's on Queens Parade, which goes to grade 2, or at St Thomas further up on McKean Street, which starts at grade 2 and goes to form 4. Most of the boys live on McKean Street, Grant Street, Groome Street and Alfred Crescent.

Nick spends his free time in the park, especially on what they call The Hill, though it's nothing more than a good-sized mound of earth covered in stones and scrub. On weekends it's overrun with kids playing Cowboys and Indians, rolling car tyres, slinging stones from shanghais, and riding roughshod on rusty corrugated sheets. Some of the Australian boys whose fathers were born in this area say The Hill grew out of a tip, and that dead babies are buried beneath it, along with horses and dogs and cats.

When they tire of scrambling up and down The Hill there's always the prospect of adventure in the Council Yard: a rectangle of land fenced by the National Can Factory at the rear, the tattered remnants of a hedge at the front, and a row of shiny-leaved shrubs at both end. Nick and his mates spend hours playing hide-and-seek among the grassy humps and dips, the tangled blackberry bushes, the strong-smelling fennel. Neglected by the gardeners who tend the park and its flowerbeds, it's become a dumping ground for all sorts of rubbish. And for more adventure, there's the timber yard, the depot with rail wagons containing briquettes and grain both loose and in sacks, the wooden footbridge spanning McKean Street and Freeman Street, and the Brunswick Street Oval, the home ground of the Fitzroy Football Club.

More than anything it's the park – the openness, the elms like the one near his house in the village, the smell of fresh-mowed grass – that draws Nick with a sense of belonging in Australia. Before long he knows the feel underfoot of every path, the softest patches of grass, the scent of different shrubs after a night of rain, the taps with the highest spurt. And he knows the monuments: the years on Captain Cook's plaque near the main entrance of the Brunswick Street Oval, the dedication on the pedestal in the circular flowerbed, the round bandstand with its columns resembling a Greek temple. On summer evenings as groups of people sit on blankets spread on the grass, talking and singing in different languages, Nick and his mates play hide-and-seek among the elms deep into the night, until, exhausted, they lie down beside their parents and gaze up at the stars. When his father says it's still afternoon in the village, Nick wonders how it could be both day and night at the same time. The night sky reminds him of *Dedo* Risto, whose features he barely recalls. The stars here are fewer and smaller than above the village. Sitting together in the courtyard, he'd point out the trill of a nightingale or the call of an owl. God has given each person their own star, he once said. When Nick asked which one was his, *Dedo* replied the visible stars belonged to the rich and powerful, and those belonging to poorer people like themselves were too small to be seen. At the time Nick questioned this unfairness and vowed to make his star visible.

And beyond the park, Nick's walked all the streets in the area, as far north and east as the lively Merri Creek, west to Nicholson Street, and south to Alexandra Parade. He knows the shops with the best chips and potato cakes, fish being too expensive. He's discovered the backdoors of factories – Weaties, Colvan, MacRobertsons – and how to sneak inside when the watchman's not on guard and grab from the conveyor belt a handful of warm cornflakes, potato chips, or a chocolate bar. He's learnt how to catch yabbies in the pond at the Exhibition Gardens, which he sells to the bigger boys, who in turn sell them to the zoo. And running parallel to every named street, behind the rows of numbered houses, there's the unnamed and unnumbered bluestone lanes, which he and the others have explored thoroughly, looking for adventure and excitement, unexpected twists and turns, trash that might contain some treasure, fruit trees with overhanging branches, factory yards where something might be found to win a word of praise from their fathers.

Living three long drop-kicks from Fitzroy's ground, he's soon drawn by the roar of supporters on wintry Saturday afternoons, when Fords and Holdens fill McKean Street. He enters the ground by crawling under the cyclone fence in the tennis courts, though not to watch the game, but to weave through the standing crowd and collect empty soft drink bottles, for which he receives sixpence a dozen. People shout and swear and call someone a white maggot, but all this goes over his head. His eyes ferret amongst shoes for the glint of a bottle, his ears echo with the chuckle of pennies, his thoughts are fixed on offering his earnings to his father, who'll smile and say how proud he is to have such a son, and how this will help pay off the house.

Relatives and friends are always stopping by their place, especially on weekends, because it's on their way to and from the tram that runs along Queens Parade and Smith Street. They let themselves in from the back gate and sit in the small kitchen which Menka keeps spotless, making sure there's not so much as a breadcrumb on the *cherga* covering the floor. Vangel's quick to offer these passers-by a bottle of beer, but most prefer

Menka's Turkish coffee, saying nobody makes it as good, with the just right measure of sugar, and alive with black froth, which they drink with a satisfied slurp. Of those who drop in regularly, Nick likes listening to *Dedo* Naum, who lives on Rowe Street. He always wears a dark suit and before sitting down takes off his hat for Nick to put in the other room. He's about sixty, pale-skinned, with ginger hair kept short back and sides. He came here as a young man in 1926 and looks and acts every bit like an Australian, so much so that he doesn't slurp his coffee, saying people here consider it ill-mannered. He tells stories about his days in the village, about serving in the Greek Army and fighting the Turks in 1922, when a bullet left a crater in his wrist, about his early years in Australia, working as a tree-cutter, clearing gum trees for farming land. Something about his storytelling – the tone and colour of his Macedonian words, the light and shade that plays over his face spotted with freckles, the lines on his forehead opening and closing like an accordion – excites Nick's imagination. It's like he's watching a film at the cinema, losing all sense of time and place, coming out of himself and entering *Dedo* Naum's world.

The kitchen's cosy, especially on rainy afternoons when his mother's cooking and the kerosene heater's glowing red. Nick could sit and listen to *Dedo* Naum for hours. They haven't got a television, like some of his friends, and maybe this is why his imagination is so lively, why these stories make such an impression. They're entertaining, often funny, sometimes sad, but in the end they are only words, and it's what he makes of them, as much as how they're said, that turns what to an Australian would be meaningless sounds into the stuff of life. When *Dedo* Naum sits cross-legged in his favourite place, there in the corner, on the chrome stool between the table and the kitchen-cabinet, when he sips his coffee, clicking his cup on the thin saucer decorated with small blue flowers, when he talks about what he's gone through, his words fall like pebbles in a pond, rippling through Nick, stirring his feelings, arousing his wonder, becoming indistinguishable from what he experienced yesterday, what he will remember tomorrow.

Things are usually quiet and orderly at home, except when Vangel's late for dinner, which Menka always sets at six, according to the green clock that sits plumply, full of ticking, on the tin containing her scissors and measuring-tape. When he's late home from The Recreation, the pub on the corner of Grant Street and Queens Parade, or, on weekends, from the Macedonian Club, Menka calls him this or that – expressions whose sting is more in how they're said, accompanied by an axe-like hand gesture, than in their meaning. She was timid around Vangel in the first few months after their arrival, maybe because after three years apart they were like strangers and needed time to know each other, but she's more outspoken these days, scolding him for the beer on his breath or the stink of cigarette-smoke in his clothes. But even on these occasions, when she's red with anger, Nick senses she's not all that angry, more just making out, as if this is what a wife's supposed to say to a husband who's late for dinner. Vangel takes it all calmly, blaming the slow service in the crowded pub or the close nature of the card game. Yes, he looks remorseful, shakes his head apologetically, avoids her eyes, yet all the time unable to conceal a smile from tugging at the left corner of his mouth. Their quarrels are short-lived and by the end of the day they're calling each other by their first name and discussing whether to buy Greek or Bulgarian fetta from the Vic Market, whose prices vary from week to week, with Vangel preferring the saltier Bulgarian, saying Greeks are better at roasting sheep than milking them.

But when all's said and done, Nick knows his parents work hard, never refuse overtime, and live modestly in order to pay off the mortgage hanging over their heads. On Saturday mornings Vangel buys a ticket from the busy Tattersalls shop on Smith Street, hoping to win the weekly prize of twenty-five thousand pound. But coming from a village, knowing only hardship and thrift, Nick doubts the win would change their lifestyle. They'd still make their sandwiches from a loaf of split-Vienna (sliced bread is too expensive), set off early for the factory, and work that extra hour if asked by the boss. With each passing year in Australia, Nick sees more clearly and painfully the sacrifice they made settling here. They left their parents and the language they were born in, for a country whose alphabet they'll never recite, where they'll always stand out as migrants. Why? So their son wouldn't have to struggle in stony fields and labour in smelly factories.

Is it because Nick's an only child that their house is so quiet? The homes of his friends are loud with squabbling and fighting among children, and sometimes frightening arguments between parents. He thinks of Dom, an Italian kid who lives on the other side of the footbridge. His father comes looking for him with a a length of timber if he's so much as a few minutes late going home from the Busy Bee: the thriving, two-storey shop on the corner of McKean and Grant Street run by Taki, a Greek the boys call Boss. This is their meeting place, where they swap football cards in winter, play nearest the wall with pennies, spin Coca-Cola yo-yos in summer, or just sit on the kerb and talk, going deep into the night during the Christmas holidays. Dom's been whacked lots of times in front of them by his father: a slow-walking man who can be heard a block away whistling the Tarantella. Nick's seen the welts and bruises on his legs, but Dom's tough, always fighting at school, and says they're nothing compared to the shiners his older brother cops from the old man.

This evening as little Archie's singing along with the Beatles' 'Will you still love me when I'm sixty-four', only mistaking the words on his scratchy transistor radio as 'Will you still love me when I'm six-foot four', Dom pricks up his ears, scowls, and runs off without a word. They know what he's heard – his ears are like a dog's when it came to that whistle – and so Nick and a few others set off after him, keeping their distance. They follow him around the dark, back-fenced end of Alfred Crescent, thinking he's going this way to avoid his old man coming up McKean Street. At the footbridge, instead of racing over it and home, Dom turns back onto McKean Street, and, using the cover of parked cars, stalks the whistler, who taps the timber on the footpath as though on an evening stroll. They watch from behind a truck. Nick's heart's beating hard, partly from concern for Dom, partly because he wants him to have it out with his father, to stand up to him the way he confronts the bullies at school. Whispering, they agree to run out and surround the old man if he so much as raises a finger against their friend. But then something strange happens right in front of Mrs Brown's shop: a sleepy little milk bar serving mainly the Australian families in the neighbourhood, who don't like what's become of the Busy Bee since the greasy Greek took over. It's dark now, but in the pale light spilling from the shop they watch in disbelief as Dom snatches the timber from his old man and raises it as though to bash him on the head. A stand-off follows. Old Mrs Brown appears in the window, shaking her head. Still whistling, the old man reaches out for the timber. Dom tenses up and swears at him in Italian. The old man casually unbuckles the wide belt around his oil-stained overalls and wraps it around his hand, still whistling, but now sharper, as if coming from between his teeth. That whistle sends a chill down Nick's spine, freezes them all, including Dom, who lowers the timber. Nick can barely watch as the old man lets fly with the belt. Dom covers his head with his arms and takes it without a word, just as he cops the strap at school, leather raining upon him, the timber prodding him toward the bridge. Crouching behind the truck, they can do no more than watch as father and son disappear in the shadows at the end of McKean Street – helpless witnesses to a violence that started with love gone wrong.

On a sultry evening brewing with an approaching storm, Nick's at the kitchen window, watching for the back gate to open. It's almost seven and his father's not back from work. He winces as lightning flickers like a snake's tongue above the factory on the other side of the lane. The table's set with fresh bread, olives, a plate of fried salt-fish, and three empty bowls waiting to be filled with lentil soup steaming in the pot on the stove. Menka's looking cross, biting her lips. A burst of thunder shakes the house, stirring the flame in the icon case. She lights it every Friday, and sometimes, like today, lets Nick put the match to the small wick floating in the glass of olive oil. The sky suddenly crumbles and falls on the kitchen's corrugated roof.

'May he get soaked to the bone and burn with fever,' she says, ladling out the soup smelling of garlic.

But Nick can tell she doesn't really mean it, because she'd have to nurse him back to health. Just as they start eating, the gate rattles open and shut. Menka threatens to lock him out, says he deserves to spend the night in the shed, but she continues eating, cooling the soup with her breath. Vangel enters with a gust of wind, wearing a clear plastic bag from head to ankles. On his shoulder, also wrapped in plastic, he balances a cardboard box. Nick laughs as he stands there, water dripping on the *cherga*.

'If you don't use your head,' he smiles, 'it gets rained on.'

He's worn the plastic all the way from the city, even aboard the tram.

'Weren't you embarrassed?' Nick asks. 'Didn't people laugh?'

'Let them laugh,' he says. 'They'll be the ones catching cold.'

'What's in the box?' Menka scowls, not looking up from her soup.

Vangel slips out of the plastic bag and pulls open the box.

'Look,' he says, as though performing a magic trick.

They've been talking about getting a television set, but he's brought home a record player instead. He stopped off in the city after work and bought it on terms, there and then, ten pound down, with twelve monthly payments of five quid each. Seventy pounds, thinks Nick, annoyed at the image of a dog sitting before a gramophone. He should have put the money toward a television which has both pictures and sound. Arms crossed tight, Menka shakes her head. Vangel turns from his wife to his son, surprised by their reaction, maybe expecting them to be dancing with joy around the record player. He removes it from the box and offers it to Menka, but she backs away, telling him to return it.

'What possessed you?' she snaps. 'You know we can't afford it.'

He replies in a calm tone that music's important to their wellbeing, maybe as important as her faith, in that it provides strength to meet life's challenges. Just as dough can't rise without yeast, so the human spirit can't rise to the demands of tomorrow without a dose of music today. Yes, it cost a lot, but what price can one put on joy?

'Joy,' Menka stops him short. 'Where's my joy, husband? For seventy pounds I could've bought a sewing machine with an overlocker – something useful, profitable. There's money in doing alterations for people and in making your calico underpants. Where's the gain in that thing? It keeps you from work and spends your money on records. Joy? Yes, it's the sound of a washing machine as it twists and turns. I'm still washing by hand, in case you've forgotten, still heating the water in that old copper with scraps of wood. Try washing on a winter's morning before setting off for the factory, then talk to me about the joy of music.'

Vangel tries putting his arm around her, assuring her she'll have all those things in time, but she shrugs him off. Nick doesn't know what to say or who to support, though his mother's eyes brimming with tears swings his sympathy her way. Unused to such tension Nick's about to leave the kitchen, when the doorbell rings sharply. He runs off and opens to two couples, Vangel's relatives, who have driven all the way from Reservoir. On such occasions the men usually sit at the kitchen table to a game of cards, where Nick likes keeping score, while the women gather in the living room. Tonight, surprised by the record player, they ask Vangel to set it up. Menka remains tight-lipped. Vangel locates a pile of small records which have come as gifts from overseas. Within minutes, a space is cleared and the men are dancing and singing in Macedonian. The women soon join in, except Menka who complains of sore legs from standing in the factory all day, until she's also drawn into the circle and her soreness disappears. For what seems like hours Nick watches from a corner of the room as they play and replay the records, dancing and clapping, forgetting the storm raging outside, forgetting the factories waiting in the dark, forgetting the language they'll never fully understand. Those familiar songs and dances lighten their bodies, raise their spirits, give them wings to fly back to the carefree days of their youth. As the storm eases so does the look on Menka's face, until a smile breaks through and she glances affectionately at her husband. When the visitors leave Nick watches through drowsiness his parents waltzing slowly to a final song. He hears his mother whisper that she'll make a bright cover for the record player.

7

Vangel now works in the Macedonian Club on weekends, starting just after they moved into McKean Street. The house cost three thousand, seven-hundred pounds. At the time Nick calculated that by saving eight pounds a week they'd pay it off in eight years, when he'd be fifteen. Menka wasn't happy him taking on weekend work, saying he should be spending more time with his son (meaning also with her), but he waved away her complaint, telling her not to meddle in the affairs of men. Had she forgotten how shameful debt was in the village? During the war, despite staring at his last handful of flour, his father refused to borrow a drachma from his well-off brother-in-law: a wheeler and dealer who wore a three-piece suit with a gold chain smiling between vest pockets, and who mixed with politicians in Salonika. His father was a proud man, so was he, and so too would be his little Kolche. The extra money from the Club would help pay off the house sooner, saving them hundreds in interest.

'We're Macedonians,' he said, pushing back his hat, 'not Australians. The ones around here rent till they die, or take thirty years to pay-off their mortgage.'

As for spending more time with his son, he eventually solved that problem very conveniently: when Nick turned ten Vangel began taking him to the Club, as his littler assistant.

The Macedonian Club's on the lower level of a two-storey building on Gertrude Street, between Brunswick and Napier Street. Behind the frosted glass façade the large room is arranged with round tables surrounded by chairs. The once gloss-white walls are now yellow from cigarette smoke. Prints and photographs hang from the walls: pictures of bearded men, soldiers with bullet-belts crossed on their chests, a map of Greece and Yugoslavia, with Macedonia circled in red. The kitchen's at the back. Apart from being a venue for cards and coffee, the Club's also a kind of home-away-from-home, a place where men come for a traditional meal of thick bean soup spiced with pepper seed, or brown lentil soup, and, on a good day, homemade pies with leeks, mincemeat, cheese and pumpkin. *Rakija* is also served, though secretly, disguised as water. The Club's owned and run by Vic and his wife and daughters. On weekdays they serve breakfast starting at five-thirty, before workers set off for the factories, followed by lunch and dinner. This is convenient for those living in rooming houses without cooking facilities. The Club's known far and wide, even back in the old country. Sometimes a man will arrive straight from Station Pier, carrying the address in one hand and a suitcase in the other. He'll soon enough meet someone who knows someone he knows. It's a first point of contact in the New World, where often accommodation and work are quickly arranged. Vic refers to the Club as the Macedonian Government: the place where decisions are made, business deals struck, marriages discussed, funerals arranged, and where the idea for the Macedonian church on Young Street was born.

Vangel makes coffees at the back on a gas stove and brings them out with glasses of water on a tray. He's also a timekeeper, recording on a small blackboard with chalk how long cardplayers remain at a table, for which they contribute to an hourly rate. Each table has its own blackboard hanging from a hook on the wall. As this requires vigilance, Vangel has taught Nick to keep time from the clock on the wall. Nick likes the quickness of the work: keeping an eye on each table, clearing coffee cups and glasses, emptying ashtrays, seeing coins flying across the table at the end of a game, listening to the winners rejoice and the losers curse. The men play various games involving points, with the winner collecting a few shillings. They talk about manilla, too, but it's played in other places, for much higher stakes. Vic doesn't allow manilla, saying this is a social club, a place where men come together for conversation not conflict, where the married can go home to their wives with their weekly wages in their pockets, and the unmarried can save to bring over family members. No, Vic insists that the Club isn't a place that ruins men and destroys families, rather one that maintains the Macedonian way of life in the New World.

Policemen visit The Club regularly, sometimes twice a day. Vic calls one of them Sergeant Tornton, unable to pronounce Thornton, because Macedonian, his mother-tongue, doesn't have the 'th' sound which is common in Greek. Greeks, on the other hand, can't pronounce 'ch' and 'sh' which are common in Macedonian. So a Macedonian of Vic's generation speaking Greek would refer to the ocean as *talassa* instead of *thalassa*, while a Greek would say fis'n'tsips, instead of fish'n'chips, even though they have a monopoly on this kind of shop.

'Good afternoon, Sergeant Tornton,' says Vic, greeting him and another officer.

They're big men, wide-shouldered, much taller than the average Macedonian. They enter with a serious look, shining shoes huge, thundering on the bare floorboards. The patrons stop talking and lay their cards face down. There are no coins or *rakija* glasses on the tables, as Vic insists, both being forbidden by the authorities. Once a patron has knocked back a shot of *rakija*, Vangel and Nick make sure the small glass is promptly taken to the kitchen and washed. As the policemen walk through the Club, looking left and right, patrons cower from their hard gaze. Nick stands in the corner, terrified by their bearing.

'I've got a good mind to book you blokes,' says the Sergeant, chest puffed out, big thumbs stuck in his belt. 'This isn't the bloody old country. You're in Australia now – we don't play cards for money in our clubs and we don't drink homemade alcohol.'

He goes to a table of four players, his hat knocking a fly-covered sticky strip hanging from the light shade.

'What are you blokes doing there?'

'Notin', just talkin' for da village,' says one of the players.

'Talking, my arse,' he says. 'I can smell the grappa on your breath.'

'We hev little drink in may house before come here,' says the man. 'Little glass for may nameday. May name Goche, George, today special for Saint George.'

'Don't get cocky with me, mate.'

'I tell you for sure, may name George. Ask Mr. Vic, ask may friends.'

'Look, I don't give a stuff about your name. I want to give you some friendly advice. I want to give you all some friendly advice. Now listen good. You blokes shouldn't be in here on a Saturday afternoon. How are you going to become good Australians speaking nothing but your lingo, drinking your grappa, and playing them foreign card games? To become good Australians you got to get away from these places, mix with Australians, speak our language. You got to go down to the Brunswick Street Oval and barrack for Fitzroy. Carna Roys! Can you say that?'

'Carna Roys,' says the man called George.

'Good,' says the Sergeant. 'Now I want you all to say it. Carna Roys.'

'Carna Roys,' the patrons chorus.

'Louder.'

The Club fills with a roar.

'Like a real bloody cheer squad,' he grins. 'Like real bloody Australians. Say, Vic, I reckon I need to come here each week to give these blokes a few lessons in becoming Australians.'

He gives a loud chuckle and they disappear with Vic in the back. The patrons relax a little, a murmur rising from the tables. Several are asking each other what Carna Roys means, and whether it's English, as they haven't heard the words before. A man with a silver front tooth, who speaks Macedonian, but comes to the Club with a Greek newspaper tucked under his arm, explains it's what football fans cry out supporting their team. The policemen sit down to a meal of cheese pie, fried liver and a few shots of *rakija*, after which Nick sees Vic slip the Sergeant a ten-pound note. The patrons are subdued as the policemen eat in the kitchen. When they come out again George shouts Carna Roys. The Sergeant bellows his approval.

'I'll have you all barracking for Fitzroy. Don't forget, Vic. Keep the Club clean, keep the machines out, keep gambling out, don't go down the track of them dago espresso bars – they're dens of vice and we're coming down hard on them. We raided one last week on Brunswick Street, pulled out the machines, smashed them to bits there and then, right on the footpath, reporters had a field day.'

As they make their way to the front door, the Sergeant fixes Nick with a steely look that almost makes him piss his pants. Nick's seen him before, but never as mean-looking as today. He points to Nick and draws him with a hooked finger. Nick shrinks before his own reflection in the policeman's belt buckle.

'How old are you, sonny?'

Nick's throat tightens, his words catch, he turns to his father, who raises his eyebrows, encouraging him to answer.

'Ten in October,' he falters.

'Ten in October – what?'

'The eighteenth,' he says.

'Ten in October – Sergeant Thornton,' he growls.

'Ten in October, Sergeant Thornton,' Nick repeats in a broken voice.

'And what are you doing in here, young fella?'

He turns again to his father.

'He may son, Sergean'. Ay workin' here. The boy wait for me go home.'

'Gertrude Street's no place for children, mister. Want to make a delinquent of him? Want him to pick up bad habits? Want him ending up in jail? Then keep him at home or I'll have you before the courts for being a bad father.'

Vangel turns pale at the mention of court and bad father.

'He no go out on street. He good boy, stay here. Ay watch all time.'

The Sergeant thinks for a moment, removes his hat, and runs his wide palm over his short back and sides.

'You look like a pretty sharp nipper,' he says. 'What's your name?'

'Nick Mangos, Sergeant Thornton.'

'Well, Nick, how'd you like to earn yourself two bob?'

Nick nods. Vangel looks more relaxed. The patrons are silent with curiosity.

'Are you a fast runner?'

Nick nods.

'Run this fiver up to the Champion – know where the Champion is?'

Nick knows it's the pub across the street. He's seen drunks staggering out of its doors, men with blue and red tattoos having a punch up, and black people, men and women, drinking inside.

'Good boy. Ask for Mick, the barman. Give him this and tell him Horny Thorny wants two quid on horse five in race three, and three quid on horse two in race five. Can you remember that?

Nick repeats his instructions, at which the policeman ruffles his hair, hands him the five-pound note and two-shilling tip.

'Bright kid,' he says to Vangel. 'Fair-haired, blue-eyed – doesn't look like your typical wog, could pass for one of us.'

Nick races out the Club, leaps over the cobbled gutter, and dashes across Gertrude Street, saying aloud the instructions over and over. He slows down in approaching the Champion. It and the Rob Roy on the corner diagonally opposite are places he always passes with trepidation, even fear. On the corner an elderly couple is screaming and calling each other names. Men come out from the pub and form a ring around them. The man's skinny, in baggy trousers, with large ears. The woman's big, straining a floral dress, flabby armed. At one point she grabs the man by the ear and pulls him away. He grimaces like a child, while the audience howls in laughter. Nick's nervous about entering the pub alone – he's been in others on his paper rounds, but they're in North Fitzroy, and quiet compared to the two at this intersection. The Sergeant's look drives him inside. The bar's crowded with drinkers. A jug of beer passes over Nick's head, froth spilling on his shirt. He brushes it away, but his hands now smell of beer. He's beginning to question accepting the policeman's offer, but there's no turning back. Spotting a likely opening to the bar, he taps the back of a man in a green suit and matching hat.

'What is it, sonny?' he asks, sharply.

Nick hesitates, at which the man raises his glass and drinks in a way Nick's never seen before: he throws back his head and pours the beer down his throat as though down a drain.

'A lemonade, that what you're after?'

'Hey, Mick,' he shouts to the bartender, 'a glass of lolly-water for squirt here. Gotta look after our street-kids, mate. The little beggars will be the ones defending us from the Japs next time round. Live round here, son? In the slums across the road? Well, you won't be there too long. The government's bulldozing everything down – shops, houses, factories – to make way for brand new flats, twenty storeys high, you'll be out of the gutter and up with the stars.'

Mick places a glass of red lemonade on the counter.

'Scuse me, Mick,' says Nick.

'What is it cobber?

'Sergeant Thornton sent me ...'

'Horny Thorny?'

Nick takes the note from his pocket and raises it to the counter.

'Squirt's a runner for Horny Thorny,' says the man in the suit.

'What's he want? The daily double, trifecta, quinella?'

With Mick's beefy face beaming over the bar and everyone staring, Nick suddenly become nervous, confusing the amount of each bet, the number of the horse, the race.

'Come on, cobber,' says Mick, taking a pencil from behind his ear and a scrap of paper from his shirt pocket. 'I gotta run the bet upstairs before the bloody races, not after 'em.'

The place fills with laughter. Nick can feel his face turning red as the lemonade on the counter. He stops the numbers swirling in his head and settles for what seems right.

'He wants three quid on horse five in race two, and two quid on horse three in race five.'

Mick scribbles the numbers with his left hand and marches off to place the bet. Nick's gripped by uncertainty. Women in colourful dresses and make-up and puffed-up hair are talking and laughing in a room on the other side. There's still time to call Mick back, tell him he might have confused the numbers, but he doesn't want to appear a fool, not in front of all these drinkers, who'd drown him in laughter. When Mick dashes up the stairs, Nick turns to go, sensing a cloud settling over him, darkening the surroundings.

'Your lemonade,' says the man in the suit, resting a hand with several rings on Nick's shoulder.

But his words are distant, meaningless, and in the swirling cloud all he can hear is Sergeant Thornton's thunderous voice repeating over and over: two, three, five – three, two, five – two, five, three – three, five, two.

When his father asks whether he delivered the Sergeant's message, Nick nods, without looking him in the eyes. The afternoon passes in a blur, with the numbers sounding in his head. He considers asking his father if he remembers what the Sergeant said, but this will only make him suspicious. He can still see the numbers Mick wrote on the scrap of paper, but how to ascertain what the Sergeant actually said. The patrons, he thinks, they all heard it. He could ask one of them when his father's not around. The man called George, he's sure to know. When Vangel goes to make coffee, Nick approaches George and picks up his full ashtray. But how to begin without betraying his uncertainty?

'The Sergeant's a big man,' he says.

'Vic learnt to fatten pigs in his village days.'

'Do you think his horses will win?'

'They'll win, alright. The bastard's got contacts everywhere.'

Nick senses the Club darkening with the colour of the Sergeant's uniform.

'Kosta was sharp,' says one of the others at the table.

'I should've gone with him,' says George.

'What did he do?' Nick asks.

'Wrote the numbers as the pig was telling you and went to place a bet.'

'Did he get them down right?' Nick asks, swallowing his words.

'Horse five, race three, and horse two, race five,' he says, holding up a tram ticket.

For an instant Nick sees the Sergeant's big black shoes coming down on him, crushing him like a beetle. He takes the ashtray and empties it in a metal bucket in the kitchen and, seeing the bucket's almost full, carries this out to the small backyard. Everything sways around him: the ground paved crookedly with red bricks, the toilet in the back corner of the yard, the adjoining buildings, the row of dingy houses across the lane, chimneys smoking, clothes hanging on crooked balconies, the woman in a green dress and cream coloured high-heels leading a man up a flight of stairs to a wooden landing where another man is reading a newspaper. What should he do? Tell his father? Cop a tongue-lashing? He can hear his reaction: how many times have I told you, write things down, don't trust your memory, the pencil's a man's best friend, black on white – nothing is surer than that. No, he can't face his anger, especially in front of the patrons. Needing time to think he goes to the toilet and sits on the wooden seat. A calendar advertising television sets hangs on the door, above a container with newspaper cut in squares. Nick takes a square and reads part of a headline: KRUSH ORDERS. Below this is a picture of a round-faced man wearing a white hat. He wipes himself with the newspaper and pulls the chain on the overhead cistern. Having resolved nothing, he empties the butts in a rubbish bin and goes back inside.

The afternoon passes in a smoky haze. His father prods him with a sharp look from time-to-time when he becomes absorbed in thoughts of the Sergeant. It's now five, knowing the last race has been run, Nick feels his heart drop whenever the front door opens, expecting to see the Sergeant storm in and demand his five pounds back. He urges the clock on the wall to move faster, so they can go home before he arrives

The door opens just after five-thirty and the Sergeant enters, alone this time. Nick's in the kitchen stacking washed coffee cups. His first reaction is to sneak out and run off down the back lane, but he freezes at the sound of his voice.

'Vic,' he shouts, 'where's that little fella?'

'What's a matter, Sergeant Tornton?'

'Is he still around?'

Vangel goes to the back and, in a whisper, asks Nick what he's done, calling him *miskin* – a word that gives an edge to his suppressed anger. Before Nick can say a word, Vangel takes him by the arm to the Sergeant, whose dark-blue presence fills the Club. The Sergeant reaches into his coat pocket and, instead of handcuffs, pulls out a two-pound note, which he waves in the air.

'We Aussies don't forget our mates,' he says, extending it toward Nick.

He's dumbstruck, nailed to the floorboards, until his father pushes him forward.

'My horses came in,' he says. 'Put this in your moneybox.'

'Thank you, Sergeant Thornton,' Nick says, taking the crisp green note with a trembling hand, yet still fearing this might be a ruse to double the impact of his punishment.

'Forty quid,' he grins, 'not bad for an afternoon's work. You blokes have to work a month for that kind of money.

A murmur rises from the tables at the size of the winnings. Nick can hear George cursing, whispering he should have gone with Kosta.

'Mick says you did a good job with my numbers,' he grins. 'You were spot on, exactly as I said.'

Nick's still bracing himself for a backhander.

'Remember this, you blokes,' he says, clapping his big hands for silence. 'Look after your mates on the way up and they'll be there for you on the way down.'

With that he winks at Nick and leaves. Vangel slips the note from Nick's hand and puts it in his pocket for safe-keeping. The Club fills with lively conversation about the Sergeant's show of generosity.

'He might be a pig,' says George, 'but he's got a big heart.'

'That's the thing about Australians,' says Vic, who's been here since the twenties and knows them well. 'They mightn't be as hardworking as us, but they're more honest and loyal to their friends. An Australian will stand up in a tram and give his seat to a woman, while we wouldn't think of such a thing. An Australian will find a wallet on the street and take it to the police station, while we'd pocket it without a second thought. That's the Balkans for you – wars, oppression, hardship – it's made us sly and shifty, so that we trust no-one and respect no-one.'

As Vic's delivering his speech, Kosta opens the door with a frown.

'I've had it with the damned horses,' he says.

'Look at him,' says George, 'putting on a loser's face so not to shout a glass of *rakija*.

'I lost, I tell you – two quid, my overtime, gone.'

'But the Sergeant was here ten minutes ago – he won forty quid.'

'Which numbers did you bet for him?' Kosta asks Nick.

'Same as yours,' Nick says, concealing his bewilderment.

'There, you must've won, you stingy snake,' says George.

'I swear on my mother's eyes,' he says.

'Show us the tickets.'

'I tore them to shreds after race five.'

In the end the patrons are left wondering and offering possible explanations for the series of events, the most plausible that George is lying or that he mixed the numbers in placing his bet.

Crimson twilight fills the sky at the city end of Gertrude Street. Waiting at the tram stop, Vangel's whistling a Macedonian melody, while Nick tries to remember whether *Dedo* Risto whistled like that. They've been in Australia almost four years and his memories of the village seem like a dream, sometimes like the feeling left by a dream he can't remember. His father's whistling becomes sharper, accompanied by coins rattling in his pocket. The angle of his hat tells Nick he's pleased with the afternoon's earnings. But Nick's still puzzled by his earnings. As a police siren sounds in the distance, he sees again the Sergeant's wink and wonders at its meaning.

8

Nick senses his father's now serious when talking about an addition to the family. It's coming soon, he says, pushing back his hat. Coming? How? Where from? Why didn't they ask him if he wanted a baby brother or sister? The questions hover over Nick's head day and night, spoiling his happiness, finally becoming a dark cloud when his mother's stomach begins to bulge. The darkness is made even worse by the fact that their street's being resurfaced and the smell of steaming bitumen thickens the air. Where he used to enjoy going shopping with his mother, holding her hand in walking along Smith Street, going into Foys with all those canisters whizzing along on wires full of money and receipts, he's now embarrassed to be seen in public with her.

This Friday evening, in lighting the icon lamp, she turns to him with the look of *Bogoroditsa* in the big icon at *Evangelismos* Church. She makes him promise he'll say a prayer every night for the coming baby. She takes his hand and places it on her round belly.

'Promise me,' she says, the little flame bright in her eyes.

Nick freezes at the movement inside.

'Promise me, Kolche.'

Another movement, this time sharper, like an elbow or a knee.

Feeling betrayed, unable to utter a word, Nick simply nods and walks away, just managing to hold back his tears.

In the weeks before its arrival, they buy a deluxe blue-and-white pram with a chrome handle, rubber wheels and a folding hood. Vangel's not happy with the colour: it reminds him of the Greek flag and he doesn't want the newborn growing up thinking itself Greek. But Menka likes it and points out that he can have his way when he carries a child for nine months. Thirty pounds, Nick broods, more than they've ever spent on him. He keeps asking for a Malvern Star bike and all he gets is: we can't afford it. Well, couldn't they have bought a twenty-pound pram and used the rest on a bike. Doesn't he deserve something? They've also bought a wooden cot, which has been set up beside their bed. How are they going to pay off the house with all this spending? Yes, he resents these things, especially the pram, which they've put in his room, where his toys and comics stayed.

Nick's noticed the change in his mother. Her thoughts seem to be elsewhere, her faraway look reminds him of the day they left the village. Having to call two or three times to get her attention, he feels she's ignoring him. He's now uneasy in approaching her. It was never like this before she started showing. He used to be the centre of her world, now the centre's somewhere else. This afternoon she appears less preoccupied so Nick raises a little false enthusiasm to ask where babies come from.

'A woman's armpit,' she replies, without looking up from knitting a small yellow cardigan.

Her answer puzzles him: despite his vivid imagination he can't see how a baby could possibly come out from that part of the body.

The darkness gathering over him seeps into his being when his mother's taken to hospital. It's the first time they've ever been apart. He goes to a relative's house after school until his father returns from work. The woman keeps saying how much fun it will be having a baby brother. But why is she so certain it will be a boy? Has she got secret powers? Can she read the future in the symbols on the bottom of a coffee cup? What else does this witch-of-a-woman know? The baby's name? The colour of its eyes? Nick doesn't like her at all, especially the way her face lights up at his unhappiness.

Vangel picks him up from school and they catch the 88 tram to the Queen Victoria Hospital on Lonsdale Street. He's heavy-eyed, wearing a black hat, and unshaven, which strikes Nick as odd because it's his habit to shave first thing in the morning, even when staying indoors all day. But maybe it's a village custom for fathers not to shave on the birth of a child. They sit in silence for a few stops, Nick's heart thumping against his crossed arms, both wanting and not wanting to know if it's a girl or boy. He looks up from twisting the flimsy ticket. They're passing the twin gasometers on the corner of Smith Street and Alexandra Parade. For some reason the huge steel cylinders suddenly remind him of a pair of huge lungs, rising and falling so slowly it's not noticeable, now one then the other, pumping out gas to every house for miles around, to their small kitchen as his mother stands at the stove, heating a pot of rice and milk for his favourite pudding, which she serves sprinkled with cinnamon. But she won't have time to make this with a baby to feed. He tears the ticket and asks his father if it's a girl, thinking his silence might be from disappointment at not having another son. Vangel places his arm over the boy's shoulder and says the baby died, before it even came out, and his mother will have stay in hospital another week. Nick's dazed, confused, relieved there's no baby, but upset his mother will be away from home so long, and then realising how sad she'll be not having the little body she carried in her belly so long. Suddenly it's like a bad dream. He'll wake when they reach the hospital. His mother will show him the baby and he'll kiss it on the forehead. But his father's words echo in his head and the thought of his mother's sadness is too much. Tears spring to his eyes, blurring and dissolving the gasometers. His father pulls him close. He doesn't deserve his love and comfort. He never wanted the baby, never prayed for it as he should have, and now it's dead. His not wanting the baby kept it from coming into the world. It's his fault and nothing in the entire universe will ever undo his wrongdoing.

Menka's in a large room with five or six other women, lying in a bed next to a window overlooking Lonsdale Street. She raises herself a little as they enter and greets them with weak smile. Vangel removes his hat and places it on the end of the bed. Nick glances up from the black swirls in the floor covering, just long enough to notice the purple shadows under his mother's eyes, and then looks down again, holding back from crying. They exchange a few words and a pale hand rustles out from under the sheet and reaches out to Nick. How can he take it knowing he's the cause of her suffering? Its warmth draws him and he kisses her on the cheek. She asks how he's been, but he's choking with emotion, unable to say a word.

'Your prayers, Kolche,' she says, forcing a smile. 'They weren't enough to save your little brother.'

Nick breaks down in a mess of tears and apologies, blaming himself for everything, burying his face in the pillows under his mother. It's all a blur after that, with his father pulling him away, saying it's nobody's fault. God took back the child because it wasn't meant for the world.

A few weeks later Nick learns more about what happened to his little brother. He's arranging footy cards on the kitchen table as his mother and the woman who looked after him are talking in the living room. His mother says the cord got wrapped around the little one's neck, strangling him. Nick thinks of the nooses in Westerns, unable to imagine any kind of rope or cord in her belly. When the woman asks if they'll try for another, Menka looks down into her coffee cup and shakes her head. The woman reminds her of how things were in the village: women lost children in the womb all the time, but they didn't give up. No, they wrapped their little things in a cloth, buried them under a rock in the hills, and went on to have another. That's the way it was and that's how it will always be for women. She's the oldest of six, but her own mother lost three before she was born.

'Tighten your heart, woman, for the sake of your husband and child.'

'Tighten my heart, yes, because I can't have another.'

'What are you saying?'

'The one I lost has taken them with him.'

'Is that from the doctors?'

'From the doctors.'

Menka returns to work in the shoe factory, looks after the large house, and stays up late at night making things on the new sewing machine Vangel bought just after she got home from hospital. The light in her eyes returns and she even manages to persuade Vangel to see the occasional Greek film at the Westgarth Cinema on High Street. Yes, she smiles again, but for Nick it's nothing more than a flutter. They play his favourite games, but she becomes silent and forgets to move a piece. The songs she sings over the sewing machine are slower, sadder, often trailing off to a hum.

On Saturday evening Nick joins his Catholic friends as they head up Queens Parade, on their way to confession at St John's. The bluestone church with the pointed steeple is different from the churches he knows. It's bigger, has no altar screen, and there's no icon in sight. The colours in the stained-glass windows glow in the dark. Following the others, he dips his fingers in the holy water near the entrance, crosses himself with four fingers, not three, and kneels for an instant before the altar. As one after another enters and emerges from the confessional box, he sits on a pew at the back, wrestling with the idea of confessing, yet scared the priest might know he's not Catholic. And if he were to pass for Catholic would his sin be forgiven by saying a hundred Our Fathers and seventy Hail Marys? No, that's what kids get for small sins like swearing or not helping around the house or stealing fruit from backyard trees. His is more serious, needing serious punishment, maybe the fires of hell. These boys know about God and sin and punishment because the Brothers at their school are like priests and they're always teaching them about these things. Tony says hell is where really bad sinners end up, people like Hitler, who killed millions of people in the war, including children. But why did Tony mention children? Is there something in Nick's eyes that betrays what he's done? If Hitler's burning in hell, then he's doomed to burn as well because his sin's worse, not in terms of number but in terms of going against the bond of brotherhood. Hitler killed strangers, people he never saw, maybe names on a list, whereas he killed his own brother, the innocent little body he felt in his own mother's belly. No, an eternity of fire will never burn away that sin.

Finally, taking several deep breaths, he stands and enters the confessional. The priest's sharp profile is visible through the small puncture holes in the dark screen.

'Talk to me, my son,' says a strong voice.

For an instant Nick sees himself standing on the end of the diving board at the Fitzroy Baths. He's just learnt to swim and the boys are urging him to take his first dive. He reads the words AQUA PROFUNDO and the depth is suddenly deeper because of the Italian. He's looking down at the blue water laced with light, rippling with black lines that look like eels waiting to wrap themselves around him. And then the water becomes crimson, burning lava, the fires of hell. He sweeps aside the curtains, races out of the confessional, past his friends waiting at the entrance, and flies across the street. They call out for him to stop, but he's sprinting down Queens Parade, against the rush of red maple leaves driven by the wind, with the words 'bat out of hell' shouted by one of the boys swirling in his head,

He stops at the entrance of their back lane. Old Mrs Knight, a wisp of a woman who lives alone in the corner house, is standing at the gate in her dressing gown, calling her cats by name in a high-pitched voice, threatening to lock them out if they don't hurry home. She keeps to herself mostly and her blinds are always drawn. Some of the boys say she's strange, maybe even a witch, because of all her cats. She looks scary to Nick, especially tonight, her thin bird-like nose longer and sharper than usual. She asks Nick if he's seen Sooty.

'No, Mrs Knight,' he says, still breathing hard.

'Such a naughty cat, he is,' she says, twisting the handle of the gate. 'More interested in girls than his dinner. Well, he'll just have to get fixed if he goes on misbehaving like this.'

Nick doesn't know what she means and thinks maybe she's a little mad.

'And why are you late getting home, Timmy?'

He's told her his name lots of times, but she keeps calling him Timmy.

'Haven't been out chasing girls, have you?' she giggles.

'I've been to church,' he says.

'To confession?'

He nods, thinking of the flaming pool. A hand wearing a glove with half of each finger showing pats him on the head. Her clothes smell of mothballs.

'You're a good boy to be going to confession,' she says. 'Yes, Timmy, stay away from girls so you don't go without dinner.'

She giggles again, covering her mouth with the half-gloved hand. Nick says goodnight and continues into the darkness of the lane. But she's added to his unease, and as he approaches his gate a black cat scurries across his path.

He washes his hands with cold water in the laundry trough, keeping the flow to a trickle so the tap doesn't whistle so much. Its silver coating worn thin, the mirror on the wall spots and blotches his reflection. The mouth of the cast-iron heater's open, still full of ash and burnt scraps of wood from this morning's wash. He looks up at the sky for a moment before going inside. The wind's thrashing the apricot tree, scattering leaves over the backyard. He finds the bright Pointers just to the right of the factory's water tank, then the Southern Cross, steadying himself on its unchanging shape.

Dinner's late this evening because Menka's been baking and preparing for tomorrow's church service. As Nick enters the warm kitchen she takes from the oven a tray with three small, round loaves stamped with symbols. The door to the living room is partly open. Vangel's sitting in there, replying to a recent letter from the village, a bottle of beer beside him. Nick usually collects the mail after school and places it on the kitchen table, except when there's something from *Dedo* Risto, which he keeps until his father comes home, surprising him by raising it and shouting *muzhdi* – news – for which he's rewarded with sixpence. When replying, his father would call him to the table and trace the outline of his hand to show *Dedo* and *Baba* how much he's grown. Tonight, though, Nick can tell he's in no mood for games. A change has come over him since Menka came home from hospital. He was concerned for her health at first, even helped her with the washing and cleaning, until a silence settled over him, when he'd just sit and drum the table with his fingers. Having never seen him like that, Nick thought it was just his way of coping with disappointment, and that it would pass with time, but it hasn't. He's taken on more work at the Club, which Menka doesn't like. In the last few weeks his silence has given way to anger, maybe fuelled by the fact that he's drinking more. He snaps at her for nothing, for being told to take his empty bottle outside. Nick hates the icy silence between them, hates even more when his father gets angry and they argue. He can't get a recent argument out of his head. The kitchen window was open and they didn't know he was in the backyard.

'What are we going to do?' he asked, his voice sounding of beer.

'There's nothing we can do,' she replied.

'I wanted children – that's why we bought this big place.'

'You know what the doctor said.'

'I wanted brothers and sisters for Kolche.'

'So did I, but it can't be.'

'Women in the village ...'

'Women in the village didn't work in a factory nine months pregnant.'

'They worked in fields, sometimes gave birth in fields.'

'What are you saying?'

'You've turned my dreams to ash.'

Their voices rose, tempers flared, then his mother broke down and cried. And so did Nick, going off to the shed where he wouldn't be seen. If only he'd said a nightly prayer for his little brother, a few tender words, God would've brought him safely into the world and his father wouldn't be drinking and saying those things.

Needing to be alone with his mother, Nick quietly closes the door to the living room. A flame's burning before a small icon of *Bogoroditsa* cheek-to-cheek with baby Christ. His mother bought this in her pregnancy, setting it in front of the larger icon of Saint George. Menka places the loaves on a napkin she embroidered back in the village.

'Six weeks,' she sighs, 'how quickly it's passed.'

'Why is bread taken to church?'

'In memory of the dead.'

Nick knows the bread's cut up and placed in a basket and people take a piece on the way out, but he can't see how it helps remembering the dead, unless it's to do with the symbols stamped on the crust.

'Why is there a flame in the icon case?' he asks.

'To keep us from harm,' she says.

'Is fire from God or the devil?'

'Everything's from God.'

'What about the fire of hell?'

She looks at him without replying.

'Fire comes from the devil,' he continues, becoming worked up. 'It's used to punish us for our sins.'

Her initial look of surprise gives way to a tenderness he hasn't seen in a long time. She pulls out a chrome-backed chair, opens her arms, and cuddles him on her lap. It's one of those moments Nick knows he'll remember forever. Remember how the small flame suddenly loses its prod and becomes more rounded, how it glows with gentleness, drawing the icon closer to him, highlighting the love of mother and child, adding to the human warmth of the kitchen, the fullness of the loaves on the napkin, the meaning of the symbols on the golden crust, shining on his hands with forgiveness. Overcome by emotion, he buries his face in her breasts and confesses everything: his terrible sin, his fear of hell. But instead of scolding him, instead of blaming him for his little brother's death, she calls him her darling boy and kisses him on each cheek.

'You're not to blame for what's happened,' she says. 'And if you didn't say a prayer when he was in me, pray for him now that he's in heaven.'

Nick breathes easier after his confession. Guilt loosens its grip and he feels close to his mother again. Still, he can't help thinking if he wasn't responsible for his little brother's death then who was? His mother says God wanted him in heaven. Why? Surely his parents had more right to him than God. And what's the purpose of earth if heaven's such a wonderful place? No, there's something selfish in God's action, and yet he's taught in religious instruction class not to be selfish. Unable to square God with his brother's death, he vows to ease his parents' suffering by being a good and loving son. As for the little brother with whom he never played in the park, nothing will ever bring him back to life, but Nick promises *Bogoroditsa* that one day he'll become a doctor and help bring children safely into this world. He'll use all his skill and knowledge against God's selfishness, in a struggle between earthly love and loveless heaven.

The silence at dinner's uncomfortable for all. Vangel's knife and fork clatter against his plate. Menka slices one of the loaves and places it on the table. It's warm and heavy and Nick can feel the impression of the symbols in the crust. Biting into the strange crosses and notches, he wonders at their meaning, and whether it will somehow become clearer after eating them, or maybe reveal itself in a dream. And then it occurs to him that learning happens mainly by seeing and hearing, but what if it could also happen through eating? What if, instead of reading a book that takes days and weeks, we could understand it all just by eating its pages, like eating thin filo pastry? The word as both nourishment and knowledge, he thinks, remembering the line from his religious instruction teacher: the word made flesh.

He's pleased to be in his room, preparing for bed, feeling better after the talk with his mother. Standing in front of the pram, his reflection wrapped around its chrome handle, he raises the little mattress and takes out his *dekara*. Before this evening's confession he felt like a criminal, cut off from his parents' love, alone in a black hole with no way out, his despair made unbearable by the thought of the cord around his little brother's neck. One evening, in his despair, he took the sash from his blue dressing gown and wrapped it around his neck, at first just to place himself in the baby's position, but then he began slowly pulling on the tasselled ends, harder, hurting like his little brother must've hurt, gasping for breath, feeling his eyes swell. He might have gone all the way if not for the dead girl in the village. She was standing near the door, wearing the same white dress, short white socks and sandals, looking as if about to run off and join her friends in the Easter festival. As his vision started blurring and the gasping became louder, the girl reached out with her left hand, whose palm seemed strange because it didn't have a single line. Suddenly, things began swirling: the look on the girl's face, the thought of adding to his parents' sorrow, the horrible noise of his choking. He stopped pulling on the sash and the girl suddenly vanished. Still gasping, he gripped the pram's handle, sobbing, tears dripping on the mattress. The *dekara*, he thought, and took it from its hiding place in the cupboard. He looked through its hole at the light, thinking he might see the girl and his little brother dancing around the bare globe. This calmed him and he thought to place the coin in the pram. Why? Maybe because they didn't have a funeral and a coffin and he couldn't offer a coin so his little brother's soul would go to heaven. At that instant the pram became the coffin and he imagined him inside, peaceful, his small hands folded on his chest. He slipped the coin under the mattress, which became its new hiding place. And now, on the eve of his little brother's six-week memorial service, having eaten the symbols on his bread, Nick feels happy again. His mother's hug has freed him from his sin and he's at peace with his little brother, and, in a strange kind of way, with the little girl, as if the two have somehow come together through the hole in the *dekara*.

The following afternoon, having been to church, Nick's at the corner shop with the boys. They're throwing pennies on the footpath and the one whose coin lands closest to the wall collects all the others. The Boss comes out in his white apron and, in a good-natured way, tells them again in broken English to quieten down. His wife, who suddenly appeared in the Busy Bee about two years ago, and looks young enough to be his daughter, is always opening the upstairs window and hissing out in Greek for them to lower their voices because her baby's asleep. When this fails she sometimes comes out with a broom, but Boss takes it from her, doing his best to balance concern for their newborn with the needs of his business. The boys are a large group and he's careful not to upset them, for they could react by taking their pocket money to the shop down the street. Feeling for the wife and the sleeping baby, Nick tries to talk the others into playing in front of the small factory that makes ballet shoes. They ask if he's alright and why he ran out of church like that.

'Sore stomach,' he replies.

'Bullshit,' says Frankie, 'got scared, didn't you?'

'Scared of what?'

'Confessing in a Catholic Church.'

'I wasn't scared of that.'

'Yeah,' says Chris, 'because it's a sin for Greeks to enter a Catholic Church.'

'I'm not a Greek anyway.'

'You were born there, weren't you? You speak Greek, don't you? You're Orthodox, aren't you?'

'You're both wrong,' laughs Dom. 'He got shit scared 'cause the priest cracked a fat and pulled it out.'

'Must've been huge,' says Lance, 'to make him run like that.'

At the burst of laughter the Boss's wife opens the window and throws out a tub of water in which she's washed nappies. The quicker boys see it coming and run aside, the others cop it, swearing and complaining their clothes stink of a shit. The Boss comes out with a towel, apologising for his wife's behaviour, saying she was up all night with the baby, inviting them all in the shop for an ice cream of their choice. At that moment Nick happens to notice his parents and another couple coming out of his house with the pram. Panic-struck he sprints across the street as the boys call after him. His father's shaking the man's hand, saying he's getting a real bargain, while his mother wipes her eyes with a hanky, wishing the very pregnant woman a light and safe delivery. As the man pushes the pram onto the footpath Nick blocks his way and searches under the mattress.

'My coin,' he shouts, 'where is it?'

The couple look at each other in surprise.

'Get away from there,' snaps Vangel.

'It was under the mattress.'

Menka reaches into her apron and raises the *dekara*.

'What's that?' says Vangel.

But just as he is about to take the coin, Nick snatches it and, ducking a clip over the head, runs inside. Rummaging about in the back shed, he finds a bag with different coloured shoelaces Menka has brought home from the factory. He passes a black one through the coin's hole, ties a double knot and slips it over his head, vowing never to take it off.

9

Nick slept fitfully last night, not only because of the stifling heat, but a mosquito that teased him for what seemed like hours, avoiding his claps, until he silenced it with a slap on the wall, where in the morning he found a splotch of his own blood. It's the seventh of January, St John's Day, scorching, but still not hot enough to deter Vangel from insisting they visit a dozen relatives named John. They start by training it to Reservoir, doing the round there, then coming back to Johns in Fitzroy and Collingwood, before tramming it to more Johns in South Melbourne and Albert Park. After the third John Nick didn't want to see another piece of fried cabana or glass of lemonade. He doesn't know how his father does it: a couple of shots of *rakija* to the health of each John, followed by three or four glasses of beer, and he's still able to walk a straight line and whistle in key. When Menka says it's getting late and complains about visiting yet another John, a man they barely know who lives near Station Pier, Vangel darts a castigating glance.

'*Zheno,*' he says, stretching out the last vowel in a gruff voice, '*stramota.*'

Like many Macedonian men, he often calls his wife *zheno*, woman, as though it's her name. Nick's also observed that most Macedonians live in fear of the word *stramota,* which, he thinks, means something like embarrassing and shameful. It's *stramota* for a husband to hold his wife's hand in public because it's not the done thing. It's *stramota* for a boy to go to school with unpolished shoes even though his pants are patched. It's *stramota* if a woman can't make a Turkish coffee with just the right amount of froth, or if there's so much as a strand of cobweb anywhere in her house. *Stramota*, shame on you, what will people say. Maybe this word mattered in the village where everybody knew each other and gossip abounded, but it doesn't matter here in Melbourne. Both their neighbours are Australians, and it's not *stramota* for the women to have a beer in the Ladies Lounge of the pub. It's not *stramota* that Danny's mother has never swept their front yard. It's not *stramota* that Lance's father sees his brother once a year, even though they're on good terms. But for his father it's a terrible *stramota* not to visit some John on his name-day, no matter how hot, how tired they are, how far away he lives, because what will John say when they meet somewhere or another six months from now. Nick vows it will be different when he grows up: *stramota* won't rule his life.

It's around midnight and they're among the last visitors to leave the South Melbourne home of the last John. Too late to catch a tram, the only way of getting home is by taxi, so the group of adults and children is about to walk to Clarendon Street when one of the visitors, a man called Kocho *Kokoshkaro* – the Chicken-man, because he sells live chickens from the back of a ute – offers to drive them as far as Fitzroy in his light-blue Zephyr. Nick watched *Kokoshkaro* during the visit: he spoke in an excited manner all evening, thumping the table with both hands, but this didn't stop him pouring glass after glass of beer down his throat, so by the end of the night his eyeballs bulged to the point of bursting. Saving a quid in taxi-fare, the men, all nearly as drunk as the driver, are quick to accept his offer, but the women hold back. A squabble breaks out, tempers rise, the women call their husbands drinkers and pumpkin-heads, while the men assure them *Kokoshkaro* isn't drunk, and even if he were a little tipsy, he's been drink-driving for years without an accident, without so much as hurting the feather of a chicken. A neighbour throws open a flyscreen door and storms out on the porch in her dressing gown, threatening to call the police.

'Foreigners,' she hisses. 'At least have the decency to argue in English, not in double-Dutch.'

Menka releases her grip on Nick's hand and he sprints to the Zephyr, followed by half-a-dozen children his age and younger. Three men squeeze in the front with *Kokoshkaro,* the rest climb in the back and sit on a blanket smelling of chicken shit. He sets off with a screech that makes the women scream and the children laugh. Driving past the neighbour leaning over the front fence, he blasts the horn in a way that sends her reeling backwards onto the front steps.

Approaching Clarendon Street, *Kokoshkaro* is so busy talking he turns right toward Albert Park, instead of left toward the city. When the men point out his mistake, he thrusts his head out the window, spits at the wind, which pushes the spit back onto the side-mirror, and roars with laughter, saying he's taking them for a joy-ride around Melbourne, free of charge. The women are alarmed, the men whistle in approval, Nick and the children clap and cheer. He then erupts in a Macedonian song, setting off Vangel in the back and the men in the front. They sing at the top of their voices as the ute speeds down the quiet street, swerving now and then to avoid a cat, or because *Kokoshkaro* has leaned out the window and craned his neck in joining the chorus in the back. Pavle, a short, wisp of a man, opens the black case he's been carrying all night and takes out a cornet. The children clap in delight at the sight of the shining instrument. Raising it to the night sky, he plays a few shrill warm-up notes. The women curse him, calling on the earth to swallow him, roosters to pluck out his thinning hair. Nick's seen the little man at other functions and asked his father about him. He lives alone, his family being back in the village, and plays the cornet as way of connecting with people. His desire to play exceeds his ability, his father said. And now, standing in the back of the ute, kept from swaying by Vangel and another man holding him by his belt, Pavle picks up the tune the men are singing, fingers a few familiar notes, loses his way, becomes muddled, and then sounds a completely different tune. But this doesn't bother the singers, who encourage him to keep playing, while the women and children wince, blocking their ears against the jarring notes. A man in the front produces a bottle of *rakija* which goes from mouth to mouth. *Kokoshkaro* takes a long swig and passes it from the window to Vangel.

The bottle does the rounds in the back, causing more arguments between husbands and wives, until returned to the driver's outstretched arm.

By this time they're cruising on the road along South Melbourne beach, heading toward Port Melbourne and the twinkling lights of Station Pier. All the men are now on fire with *rakija* and music. A honk from the occasional car going past is given three in return by *Kokoshkaro.* As the women's concern rises above the singing, the driver swings to the left and stops abruptly, sending those in the back crashing into each other. Saying he needs to take a leak, he jumps out and with a flying leap disappears over the beach-front wall. With Pavle still playing and the men singing, they follow him over the wall. The women make the most of the opportunity to stretch their legs, saying they're better off walking home. The children run around playing tiggy on the wide footpath. Suddenly the cornet and singing stop, and Nick turns to the sound of trickling coming from the other side of the wall. The women curse the men, saying they have no shame, telling the children to block their ears. One of the boys climbs onto the wall and, pointing down, begins singing seven little dickey birds pissing in a line. His mother whacks him on the legs, propelling him onto the other side. After a moment's silence the cornet sounds again, followed by singing. When Nick looks over the wall, the men are dancing in a circle on the sand, with *Kokoshkaro* leading the way and Pavle playing in the middle. They wave for the others to join them. A man calls out it's the first Macedonian dance on an Australian beach and everyone should celebrate such an historic occasion. One of the women questions why those good-for-nothing drinkers should be having all the fun. The others agree. Finding an opening in the wall, they take off their high-heel shoes as the children run off toward the dancers, kicking up showers of sand. Soon men and women are dancing to Pavle's shaky notes in one big circle. The boy who climbed on the wall is sent to get the *rakija* from the car, and before long the bottle's empty and everyone's happy, including the women, whose anger has dissipated with the dancing. Excited by the surroundings and the water, the children take off their shoes and socks and step in ankle-deep. Nick's been in Australia four years and this is his first time at the beach.

Macedonians do things in strange ways, he thinks. Instead of coming to the beach to cool off on a hot day, like his Australian friends, here they are at one in the morning, a reddish crescent moon in the sky, and the water dark and scary.

Menka calls Nick away from the water's edge and they return to the car, the men unable to walk a straight line, *Kokoshkaro* still talking, now arguing with Vangel about whether the Jack of Hearts has a moustache or not. They continue even after setting off, with the driver's head out the window, insisting on a thin moustache, while Vangel leans over the edge, shouting he's clean shaven. The others are now quieter, tired from dancing and running around. Pavle keeps the cornet warm under his arm, every now and then blaring out a couple of notes.

Having dozed off on his mother's lap, Nick's startled by screaming and shouting. The car's speeding erratically on the wrong side of St Kilda Road. He can see through the back window one of the men struggling with *Kokoshkaro* for control of the steering wheel. The smaller children are crying and the women cursing as *Kokoshkaro* yells at the man to keep his hands off the steering wheel, swearing he didn't fall asleep and knows exactly how to get back to Fitzroy. Those in the back are holding onto each other, bracing for an accident. Nick becomes alarmed when one of the women crosses herself. All are now huddled on the floor, Menka pressing Nick close to her, Vangel holding them both, when they're shaken by a terrible jolt. Nick fears they've hit a brick wall, but the car's still moving, and when he looks up, they're driving through a park, on the grass, swerving to avoid trees, heading for the Shrine of Remembrance lit up on the hill-top. As the men continue wrestling for control of the wheel, the car skirts the Shrine, when suddenly Pavle sounds a stuttering version of the cavalry attack tune. Two soldiers on sentry-duty leave their posts, take cover behind a wall, and aim their rifles at the approaching car. Vangel snatches the cornet from Pavle.

'No shoot, no shoot,' he shouts, 'we friend for Australian soldier.'

The car comes to a shuddering halt at the foot of the wide stairway rising up to the Shrine. *Kokoshkaro* stumbles out, followed by the men in the front. The others climb off the back, crying and shaken and comforting each other. Rifles aimed, the soldiers order the men to sit on the step with hands behind their heads. They direct the rest to sit on a higher step.

'Sorry, sorry,' says *Kokoshkaro.* 'Too much *rakija,* mix 'em up street for go home to Fitzroy.'

'Sorry, sorry, *me razboli,*' says the woman sitting next to Menka, rhyming sorry with the fact that the driver's stupidity has made her feel sick.

'Where are you from?' one of the soldiers asks, squinting through the rifle's sight.

'Macedonia,' says *Kokoshkaro.*

'Banitsa,' says Vangel.

'Vevi,' says Mum.

The other soldier puts down his rifle and approaches Menka.

'Lady, did you say Vevi?'

'Vevi, Vevi,' she repeats.

'The old man fought the Germans there,' he smiles. 'The Battle of Vevi, April 11th and 12th, 1941. He was in the Second, First Anti-Tank Regiment.'

'Yes, yes,' says Vangel, springing up. 'Australia soldier come to fight German. Very cold for Australia soldier. My father give 'em *rakija,* you know, whiskey, to drink for warm 'em up.'

'Jeez, was that your father, mate?' says the soldier. 'The old man tells the story of how some local brought them some home-brewed whiskey.'

'May father, he take 'em *rakija,*' says Vangel, shaking the soldier's hand. 'You know, whiskey, and Australia soldier say him tenk you.'

'Well, I'm real pleased to meet you,' says the soldier. 'I'm sure the old man would love to see you and thank you for your father's kindness.'

The soldier writes Vangel's name and address, promises to contact him, and helps the women and children onto the back. Standing either side of *Kokoshkaro,* they warn him about speeding, saying they'll report him to the police if anything should happen. Menka takes the initiative and sits in the front, together with Vangel and Nick, snarling at the driver when the speedo so much as nudges thirty.

10

Late January, a scorching afternoon, Nick and his friend Charlie are leaving the Fitzroy Baths, complaining of the walk home. The hours spent cooling off in the pool, doing bombs and belly whackers off the diving board, seeing who can swim furthest underwater on a breath – all this evaporates the moment they step out onto the footpath softened by the shimmering heat. With damp towels on their heads as protection from the sun and thongs clapping at each step, they hurry from shade to shade, stopping here and there to adjust their turbans, or count their coins to see if there's enough for an ice cream from the little corner shop opposite the gasometers. Along with Charlie and the other boys, Nick's already endured the summer ritual of sunburn. For three long days and three sleepless nights, his body blazed red and raw. He tried all sorts of remedies to ease the burning: cool towels, a rub of olive oil and vinegar, a spread of cold yoghurt. In the end, though, it was a matter of putting up with the pain until the body's glow subsided and the peeling began. And then, in the shade of the Busy Bee, the boys would tear strips of skin thin as cigarette-paper from each other's backs and shoulders to see whose burn made the largest piece.

Friendships are strange, Nick muses, glancing at curly-haired Charlie. They develop for no reason, some lasting a summer and then fading away, while others grow slowly and hold for a lifetime, like many of his father's friends who go back to his village days. Charlie lives around the corner from

Nick on Grant Street, and though they're often together outside the Busy Bee, or playing group games in the park, Nick doesn't know why they've struck up such a close friendship these holidays. It may be the new bike Charlie got for Christmas. He was riding it in the park one afternoon and asked if Nick wanted a ride. Before long they were exploring back lanes as far off as Abbottsford, taking turns dinking each other. One day they rode all the way to Luna Park in St Kilda, though they did get off and walk up Punt Road just over the Yarra River. Having no money for a ride on the Big Dipper, they went to the beach instead, where they drank a handful of sea water, and rode back, all before their unsuspecting parents got home from work.

As they walk past the kindergarten's fence, Nick notices a large white rabbit nibbling the long grass in the yard. His first thought is: a fur jacket for his mother and a meal for dinner, like the skinned rabbits his father brings home from the market for onion stew. Charlie tries talking him out of it, but the idea's taken hold, especially the soft jacket. He asks Charlie for a boost up, promising to give him the fur of one of the legs, because rubbing it brings good luck. With Charlie's knee and shoulder as stepladder, he manages to climb the cyclone fence to the top. But once there, arched like a cat on the hot cross-iron, he's thrown off balance by one of his thongs slipping off. He sways for what seems ages, his grip tightening, though more in bracing for a fall than anything else. Suddenly his feet give way, followed by a desperate scramble, and then, instead of the dreaded fall, he's hanging from a tip of wire piercing his forearm. He cries out to Charlie, who unhooks him like a lamb in the freezer of a butcher's shop, and helps him down. The wound's deep, fleshy, and makes them both feel sick. Nick grimaces, saying it needs stitches, maybe six or seven. And then Charlie points to the rusty wire and says rust causes tetanus, a deadly disease. Nick steadies himself on the fence against a surge of nausea. Seeing him change colour, Charlie advises him to quickly piss on the wound as a way of stopping the tetanus germs, which he learnt in Cubs. Despite Nick now moaning in pain, Charlie's chattering about Cubs, how he's learnt to treat spider and snakes bites, and that he wants to become a Scout but his parents won't let him because they can't afford the uniform. He then holds up his towel, screening Nick, who, facing the fence, struggles to pull down his wet shorts and togs with one hand. Looking around in case he's seen, he lowers the injured arm and tries to summon a stream, but nothing comes. Charlie tells him not to worry about being seen, to close his eyes and try harder. Nick concentrates, recalling how effortlessly it comes in the Council Yard and exploring new back lanes. Still nothing. When Charlie says he'll die of tetanus if he doesn't piss, a golden stream suddenly arcs hot and stinging onto the wound. Charlie urges him to keep pissing, saying it's supposed to sting because it's killing the tetanus germs. As Charlie wraps the towel around Nick's arm, the red-eyed rabbit continues nibbling with what appears a grin.

At home Nick's spared a hiding from his mother by his intentions regarding the rabbit, but he can't avoid a tetanus injection and three stitches on the inside of his right elbow, which, he thinks, will probably mark him for life – a little pink curve with three dots on either side, just like the mouth of that tempting rabbit.

Most of the neighbourhood boys have taken up breeding pigeons as a hobby. Nick resisted at first, but was eventually drawn in by Charlie, whose father, like lots of Maltese, keeps a large flock of racers, not to mention an impressive collection of show birds like Jacobins and crests and tumblers. As news of President Kennedy's assassination hisses on transistor radios – later on this Saturday, death will enter living rooms in black and white, unreal yet compelling, coming as it will through the same screen as all those other shootings in favourite westerns set in Texas – Nick gets up early without having to be woken. He hates going with his father to the Victoria Market, hates walking around, listening to him haggle, waiting on corners with shopping bags, and bringing stuff home by tram. But after begging for weeks about getting his own birds, when his father would put on that imperturbable look, Nick was surprised by how casually he assented. He's often expounded the character-building virtues of tending flocks of sheep and goats, as he did in his youth, but as this was not possible in their narrow backyard the next best thing for his son's development would be tending a flock of pigeons.

Entering from Elizabeth Street, Nick's confronted by gum-booted fishmongers trying to catch customers with their cries, butchers enticing them with raised legs of lamb, and further on fruit and vegetable vendors singing in English thick with operatic Italian. Bargain hunters push through the crowd, those who've finished strain with the weight of home-made shopping bags, here and there disputes flare over goods and prices. After a tour of inspection of the entire market – Vangel says it costs nothing to look and compare prices first – they settle on a smelly stall run by a Chinese man. Having accepted he's allowed two pigeons, Nick's unable to decide. He studies the restless birds cooped in wire cages and finally chooses a sandy-coloured pigeon with brown bars on its wings, and a good-looking black and white. Both are fairly young because, as he's learnt from Charlie, their beaks are pink and still uncrusted.

'Which one man?' asks Vangel, shouting in the vendor's face.

The vendor feels between the legs of both birds and points to the black and white. Charlie has shown Nick his way of telling them apart: hold the bird by the beak and if it flaps it's a male.

'This one lady?' Vangel shouts.

The vendor feels again and nods. He places them in a shoe box with holes in the lid and ties it with string. And now Vangel comes out with his old haggling trick, which never fails to embarrass Nick. He agreed to the vendor's price when the birds came out of the cage, but now that they're in the box and about to be handed over, he tells the vendor his price is too much, that he can get them two shillings each cheaper at another stall. As the vendor flares up in Chinese, Vangel takes Nick by the hand as though to walk away. Passers-by are laughing, the caged pigeons start flapping, ducks honk, canaries and budgies fly around in a frenzy.

'All light, all light,' says the vendor.

'Orait, orait,' Vangel laughs.

He hands him the money and Nick gets the shoe box, barely able to hold it from a tremor of excitement and embarrassment.

'Why do you do that?' he says, face burning.

'It's the market,' says his father.

'But you agreed on the first price.'

'It's part of the game.'

'You upset the poor Chinaman.'

'He was playing the game, too.'

'You mean, you were both testing each other,'

'That's business, my boy.'

On the way home Nick holds the box tightly under his arm, feeling the weight of the pigeons, the scuttle of their clawed feet. The familiar conductor paces the tram, peering over the top of his glasses, crying out to amused passengers.

'Money, money. I want your money. I need your money. Give me your money.'

On Saturday mornings his face is more flushed than usual, his anger somehow sharper, maybe because the tram itself resembles a market, with onions and potatoes spilling from shopping trolleys, boxes blocking doorways, lamb shanks and pig trotters pushing through soggy butcher's paper, fish heads popping out of newspaper, live chickens flapping and squawking in net-like carry bags, fouling the floor with green watery shit. Nick embraces the box against the conductor's crimson anger, fearing he'll take it from him and release the birds.

At home he places the pigeons in a cage made from a packing case whisked away from the National Can Company. His excitement at having his own birds is suddenly dampened by the two options for making homers of them: keep them confined in the cage for three long weeks, or use his mother's sewing scissors to cut off the lower section of their wings. He's seen Charlie do this to strays drawn in by his flock. Holding the bird between his thighs, he spreads the wing and cuts in half about six long end-feathers. It seems cruel to Nick, but Charlie sees it differently: the bird knows it can't fly, so it accepts its condition, grateful that at least it can wander around in the backyard until the feathers re-grow, by which time it will get used to its surroundings and become a homer. The other way, according to Charlie, is much crueller: the bird knows its wings are whole, knows it can fly, is desperate for its freedom, but has to suffer the hell of being cooped up in a cage for three weeks. Nick can still hear the sound of Charlie's scissors cutting the wing feathers – it sends a shiver down his spine and he settles on the cage.

Exactly three weeks later – images of a nation still grieving for its President vacillating with the sight of two common pigeons desperate for flight – Nick's both eager and afraid to release the birds. What if they don't return? His father would never consent to buying another pair. Should he wait another week? But Charlie swears on his mother's grave, even though she's alive and well, that three weeks is enough, any longer would be torture for the poor birds. Nick takes them from the cage, first the male, then the female, and throws caution to the wind. Long-folded wings scatter from his hands, clapping hard their freedom, covering blue distances with a single flick. They circle the house several times and disappear in the direction of Clifton Hill. He spends the afternoon high in the backyard apricot tree, scouring the sky, following Charlie's big flock, dozens of birds moving as one. He swallows back a fear his might become someone else's strays. But just before sunset, his heart springs at the sight of two dots in the clear sky. His pigeons return with a happy rush, perching on the back fence, sounding a few coo-coo-coos, then fluttering down into the yard. More coo-coos and they whir up onto the ledge in front of the cage. Nick watches nervously as they strut back and forth before going inside. He clips shut the cage door, overjoyed they're homers.

The birds mate, eggs appear, chicks hatch. In time two become four, then eight, and before long Nick has a respectable flock of fairly common birds, with the odd feathered foot and fantail. Breeding has become not only a hobby but serious business as well. Just as there's a pecking order among pigeons, so a boy's standing in the neighbourhood is measured by the size of his flock. A late starter, but competitive by nature, Nick's determined to make up lost ground. There's a brisk trade in birds among the boys. They buy and sell, trade and barter. Some boys risk their lives climbing buildings and bridges for chicks, while a few wouldn't think twice about stealing from other neighbourhoods. And he's now fascinated by the courtship ritual of pigeons. He observes how the male's throat throbs in crooning and croaking, the way he puffs and swells his body and fans out his tail, how he bobs up and down in circling the female showing no interest in his show of affection, sometimes even strutting away angrily from his advances, though rarely flying away. But eventually the female relents and places her beak in the male's, like a sort of kiss. And then that startling moment that takes Nick's breath away: as the female squats on her underside the male mounts her, chest thrust out, head high, shuddering and flapping his wings, as though showing off his strength while at the same time trying to remain upright in this awkward position. But the moment passes before he's able to fully grasp it: the flurry of feathers stops, and male hops off, becoming his usual size again, then flies off, sounding a couple of happy claps with his wings. The female remains squatting for a few seconds, then she, too, springs up and trots off a little unsteadily, as though dazed by the experience.

Yes, Nick's excited when the male courts and mounts the female. It signals the birth of new birds, the growth of his flock. But this excitement might also have something to do with changes taking place in him. The mating of birds mirrors what's being discussed in all kinds of detail by boys in the schoolyard and at the corner shop. Recently one of them told Nick how his older brother wore a franger in rooting a girl so she wouldn't fall pregnant. When Nick asked what a franger was, the boy said it was made of thin rubber and looked like a balloon. Nick still can't imagine how it's used. Maybe the franger's blown up like a balloon and placed between stomachs to keep a couple apart.

On this wintery June day Nick and Charlie are on the bike, weaving through a noisy crowd on Bourke Street. They happen to pass the Southern Cross hotel just as the Beatles appear on the balcony. The crowd suddenly goes wild, girls scream and shake in a kind of frenzy, young men surge toward the hotel, mounted police struggle to contain the chaos. Here and there people faint in the crush and are carried to safety. Being followers of Elvis rather than these mop heads, the boys barely glance at them. They are more excited by the prospect of pigeon chicks waiting for them down at Spencer Street. When they get there Charlie points to a railway bridge running along the Yarra, which here widens in flowing out to the bay.

'Up there,' he says, having done this before.

He points to the gap in the bridge separating the outbound and inbound lines. Nick's heart sinks: he's afraid of heights, but too embarrassed to tell Charlie who'd call him chicken. Bracing himself, he follows Charlie up a series of metal rungs fixed into a brick pillar shouldering the bridge. Trains rumble past on either side as they stand on the top, an icy wind howling through the gap. Charlie indicates the pigeon nests on the steel flanges, but in order to get to them they must walk with a foot on each flange, the broad brown river shivering below.

'Let's go,' says Charlie, and sets off lightly, side-stepping from flange to flange.

Unsettled by the height, Nick feels light-headed, barely able to look down at the wrinkled water. He must think quickly to save face.

'Hey, Charlie,' he calls out, 'what's today's date?'

'The fourteenth, I think. Why?'

'Shit!' he pretends.

'What's up?'

'It's Saint Trifon's Day,' says Nick, grasping at the first saint who comes to mind.

'Saint friggin' whose Day?'

'Saint Trifon. It's bad luck for Macedonians to climb heights today. Back in the village, boys weren't allowed to climb trees, men didn't set foot on ladders, and women stayed away from balconies.'

'You scared, or what?'

'It's alright for you to talk,' Nick says, offended. 'You're Catholic – you don't believe in Saint Trifon so nothing bad will happen to you.'

'Alright,' says Charlie. 'Wait here.'

He tucks his jumper into his trousers, tightens his belt and, as though hop-scotching, makes his way along the flanges to the nests. Brushing aside adult birds flicking wings in defending their young, he plucks the chicks from their nests and shoves them down his jumper. When he's collected seven or eight, he pisses into the river, just missing a boat which lets out a shrill blast. He turns and trots back to the pillar in a way that makes Nick fear for his safety.

'Here,' he says, pulling out trembling chicks. 'Half each, right?'

Nick puts four inside his jumper and follows him down. Eager to get the chicks safely home, they avoid Bourke Street and the Beatles, riding instead down La Trobe Street and turning into Rathdowne.

The other pigeons resent the chicks, flicking them with their wings, driving them trembling into a corner of the cage, ignoring their hungry little squeaks. Nick fears for them until Charlie instructs him to pour a mix of crushed wheat and milk into their beaks. This swells their gullet and weighs them down so they can barely walk. Nick's concerned by the deformed-looking chicks, but Charlie urges him to persist, saying he's done this lots of times. In a couple of weeks, to Nick's surprise, the chicks begin to develop, fend for themselves, and soon became one with his growing flock.

There are times, though, when Nick questions why he's a pigeon breeder and not, say, a breeder of hamsters, like Neville up the street. Maybe it's because he sees himself as an extension of the flock, especially in those moments when they arc as one across the late-afternoon sky, though not in search of food, or from fear of sparrow-hawks, or in racing to get home before dark, but simply in the playfulness of flight and speed. Apart from this, it may also have something to do with the fact that pigeons resemble doves, and through this the feathery aspect of angels and the air-born Holy Spirit. As a boy in the village church, he remembers staring at the dove carved from dark wood above the central door leading into the sanctuary. Its wings were spread and a lighted oil lamp hung from its beak. The side entrances to the sanctuary were painted with icons of archangels: Michael on the left, Gabriel on the right – both with wings wrapped around their slender bodies.

Ever resourceful Nick and Charlie have started their own business: selling wheat as pigeon feed. Once a fortnight, on a Sunday evening just before nightfall, they throw an old blanket in Nick's billycart and sneak off to the park, but veer left past the Council Yard, to the locked gate of the National Can Company. They leave the cart on the grassy footpath and slip under the wire fence, into the rail depot under the footbridge. They look in the carriages covered in tarpaulin, find one containing sacks of wheat, and drop a sack over the side. They drag it to the cart, cover it in the blanket, and, making sure no-one sees them, push it to Nick's place. Keeping their source a secret – Nick tells his parents Charlie's uncle gets the sack from his work – they use scales to fill paper bags against a black two-pound weight, selling them for a shilling each. Boys come from as far as Northcote and Collingwood, demand soon outgrows supply, and they're driven to increase business by visiting the depot every Sunday.

Business is running smoothly, making a pretty penny from each sack of gold, when Nick's struck and knocked off course by something the Religious Instruction teacher says. A tall man in a grey suit and thick glasses that magnify his eyes, he comes for an hour a week and tells the class stories from the Bible, explaining their meaning and asking questions. Nick doesn't mind the hour – some call it a bludge hour – because all they do is sit and listen. Nick's listening and thinking about his birds and scheming about another sack of wheat, when the teacher looks him straight in the eyes with his huge eyes and says God sees and knows not only everything he does but everything he thinks of doing. Nick doesn't know why he's staring at him – he's done nothing to attract his attention – but his look goes right through him like a sword. The teacher goes on to say that God rewards or punishes people for the things they do. These words are like a slap on the face and he feels his cheeks burning. His words echo in Nick's head all day and keep him up at night. He tosses and turns, feels a fever coming on, dreams of being buried up to his head in burning wheat. On Sunday, when Charlie comes over to discuss evening business, Nick tells him what the teacher said.

‘It’s all bullshit,’ he laughs. ‘Don’t believe a word of it. The old man reckons God’s been invented by capitalists to keep the poor in their place.’

‘What’s a capitalist?’ Nick asks, shocked by his words.

‘A rich person – an owner of a factory, a wheat merchant.’

‘But how can a capitalist invent God when God created man?’

‘That’s a fairytale,’ he says. ‘The old man’s a communist and …’

Nick’s heard his father talking about communists in stories about the Greek Civil War.

‘What’s a communist?’

‘Someone that believes man is God, and all men are equal, and the poor have got a right to a sack of capitalist wheat.’

Something in Nick can’t dismiss God the way Charlie has – maybe it’s his experiences in the village church, or his mother lighting the icon every Friday night, or the candle they bring home alight at Easter time, or the death of his little brother. Maybe all these things, and more, have fixed God in his mind in a way that He’ll always be there, even when he grows up and becomes a man and maybe stops doing his cross and going to church at Easter. In the end, he tells Charlie he’s leaving their business.

‘Suit yourself, but remember,’ he says, ‘God won’t feed your pigeons.’

Charlie continues doing business on his own, borrowing Nick’s billycart, offering a bag as payment, which Nick declines, though they still remain friends. He’s right, Nick thinks, God won’t feed his growing flock, so in order to support his hobby he goes back to helping his father in the Macedonian Club on either Saturday, when it’s not footy season, or Sunday afternoon. He also becomes a paperboy for a while, selling The Herald and the pink Sporting Globe on Saturday nights. He stands at the traffic island on Queens Parade, at the intersection of Michael and Gold Street, selling to city-bound traffic. It’s winter and cold and the leather strap hurts his bony shoulder and his hands are black from the print and it’s not the best spot for selling and he keeps his eyes on the arm of the traffic signal as it sweeps around the red-green-orange face, timing his moves so he’s back on the island as the arm reaches the narrow orange band. He comes home blue with cold, sometimes drenched despite his father’s raincoat. After two weeks his mother intervenes, saying they haven't come to this country for her son to freeze to death for a handful of pennies. His father insists it will teach Nick the value of money, make him work harder at school, so that he gets a good job, maybe in an office or bank. Menka gives him her sharp look, making him raise his eyebrows and pull a face that tightens his mouth.

Nick's hobby ends abruptly a year after it started. By this time, his flock's outgrown not only the coop but their small backyard. His mother complains that, along with pigeons, he's also breeding rats and mice because of the wheat. Not only this, she's tired of hosing pigeon shit from the yard and wiping clean the washing line and trying to rid Nick's hair of lice. He offers to reduce the size of the flock, but she remains firm: it's time for a thorough clean-out. And this happens in the summer holidays, while they're at a picnic. When they return at sunset, the pigeons are gone, the entire flock stolen. Nick's sure it is the work of the Celebri brothers who live over the footbridge on Freeman Street, but he isn't game to go snooping around in their back lane as they're the sort of characters who'd knock you out first and ask questions later. Still, Nick's surprised at how quickly he gets over the theft, as though outgrowing his interest in pigeons. A few days later, when his father takes an adze and smashes the cage for firewood, Nick helps him stack the pieces in a neat pile behind the laundry shed.

11

Having attended the wedding ceremony at *Evangelismos* church on Victoria Parade, many of the guests are now walking along Smith Street to Allan's Photo Studio. They're on the Fitzroy-side of the street, in the shadow of closed shops, banks, furniture stores, Raven's Funeral Parlour. A hot northerly tosses about coats slung over shoulders, grabs at bags and hats trimmed with lace, fills the eyes of children with grit. The men are leading the way, followed by the women, and the kids straggling behind. The talk's loud, often sounding like an argument, which is how Macedonians speak. Nick finds church and photos the boring parts of a wedding. The reception that follows is more fun, especially when in a spacious venue, and no venue's bigger than the Fitzroy Town Hall.

Nick doesn't know the couple getting married, but they're both from his village, so just about everyone who's from there has been invited. The bride came to Australia with a passport-size photo of the man she was supposed to marry – a handsome man, with shapely eyes, thin moustache, and a cigarette between his fingers. The person who greeted her at Station Pier with a bouquet of wilted flowers turned out to be not only much older, but instead of having two eyes looking lovingly at her, one looked east, the other west, missing her completely. Not one to hold back, she accused him of deception and rejected him on the spot. Having paid for her fare, the man saw this as payment for her and insisted she was legally his. Outraged, the young woman threw the flowers in his face and set off on foot, holding a scrap of paper with the address of the Macedonian Club. She walked straight in and asked Vic for a room to rent. Impressed by her spirit Vic found not only a room but a job in the cotton mills near the Yarra Falls in Collingwood. A proud girl, the thought of the fare played on her mind. Determined to pay it back without delay, she cut off her long blonde hair to the roots, wrapped a scarf around her head, and worked day and night. When asked why she'd spoilt her looks, she replied it would keep her from socialising and attending dances at the Fitzroy Town Hall until the debt was paid off, by which time her hair would grow again. And when that time came, she dressed in her finest clothes, braided her thick hair, and visited the man, who ran a dirty milk bar in Abbottsford. Her face glowing, eyes flashing, she threw the money in his unshaven face and left without a word. Free of debt, she was also free to choose her own husband, and this afternoon there she was, dazzling in white, leaving the church arm-in-arm with the groom in a suit cut from a priest's shadow.

Nick and several boys stop at a furniture store, where they press their foreheads against the window, smudging the glass in admiring the dozen or so televisions on display. The screens are cased in polished wood, with gold and silver dials and trimmings. Those with darker wood remind Nick of the coffin he saw in church not long ago. It was just as shiny and about the same depth, only he was too scared to walk past and look inside. They point to this or that television, saying their father will buy it for them next payday, making bets on who'll be first to get one. Nick goes along with the others, knowing it's nothing more than wishful thinking, because they can't afford one, not until the house is paid off, which is still years away. He focuses on the most expensive, the pound symbol large and loopy, like the sign at the beginning of a piece of music. Staring at the grey screen and the reflection of boys in white shirts and shorts, Nick wonders if a television will be invented that captures every passing moment in every place in the world, like these boys on their way to a wedding, the number 88 tram grinding to a halt because its thin arm has jumped off the overhead cable, a pink newspaper rustling in the illiterate wind. Yes, everything captured and held in the television's memory, so people can watch themselves, like they watch old cowboy films, in a hundred years from now.

When he looks around the other boys are running to catch up with the leaders: a line of people stretching more than a hundred yards, all somehow related, one loose family going back to great-grandparents, maybe even further back to Alexander the Great. They're a family of sorts, he thinks, especially the adults, who are drawn together by village customs and the need to feel secure in this new country. But differences are already appearing in this extended family: where the adults speak their earthy Macedonian and look forward to tonight's traditional dances, the children speak fluent English and run from the sound of folk music, as though pierced by the clarinet's notes.

The bridal party and guests squeeze into the studio's foyer and up the narrow stairs to the second floor, just as another group makes its way down, their faces flushed, sweat glistening on foreheads, tempers short. The photographer, a middle-aged man with silver braces around his shirt sleeves and a spike of hair defying oil's grip, directs the new arrivals into a large carpeted room with heavy blue drapes on three sides. Mounted lights beam heat at rows of bare benches along the back. The three-legged camera stands between them, its head covered in a black cape, unfussed by the chaos swirling around. Dashing about in a frenzy, clapping for attention, constantly brushing down the stubborn spike, the photographer calls on the immediate relatives of the bride and groom to remain standing, while directing friends and more distant relatives to the back benches. Unhappy about being positioned furthest from the camera, people begin ranking their relationships to the bride and groom, going back to great-grandparents and beyond. It must be some kind of honour to stand close to the bride and groom, thinks Nick, because some of the guests are shouting abuse at each other, denying being third or fourth cousins, claiming to be at least second. Suddenly Macedonian words for family connections start flying around the hot room, and Nick's struck by the richness of a language he's come to consider poor, almost peasant-like, compared to English. He hears familiar words as though for the first time. *Baiko* – an uncle on the father's side, *vuiko* – one on the mother's side, *tetinko* – the husband of a maternal aunt, *teta* – an aunt on either side, *vuinya* – a *vuiko*'s wife, *dever* – a woman's brother-in-law, *yiatrva* – a woman's sister-in-law, *zolva* – a woman's brother-in-law's wife, *bajanatsi* – husbands of two sisters. And so, as these words flutter overhead, as the six bridesmaids gather around the bride and arrange her sprawling dress and veil and bouquet of flowers, as the black-suited groomsmen wrap the thin-faced groom in chains of cigarette smoke, as children run around the room and behind the drapes and pull faces at the still camera, the photographer's beside himself, shouting and pushing people toward the benches, threatening to call off the session if they don't take their places at once, saying another wedding party is arriving at four, Maltese, far more civilised than Macedonians because they've had the good fortune of being part of the British Empire. Ordered by him to do something useful, the groomsmen toss their butts in a tin filled with sand and start herding people to the benches, the more nimble at the back, the children seated cross-legged on the floor in front of the bridal party.

The heat's now intense, with all lights on, beaming at the assembled. Despite this, a restless murmur persists. A woman at the back complains she should be closer to the bride, because back in the village their grandmothers had been best friends, if not third cousins. An elderly man in a thick woollen suit meant for village winters calls out to the photographer in Macedonian, imploring him to hurry before he explodes.

'Not from the rear end,' says a man behind him. 'Those beans you had for lunch will smell us out.'

A burst of laughter threatens to reduce everything to chaos, but the photographer's quick to clap his hands and shout for silence.

Nick and the boy next to him are comparing the length of hairs on their forearms when from halfway up the back he hears his mother whispering, telling his father to remove his hat for the photograph.

'People won't recognise me without it,' he chuckles.

'It's disrespectful to the bride and groom,' she says.

'She's right, Vangel,' says a man's voice.

'Your hat's blocking my face from the camera,' says another man.

'A face like yours needs blocking,' Vangel snickers.

Another burst of laughter unsettles the gathering. The photographer releases a long, loud shhh that's picked up and echoed by others. The next instant Vangel's hat flies across the room and lands at the feet of the camera. Nick's first reaction is to get it, but holds back, embarrassed. An exchange of heated words follows, tempers flare. An old woman loses her balance, causing those around her to lose theirs in attempting to hold her up. The photographer throws up his arms, smooths back the spike with both hands, and picks up the camera as though to leave. The groom's father is a thick-set man weighed down by a brooding moustache, and known as Tsanko *Ofcharo* because he was a shepherd back in the village. He now stands on the bench, wipes back the whiskers from his mouth, whistles piercingly as though to a flock of recalcitrant sheep, and pleads for everyone's co-operation in these extreme conditions. The chatter and restlessness subside, though Nick hears his father calling on him to retrieve his hat. As he crawls toward it, the photographer kicks it aside and orders him back in his position. His embarrassment made worse by the lights, Nick retreats, wishing his father would stop hissing curses at the photographer and complaining his hat's been crushed.

When the photographer has set up the camera again, he slips under the cape for a moment, reappears, and demands everyone's attention by clicking his raised fingers. For some reason, and without planning it before coming here, Nick and a few boys strike up a boxing pose – fists up, left in front, right low, chin tucked in – as though challenging the photographer to a fight for keeping them in this heat so long. And then, maybe not noticing their pose, or maybe wanting to finish without more interruptions, he calls on everyone, at the count of three, to say cheese in Macedonian.

'Cheese in Macedonian,' shout a few teenage boys.

Laughter breaks out from those who understand the joke, whispers of confusion from those who don't. Face blazing as though he's eaten a hot chilli, the photographer silences everyone with a glaring look and explains what he wants said.

'*Sirenye*,' they chorus, stirring the drapes.

The press of a button releases a flash. In that blinding instant, which stills time and snatches Nick's smile from fluttering off in joyless space, he's filled by thoughts almost too big for his thin body: why's he sitting here, on this green carpet, this boy with bare legs crossed, a crisp scab on his left knee, fists the size of garlic bulbs cocked in the orthodox position, and the shine of victory in his eyes? Then another thought: why are Menka and Vangel his parents, and not the couple sitting on his right, each with an identical twin girl on their lap? And another: why has this number of people, not a person more or less, gathered here, in this upstairs studio, on this sweltering afternoon? Given the variety of clothes in wardrobes veneered in Russian birch, why has one woman chosen to wear a dress cut round at the neck, another preferring one cut square? Why has this man done all three buttons of his coat, while another has it open? Of the countless ways they could've arranged themselves on the benches and on the floor, why have they settled on this, with just that show of expression on their faces? And how has it happened that the boy sitting on his right is Louie the Fly, who's sometimes too wild for his liking, and the kid on his left is Ginger Jim, whose reddish-orange hair will never be obvious in the black and white photograph?

Nick expects another click, another flash, but the photographer has finished. He pulls out the black plate from the camera, hides it behind his back, and orders everyone out, except the bridal party. Children spring away, those on the benches make their way down, the bevy of bridesmaids gather around the bride and cool her with fans. As the group moves off, Nick reflects on another thought: next month, next year, or sometime in the distant future, he might come upon the photo hanging on the wall of a relative's house, when he'll see again these faces focused on the absent photographer, note his father's peeved expression, observe the groomsman's watch showing from his coat sleeve, smile at the little bridesmaid whose floral headband has come loose. And even if he were to live an eternity, until the sun swallowed the earth, as his teacher says will someday happen, the moment captured in Allan's Studio, this gathering of Macedonians new to Australia, will never happen again.

Nick's glad to be outside, despite the hot wind stinging his bare legs and pins of light glinting off a broken beer bottle in the gutter. Vangel's friend offers to take them in his car, along with his family. It's parked across the street: a red and white EK Holden, its chrome hubcaps doubling the number of people leaving the studio, small crosses and icons dangling from its rear-view mirror, and tail-lights sticking up like shark fins. Nick tugs excitedly at his mother's bag, but she stands firm, saying she doesn't want her dress creased. Seeing himself shrunken in the hubcaps, he tugs harder, at which she turns away. He walks off disappointed. What do a few creases matter compared to the joy of riding in a flashy car? But then, recalling the last time they accepted a lift, he sees beyond the creases and grasps the reason for her refusal.

His steel-capped heels scraping the footpath, Nick's in no mood to join the other boys hop-scotching the lined footpath. He's tired and bothered by the blustering wind smelling of bushfire smoke. Turning right into Moor Street, he's suddenly eye-to-eye with the late-afternoon sun, his stretched-out shadow pulling at him as if black bubble gum stuck to the soles of his shoes. It's the time of day when that strange feeling tends to come over him. He can't put a name to it, but it's been happening more often lately, stronger each time, like the greyness rising from the grate of a bluestone drain. It's triggered by nothing in particular, and might be due to nothing more than a drop in his energy level, but it has the effect of making familiar things seem different. Like now, the way sunlight leans against that factory's redbrick wall, or that little finch on the corrugated fence expanding in song, or that man in a white singlet on the balcony, gazing through cigarette smoke. As if pulled in by this feeling, his thoughts turn from the world and become inward. He's almost eleven, can barely remember being five, and yet he's done nothing out of the ordinary. He has no talents or skills. Sometimes he thinks it's a curse being Macedonian because Alexander's always shining in his imagination, leading the way to the future. He was only a few years older than Nick when he noticed Bucephalus was spooked by his own shadow. He faced the stallion sunward, when he mounted the wild Bucephalus and rode him around Pella. When he brought him back to his father, Philip marvelled at his son's intelligence and skill. Nick's heard this story many times, but now, under the influence of this feeling, he looks at his father up ahead, hat low over his eyes, and sees himself in the swing of his arms, the angle of his step, and recalls the Macedonian saying about the pear falling under the pear tree.

12

Rising from the press of surrounding houses, the clock-tower of the Fitzroy Town Hall is crowned in light. Fading conversations suddenly pick up, tired steps quicken, wind-parched lips can almost taste cool beer and lemonade. Those who've walked the distance are relieved to be in the building's shadow sprawled over Napier Street. The guests are welcomed by the wide, columned façade and the lift of the stairs. The bridal party has arrived, their ribboned cars parked along the front. Nick likes coming to weddings here because children can play freely inside and out while the grown-ups are eating and drinking and dancing and making boring speeches.

Long tables covered in white paper have been arranged around perimeter of the ballroom, leaving enough space in the centre for dancing. Guests are free to sit anywhere, apart from the bridal table, so Vangel leads the way to the side opposite the main door, heading straight for a family with three girls. Nick tries pulling him in a different direction, but he's a good friend of the girls' father and his efforts go unnoticed. He's always uneasy around this family because both fathers tease him to the point where blush burns his face. They laugh and raise glasses to the vow they made back in the village about becoming in-laws and drink to the future groom and bride: Nick and the middle daughter. As they approach the table, Nick sneaks a glance at her: she's about the same age, front teeth missing, wearing a lemon-coloured dress with a blue-eyed charm pinned to the collar. Nick wore one of those eyes when he was younger as a way of keeping him from harm. Before setting out for days like this, his mother would pin the eye on his left lapel and a small cross on the right. He'd often wonder which had more power to keep him safe: the figure of Christ on the cross or the light of the mysterious eye. And why was the eye blue, like his, not brown or green? One day his mother explained that the eye went back to a time before the cross, when shadows were young and dressed only in white. In those days there lived a magician who had the power to harm children just by staring into their eyes. An evil force would enter the child, draw their strength, and weaken them until they wasted away in sleep. Parents lived in terror of losing their child, until a clever marble maker hit upon the idea of making an eye from glass. He advised parents to pin it on their child in a visible place, saying its beauty would attract the magician's attention first, causing the evil to reflect back into him. And it worked, the magician was destroyed by his own power, but parents continued pinning the eye on their children, maybe as a safeguard against other magicians, or maybe in memory of the nameless marble maker.

Nick's pleased not to be sitting directly opposite the girl, though he can't help glancing at the charm, recalling his mother's story. Plates of food are already on the table, while jugs of beer and lemonade are brought by relatives, men and women in aprons, acting as waiters and waitresses. Nick looks around: the hall has filled with more people than were at Allan's Studio. Kocho *Kokoshkaro* knocks back a glass of beer and attacks a plate of fetta, mashing his words white. Pavle's on the stage with the musicians, cornet tucked under his arm, arguing with the clarinet player. A waiter appears, says something to Pavle, and then, taking him by the arm, almost pulls him away, behind the curtain on the side of the stage. The man on Nick's left has a full face, with round-rimmed glasses, and a scar shining down his left temple. He speaks to Nick in good English, the best he's heard from a Macedonian. He says he's been in Australia since 1935 – almost thirty years, Nick calculates. For some reason he has trouble coming to terms with this fact. Thirty years – will he be in Australia that long? Yes, because his father hasn't once spoken about returning to the village.

The man says he was in the Australian Army, fought the Japanese in New Guinea, where a bullet grazed his head. Australia has been good to him, given him opportunities, and he wants to give something back to his adopted country.

'What do you want to be when you grow up?' he asks.

The question surprises Nick. Most of his father's friends take little notice of him when they get together, yet this stranger is talking to him as if he were an adult.

'Dad wants me to work in a bank,' says Nick.

'Nothing wrong with that – are you good with numbers?'

'Best in the grade with the times-table.'

The man tears off a piece of the table's cover, takes a fountain pen from several in the small breast-pocket of his coat, and sets out a four-digit by two-digit multiplication problem. He points to the challenge and hands Nick the pen. Eager to impress him, he performs the calculation quickly and returns the pen.

'You should be an accountant,' he says, after checking the answer.

'I'm already a fast counter,' says Nick.

'An accountant,' the man laughs, 'helping people run businesses.'

Pretending to understand, Nick slips the scrap of paper in his pocket, not knowing what to say, when a man in a black suit and bow tie calls for attention through a microphone. The band plays a lively tune as couples are announced and greeted by applause. As the bride and groom enter, waving left and right, Pavle re-appears on stage, this time from the opposite side, and, maybe knowing the clarinet player won't stop during such an important moment, begins playing the cornet, though not exactly in tune with the band. People point and laugh, the musicians shake their heads, the groom's father, furious under his moustache, signals to the waiter who escorted him off before. Suddenly there's something about Pavle that Nick admires, maybe his unusual love of music and the fact that he's prepared to make a clown of himself in front of so many people. But then again, he probably can't hear their laughter through his playing, and, with eyes closed and cheeks puffed, can't see his audience. When the bride and groom are seated, the music stops and Pavle finds himself caught between an angry band and a stern waiter. Unhappy with the distracting stage show, the groom's father signals to the waiter with a sharp, sideways movement of his head. The waiter and the drummer lunge at Pavle, who, being short and quick, springs away to the front of the stage. The guests are now howling with the laughter, the groom's father is making a throat-cutting gesture at the little man, the bride's whispering to the groom. With the right exit blocked by the accordion player, the left by the trumpet player, the others move in on Pavle like cats on a pigeon. His only escape is to jump off the stage, a height at least that of an adult. He thinks about this a second, Nick can see it in the desperate look his eyes, but he darts left instead, snatches the clarinet from where the player left it on a stand, and raises it as though about to smash it on the floor. The musicians freeze, knowing it would ruin the wedding, as Macedonian songs and dances revolve around the clarinet. A minute's stand-off follows: the laughter subsides, the stunned musicians look at one another, even *Kokoshkaro* stops talking. For an instant Nick sees in little Pavle the figure of Zeus threatening to throw a bolt of lightning at a misbehaving world. The clarinet player approaches him with extended hands, stepping as though barefoot on glass, pleading with him not to do anything foolish, saying the clarinet belonged to his grandfather, who'd formerly played the bagpipe, but sold two fine oxen in order to travel to Salonika and buy it from a Jewish nut-merchant, whose only son had left the instrument behind in running off with a gentile girl. Pavle backs away, the instrument still raised, drops of spit glistening from its funnelled end, and orders the drummer to move from the exit. Seeing his escape, he throws the clarinet to its owner, who just manages to catch it, and runs off-stage. Looking embarrassed, the groom's father instructs the band to start playing, determined to get the wedding back on track. As they take up their instruments and positions, Pavle surprises everyone by showing up at the main door and letting out a shaky version of the army retreat tune. At the sight of several waiters approaching, he gives a loud flurry of notes and disappears, the cornet still sounding, until overcome by the instruments on stage.

The night unfolds in the manner Nick's come to know from other weddings. He listens to speeches in Macedonian, with close relatives congratulating the couple and using stock expressions in wishing this happiness to other houses. The groom's mother is handed the microphone and in a high-pitched voice sings about a daughter given in marriage seven mountains away, moistening eyes here and there. The best man is honoured by starting the dances, followed by the bride and groom, and then people are called out by name to order a dance and lead the circle.

As all this is happening, the children begin by running around inside, then up to the balcony, and finally out on the steps and the footpath. The bigger boys sneak off to Gertrude or Brunswick Street, where they play the pinball machines in the espresso bars. Nick's been warned about going to those places, but, knowing his way around Gertrude Street, he encourages a few boys to follow him on a little adventure. It's just after nine as they set off. The clock in the tower glows like a full moon. Exhausted from rushing about all day, the wind has fallen to a whimper, barely stirring the flag on the tower. They go up Napier Street, past houses with front doors open for relief from the heat, people sitting on verandas talking in sun-dried voices, kids still playing on the street, in circles cast by streetlights, the occasional welcome spray from someone watering a small front garden. Stopping at the entrance of an unlit lane, Nick says they're about to enter an area called the slum of Melbourne. It's a rough place, full of drunks and criminals and Aboriginals who don't like whites walking through their neighbourhood. Some of the boys refuse to go further, saying they've heard of murders in this place.

'It's not for the gutless,' Nick says, and sets off into the dark on his own.

After a lively discussion, a few turn back and three catch up to him. They walk shoulder to shoulder to the end of the lane, coming out onto a narrow street with few lights and footpaths barely wide enough for one person. The houses are small, run-down, with front doors right on the footpath. They draw closer together at the sound of a man and woman swearing in the front room of a cottage that seems to be leaning to one side. A man sitting on a doorstep, smoking, growls for them to get off the bloody street. Nick's now questioning his own bravery, but does his best to hide it from the others. A little further on, they're all shocked by the sight of a skinny boy sitting on the bluestone kerb, sobbing and eating Vegemite from a jar with his fingers. He's about three or four, with curly-blonde hair, and wearing nothing but a dirty singlet which has slipped off one shoulder.

'Get in here you little devil,' shouts a woman leaning over a wire fence sagging at one end. The boy continues dipping into the jar, face smeared in tears and Vegemite.

'Get in here,' she shouts, throwing open the gate held up by string. The boy springs up and scampers off down the street, his little feet slapping the bitumen still warm from the day's heat.

'What are you little bastards looking at?' she yells. 'Piss off before you cop a belting.'

They run for their lives to the next corner, where they stop beside a light-pole with a sign: Atherton Street. Aboriginal kids are playing outside a house with green window shutters swung open. A girl's hopping in and out of an elastic band stretched around the ankles of two smaller girls at each end. All these places are going to be pulled down, Nick whispers, glancing into the house through the open front door. An Aboriginal woman's cutting the hair of a bare-chested man with dressmaking scissors like his mother's.

'Why are they being pulled down?' asks one of the boys.

'To clean up the area and make way for twenty-storey flats.'

'Where are those kids going to live?' asks another.

The question jolts Nick. He's known for some time about the coming demolition but without really giving it much thought. Being here, though, just taking in the heavy smell of chops frying in fat, makes it real in a painful sort of way. What will become of these families, each with its daily hardships and flicker of evening joys? Maybe people move on and re-arrange their lives to new surroundings, just as they did coming to Melbourne. But this street, these houses, this light-pole – they'll all be gone. When the twenty-storey flats go up, this here and now will exist only in his memory, in the past of that kid running away from the man, in the dreams of the Aboriginal girl skipping over the band. And in time when he grows old and his memory fades, it will be as if all this never existed. He feels a swell of emotion, a need to grasp this place, save it from disappearing without trace. Yes, there's a purpose in coming here tonight, to stamp this place in their memories so it remains standing long after it's all been pulled down. He tells the boys to remember this walk, to take something with them, a sight or a sound, so that when they meet in fifty years from now, they'll bring Atherton Street back to life.

They feel better under the lights of Gertrude Street, secure in the rumble of a passing tram. The street's quiet on a Sunday night, different from the violent, drink-driven place of a Saturday evening. The Macedonian Club's closed, but the boys give each other a boost up to see inside, only to jump down disappointed, unable to understand how their fathers can spend a whole day in such a place. Nick points out the pubs where he's seen all-out brawls, men slashed with broken beer bottles, heads bashed against bluestone gutters. They press their faces to windows: rows of old shoes abandoned by their owners, second hand furniture waiting for a home, chairs turned upside down on tables in cafés, jars of pickled onions on the counter of the fish'n'chip shop, the scale in the fruit shop with its collection of brass weights balancing the dark, the milk bar's cash register, its till left open, springy traps up, compartments empty.

They're about to turn into Gore Street when three boys appear from around the Builders Arms pub. The King brothers – Nick recognise them at once. They've all got shanghais, probably out blinding streetlights. Vic's pointed them out from the door of the Club, saying they're from a family of criminals and heading for jail themselves. They steal from shops along the street, spit at police cars driving past, and he's heard they roll drunks for their watches and wallets. Nick could take off and outrun them for sure, but his friends aren't as fast, they'd be caught and bashed. The Kings stand in the way, heads cocked to one side.

'What are you slags doin' here?' says the one on the middle, a ferret-faced kid sporting a shiner around his left eye.

Nick's friends turn to him, frightened. He's also afraid but, feeling responsible for the situation, puts on a show of courage. He thinks of Alexander – what would he do faced with these characters? Confront them? No. They wouldn't stand a chance against these seasoned street-fighters. Outsmart them, play on the hunger in their eyes, trick them with money, yes, that's what they're after.

'We're off to buy hamburgers – with the lot,' says Nick.

'Hamburgers with the lot,' says ferret-face.

'Yeah, double bacon and egg and cheese.'

The Kings exchange looks, lick their lips, swallow hard.

'With the lot,' says the one on the left, 'they're three fucken bob each.'

'How's a little dago shit like you gonna find three bob for a fucken hamburger with the lot?' says the one on the right.

'It's my birthday,' Nick says. 'My godfather's given me two quid instead of a present. We've sneaked away from the party to buy hamburgers – with the lot.'

Nick takes the scrap of paper with the calculations from his pocket and rustles it close to his side. The Kings shove the shanghais in their trousers and whisper to each other in approaching him. Certain all three will chase him like hounds after a rabbit, he whispers in Macedonian for the boys to run the other way when he gives the signal.

'Stop fucken talkin' dago talk,' says the one on the left.

'Go,' shouts Nick.

The boys dash off along Gore Street as Nick sprints down Gertrude Street. Just as he figured: all three Kings are after him, shouting and swearing and threatening to break his legs if he doesn't stop. But Nick's fast, with stamina – qualities Alexander had – and soon puts a safe distance between himself and the tiring Kings. He doesn't ease up, though, not until he turns into Moor Street and the Town Hall's in sight and the music's within earshot, by which time they've given up the chase.

Puffing and sweating, he waits for his friends on the front steps, proud of escaping what would've been a certain bashing. Groups of young men are smoking, casting glances at young women fanning themselves. The boys appear a few minutes later and run up the steps. They embrace and perform a little victory dance.

'Have you really got two quid?' one of them asks.

Nick shows them the scrap of paper. They laugh and set off down the corridor for a glass of lemonade. On the way, they vow again to remember Atherton Street – a vow now made stronger by their encounter with the feral King brothers.

The ballroom has now really heated up. Coats and jackets drape the backs of chairs. The bride's removed her veil, her face beaming, golden hair woven to look like a crown. The groom's sitting with elbows on the table, chin on hands, looking thoughtful. Tireless in their push to make old tunes new, the band's stirring the dancers, moving them anticlockwise with a lively melody. The accordion player is singing what Nick's come to know as a Macedonian favourite, *Zaiko Kokoraiko*, a song about old rabbit *Zaiko* who goes around with a big moustache and baggy trousers and refuses to marry because he's still too young for marriage chains. The words suddenly catch Nick's attention, not so much for their humour, but for what they seem to be saying. *Zaiko*'s no fool: why should he get married when he can roam free the region surrounding Salonika and enjoy himself at other people's weddings? And then Nick's struck by the thought: why are weddings such joyful occasions when what follows is unhappiness? Could that be what *Zaiko* knows? The joy of the wedding day, all this tonight – the music, the dancing, the drinking and eating – is it all a cover-up for the loss of youth and freedom? Is the groom thoughtful because he senses this? Yes, *Zaiko* might have a grey moustache, but he's still young at heart, with a mind of his own, a folk hero, someone who can stand beside Alexander.

At the table, his mother asks where he's been and why he's flushed and sweating so much. She's sitting with the mother of the three girls. Nick's pleased they aren't there. As usual at functions where beer flows freely, his father's had too much to drink and Nick can see his hat bobbing around among the dancers. Boys have emptied food into jugs of flat beer, making cocktails of cabana, olives and fetta, in order to spin the empty paper plates across the hall from the balcony. Nick fills his glass and looks around for

Pavle, half-expecting to see him spring up from under a table and let rip with the cornet. Has he really left, or is he waiting for another chance, maybe the last melody of the night, to show everyone he's a real musician?

The man on the microphone calls one of the groomsmen to come to the front and order the next dance. He reminds guests not to break off and start new dancing lines, but to respect the person who's been honoured to lead. The young man speaks to the accordion player, who in turn passes on the request to the other band members. The clarinet player taps the spit from his instrument, fingers the silver keys, and begins with several high-pitched notes. Nick knows the tune, his father's favourite, the *pushteno*: a quick, free-flowing dance, with hops and skips and, depending on the leader's skill, lots of twists and turns. The young man sets off in the open space with a dozen or so from the bridal party, all quick and light-footed on the throb of the drum. But they haven't completed a quarter of a turn when others join the line, extending its tail, then others, forming an open arc, and even more, making an ever-tighter, slower, spiral, until the floor's crowded with dancers barely moving. And then, at the end of the spiral, which is almost at a standstill, a man wearing a floppy white sombrero appears from nowhere and springs up like the tail of a rattle snake. Curious, Nick races up to the balcony for a better look. The man's old, fifty or more, in a short-sleeved shirt and green trousers with a silver buckle. His movements are too vigorous for the tight space, left arm swinging wildly across his body, squatting and leaping and slapping his high-kicking shoe. A small circle opens around him as people back away in fear of a karate chop to the head or a foot in the stomach. Nick's never seen anyone like him. A gold tooth gleams as he throws up a smile. Slowing down, almost out of breath, the lead dancer nods for the band to stop, but the character's becoming more worked up and gestures for them to continue. Nick picks up the conversation of an elderly couple leaning over the balcony.

'Look at him,' says the woman, 'no shame at all.'

'Couldn't wait forty days,' says the man.

'Forty days – it was two weeks yesterday.'

'He could've at least worn a black hat.'

'Her eyes haven't burst yet.'

'She must be turning in her grave.'

'Look at him,' says the woman, thrusting an open hand in the dancer's direction, 'you'd think he's celebrating his wife's death.'

Nick doesn't understand why they're so critical of him. Is it because he's not wearing black and mourning his wife? Should he be slumped in a chair with his face hidden in his hands? He admires the man's energy and fitness. He sees in the sweep of his arm and the spring of his body a proud defiance of death. The small space around him is an arena, a kind of battleground, in which he smiles at death, daring it to take him, or to be crushed under his heel, like the head of a snake. Nick ponders whether he'll be as fit and active at that age. Will he have the man's fighting spirit? And for an instant he sees in him the image of *Zaiko*. Who knows, maybe this man loved his wife, maybe he cared for her day and night during some long illness, and when her time finally came, maybe he felt free again, as he'd been in youth, before marriage, and his dancing now is an expression of that freedom. He compares the groom sitting heavy-eyed beside his new wife, to this high-spirited *Zaiko*-like character who's just lost his wife, and in that instant he glimpses something heroic in his dancing, a kind of noble struggle against silence and stillness. There and then, maybe caught up by the man's vitality, Nick vows never to get married.

It must be nearing twelve: most of the tables are empty, Nick's friends have left, and he's drowsy. The parents and girls have gone and he's not embarrassed to rest his head on his mother's shoulder. He asks if they can go, but she points to his father in the middle of a line of men doing a slow arm-on-arm number. The clarinet player is down amongst them, the end of his instrument close to the lead dancer's ear. A five-pound note's caught under the silver keys, other notes are stuffed in the pockets of his shirt. The *Zaiko* character is at the end, leaping high, slapping his heel, twisting this way and that. Held by a cord around his neck, the sombrero's bouncing on his back. The man at the front suddenly breaks away from the others and performs a few sharp turns. His skill's greeted by whistles and cheers. He licks a two-pound note and plasters it onto the musician's forehead.

The men begin singing along with the band, roaring out the chorus in Macedonian: Don't cry, Mother, don't mourn if you never see me again. Letting go with a piercing two-finger whistle, Vangel runs to the front, squats beside the leader and pretends to wipe the floorboards with his hat, as if cleaning a path for the man's brown shoes. The music's tempo picks up and Vangel hurries back to his position. The dancers are now kicking in and out, mincing their steps, struggling to keep up with the clarinet. Just when it seems they can't play any faster, the band finds another gear, the bass drum beats frantically in three's, driving the men forward, scrambling their steps, reducing the dance to a ragged race, threatening to exhaust and collapse them in a heap. And then, maybe sensing it has pushed the dancers to the limit, the clarinet suddenly pulls back, the drum slows, the music stops. The line breaks apart, men breathing hard, sweating through their white shirts, shaking hands, congratulating themselves on a fine effort. In the centre, standing upright and composed, the *Zaiko* character places the sombrero on his head, straightens his silver buckle, and strides to his table for a beer.

The men are still catching their breath when another name's called out. Menka sits up in a way that rouses Nick from his drowsiness. He's relieved to hear it's the last dance, after which the bride and groom will be farewelled. A man with a thin moustache speaks to the clarinet player. Standing near, Vangel turns suddenly, as if hit on the back of the head, and confronts the man.

'*Le-le*,' says Menka. 'He's going to shame us.'

Nick's now wide awake, standing beside his mother twisting her new cream gloves.

'A Macedonian wedding's no place for a *zembekiko*,' says Vangel.

'I'll order what I want,' retorts the man.

He turns to the clarinet player and speaks to him in Greek.

'No *zembekiko*,' Vangel snarls.

Nick doesn't understand why he's so against a *zembekiko*, whatever it is. He keeps telling Nick Australia's a free country, where people can sing and dance as they please, so why is he now denying the man his right to the music of his choice? A few of Vangel's friends attempt to pull him away, saying the night's almost over, but this only makes him more determined. He breaks their grip and steps between the man and the confused musician.

'Spies and opportunists,' Vangel shouts, 'that's what you and your family were. Your mother couldn't say *yiasou*, and here you are, making out you're more Greek than Onassis.'

The man turns to the groom's worried father, expecting him to intervene and sort out the argument, but Tsanko *Ofcharo* looks sheepishly from one to the other, nervously twisting his moustache. Vangel removes his hat and spins it in Nick's direction. Menka shakes her head and repeats *le-le*. Picking up the hat in case it's crushed, Nick stands next to the stairs leading up to the stage, heart pounding, terrified a fight might start, yet also wishing it happens.

'No,' Vangel continues, face blazing. 'I'll never forget that Easter Sunday in the village square. Remember? We were dancing the *pushteno* when soldiers stationed in the village stopped the music and demanded a *zembekiko*. We took a stand in front of the band, but they pulled out their guns, marched us off to their barracks and beat us white and blue. Remember? You saluted them as they led us away, saying *zito ellas*. Remember? Yes, long live the Greek army, but it's not here tonight, my friend. We're in a free country, this is a Macedonian wedding, so don't add more shame to your family by ordering a *zembekiko*. You're so thick-headed, you don't know it's really a Turkish dance, shipped to Athens in the twenties by refugees who'd lived in Turkey for generations.'

'We should've driven you from the village when we had the chance.'

'Hear that?' Vangel laughs. 'He'd still be going around with holes in the seat of his pants if it weren't for his Greek friends.'

'The Civil War ended too soon for your kind.'

'Your family prospered very nicely in that hell.'

'We should've driven you into Tito's communist Yugoslavia.'

'Yeah, so you fascists could claim our property.'

The man swings a round-arm, but Vangel ducks and springs up again, catching him in a headlock, bringing him down to his knees. The bridesmaids scream, the groomsmen scramble onto the dance floor, a circle gathers around the fighters. Men are shouting and arguing, some supporting Vangel, others his opponent. The man breaks Vangel's grip and they begin throwing punches. Nick's sickened by the thud of fist on face, afraid for his father, who's much shorter than the other. Soon the ballroom fills with chaos as the fight spreads to thirty or forty men. The groom's father grabs the microphone and calls for order and respect, his words accompanied by a screeching electrical noise.

'Please, please,' he shouts, 'it's time to farewell the newly weds.'

But nobody's listening. The fighting's now an all-out brawl: shirts are ripped, tables upturned, jugs shattered, beer puddling the floor. It seems even the groomsmen have taken sides, swearing and pushing each other. Wives are crying like seagulls, calling on their husbands to stop, saying they'll leave with the children. This inhuman explosion of anger terrifies Nick. Ten minutes ago these men were dancing together, now they're blinded by savagery. The brawl's no longer about Vevi or Banitsa, no longer about right or wrong, simply a wild desire to hurt the other person.

Tears filling his eyes, Nick calls on his father to stop, when the man lands a right flush on his nose. The sight of blood on his father's face and white shirt stuns Nick. He turns helplessly to his mother, who races over and embraces him, trying to shield him from the violence, crying and cursing her hot-headed husband. Nick pulls away from her soft, perfumed hold, thinking how she hasn't comforted him like this in ages. His initial numbness at the sight of his father's blood now gives way to a kind of rage. He wants to throw himself at the man, punch him in the face, make him bleed, but all he can do is tighten his grip on his father's hat. Suddenly, the police come to mind. The station's just around the corner, he thinks. They'll stop this madness. He's about to run out, when the cornet sounds from the main door. Pavle enters playing a familiar tune – the sad melody that signals the end of all weddings, when the bride and groom are farewelled – playing skilfully, the long notes steady and sure, sending a shiver down Nick's spine. He walks slowly through the ballroom, eyes closed, head thrown back, rosy cheeks puffed out, walks past the astonished women, into the chaos of the brawl. And then something strange happens, the way things unfold in a dream. A few women turn from the men and, in a single voice, start singing to the tune, growing in strength with each heart-felt word that tells of a young bride's separation from her mother. The fighting begins to ease, the swearing subsides, men pull away in bewilderment. More women take up the song. Pavle plays with deeper feeling, his notes faultless, blending with the chorus. Menka wipes her eyes and joins the singers, who now form a circle around the remaining skirmish, until the last fighters step back, dropping their fists in shame. Vangel covers his face with a blood-soaked hanky. The men move away from the dance floor, most joining the circle of women, some slumping exhausted onto chairs. Vangel sways toward Nick, who helps him sit, head back against the wall.

'Promise me something,' he says through the hanky.

'What, Dad?'

'Put your finger here and promise.'

Touching the moist hanky, Nick looks at his red fingertip.

'Promise you'll never betray this blood.'

'I promise, Dad.'

The cornet and singing continue, filling the hall and everyone's heart – those from Vevi and those from Banitsa, those who think of themselves as Greeks and those who call themselves Macedonian. The clarinet player joins Pavle in the circle as the newly weds are farewelled by the immediate family in the centre. The bride and groom move in opposite direction around the circle, shaking hands with their guests, finding a pound note in each clasp. When they come together again, they're escorted to the front door by the musicians and a group of singers.

The wedding finally over, Nick places the hat on his father's head and helps him to his feet. Biting her lips, Menka folds his coat and carries it over her arm. Descending the steps of the Town Hall, they meet Pavle, who's shaking spit from the cornet.

'I didn't know you could play like that,' says Vangel, sounding nasally.

'It was very moving,' adds Menka. 'Brought tears to my eyes.'

'The tune played itself,' Pavle smiles.

'What do you mean?' asks Vangel.

'It just came out of the cornet.'

Walking home between his silent parents, Nick ponders Pavle's strange words. Was he joking? Is that the only tune he can play well from beginning to end? But what if he was serious? What if some tunes exist in a place beyond musicians and instruments? Maybe in being played over the centuries, in being given breath and body by generations of musicians, some tunes rise to a life of their own, choosing the moment and occasion for full expression. Did he witness such a moment tonight? Yes, maybe the sad tune played itself through Pavle, as though by magic or miracle, and made everyone more human.

13

Saturday evening and Nick's tooth is killing him. This morning's annoying little niggle, which he eased by sucking in breath from the left side of his mouth, soon flared to full-blown agony. His mother's home-grown remedies haven't helped: first gargling a salt solution, then Aspro dissolved in water, even chewing a clove of garlic. With dentists closed on weekends, she now urges him to be strong, just like the saints, who endured torture in silence, all through the strength of their faith. He watches with growing doubt as she strikes a match and lights the wick floating in the small glass of oil. Reaching up, she places it in the icon case, this time before Saint George instead of *Bogoroditsa*, and crosses herself slowly. Instinctively he brings his three fingers together, but then tightens them in a fist, angry at God for allowing pain in the world.

'If it doesn't settle by tomorrow,' she says, 'I'll stay home on Monday and take you to the Dental Hospital.'

Two long nights and another whole day of torture, he thinks, grimacing at the fiery-mouthed dragon in its death throes around the saint's spear. Helpless before the boy's crushed look, she feels a flush of resentment toward her husband: if they had a television, like their relatives, it would've helped take the boy's mind off the tooth. And then, perhaps as a last resort, or at least a way of distracting him for a while, she suggests he goes to Stoyan's place, where his father and a few others are brewing *rakija* in the back shed.

'In the village,' she says, caressing his cheek, 'we used it for toothaches.'

'The stuff's firewater,' he winces.

'It's not so bad with sugar.'

'Will it really help?'

'It helped me when I was your age.'

'Alright,' he says, desperate for relief.

'But don't be long – dinner's almost ready.'

The wrought iron front gate groans as Nick pulls it shut and hurries up McKean Street. It's late autumn and winter's already in the air, together with the smell of burning briquettes and chops frying. The six o'clock dark has descended from the elms in the Edinburgh Gardens and spread over Fitzroy. A misty drizzle haloes the streetlights. Danny's mother is coming down the street, pulling a shopping trolley with one hand, holding an umbrella in the other. She's a chatty woman, friendly toward Nick, always asking with a smile how he's going at school and what he wants to be when he grows up. He can't tell her age because her clothes are old-fashioned: silver-rimmed glasses, a knitted hat over stringy grey hair, a dark overcoat often buttoned unevenly, and brown lace-up shoes. She could easily pass for Danny's grandmother. The pain throbbing, Nick's in no mood for conversation, but she stops him under the umbrella and, in a high-pitched voice, asks if anyone at school is bullying Danny because he hasn't been himself lately.

'No, Mrs Mason,' he says, grimacing.

She brushes the drizzle from his shoulders and asks him to look out for Danny. He's such a sensitive boy and too shy to talk about whatever's troubling him. Maybe it's partly his father's fault. He was an army man, and still is, very tight lipped, keeps his emotions in a fist, hardly speaks to the boy, except to scold him when sometimes he complains of this or that, telling him to stop acting like a sissy and take it on the chin.

'I'm running a message for Mum,' says Nick, backing away.

'You're such a thoughtful boy,' she smiles, 'always helping her, and in weather like this. She's so hard working, what with toiling away in a factory and keeping the house spotless and making time to tend the front garden with roses a joy to walk past. I don't know how she does it.'

'I'll keep an eye on Danny,' says Nick. 'Bye Mrs Mason.'

Halfway up the street he enters a lane with a house along the length of each side. Light spills from windows onto the glistening cobblestones. The lane turns left into a dark dead end with patched, rickety fences leaning this way and that. The air's pungent with vinegar. Smoke rising from Stoyan's shed swirls in the drizzle. Nick thumps the tin gate. The lively voices fall silent. A shiver goes down his spine at the thought of being watched through a nail hole. And then the gate swings open and Stoyan pulls him inside. Familiar faces are sitting around a bench, drinking, eating fried sausages. Nick's father puts down his glass and shakes his head. A kerosene lamp hangs from the rafter above him.

'Boy, don't scare us like that,' says Stoyan.

He's a big-jawed man, with a couple of gold teeth, and wearing a flannelette shirt with sleeves rolled past his elbows.

'Cops are always snooping round these back lanes,' he says.

'They caught Yanko a few days ago,' says one of the men.

'He'll get his arse burnt,' says Stoyan.

'What are you doing here?' scowls Vangel.

'My tooth's sore.'

They laugh and a bald man offers to pull it out, saying he did it to lots of goats and sheep in the village.

'Mum said *rakija* will ...'

'Yes, *rakija*,' says Stoyan, clapping and rubbing his hands. 'We'll have it fixed in no time.'

The still's steaming in the corner of the shed, heated by scraps of wood in a brick base. A pipe coiling from a copper drum runs under a tap and drips clear liquid into a large glass container. Stoyan scoops some into a small coffee pot, adds a few teaspoons of sugar, and heats it on the fire. He then sits Nick on a wooden crate at the back of the shed and instructs him to swish on the sore tooth, warning him not to swallow, but to spit it out and keep swishing until finished. He places the coffee pot and small cup on another crate and returns to the men at the bench. Nick pours some and smells it – the fumes are sharp, going straight to his head. He dips a finger and tastes – his mother's right: sugar softens the sharpness. He takes a mouthful, tilts his head to one side, swishes.

Stoyan's telling a story about a village priest who falls into a swamp and can't get out because his robes are heavy with water and mud. A villager walking past calls out for his hand, but the priest curses the fellow and continues flopping about this way and that like a fish on land. A second fellow passes and calls out: Father, please, give me your hand and I'll pull you out. Again the priest refuses the offer of help, even though he's now struggling like a buffalo in a swamp. When the two villagers relate the incident to the men in the café, a man in a sheepskin coat springs up and announces he'll rescue the hapless priest. He races off to the swamp, watches the priest kicking about like a beetle on its back, and calls out from the edge: Father, here, take my hand before you drown in your own stubbornness. In an instant the priest grasps the outstretched hand and is pulled to safety.

'Was the priest drunk?' laughs the bald man.

'Priests hold their drink better than anyone,' says Stoyan.

'Was he mad?' asks another.

'I've got it,' says the bald man. 'He's a priest, right? He believes in the Holy Trinity, right? So he wants to be rescued by the third passer-by.'

'Good try,' laughs Stoyan. 'But it's like this: the first two ask the priest for his hand, while the third offers his hand, knowing that priests are takers, not givers.'

As the men tell a few more jokes about priests, Nick's ballooning his left cheek and swishing the *rakija*, but ignoring Stoyan's warning. The sugar's made it tasty, and he finds himself swallowing more than he spits out. By the time he finishes what's in the coffee pot, the shed's tilting like a ship, the lamp's rotating above him, the men's voices sound distant and angry. He tries to stand but his legs give way and he slumps back on the crate. The thought of being drunk amuses him to the point of laughter. His father's now arguing with the bald man over whether a mule is the off-spring of a female horse and male donkey, or male horse and female donkey. Stoyan sways between them, trying to calm them down, his gold teeth flashing. Nick feels the tooth with his tongue: the pain's gone, just like his mother said. He wants to shout in joy, tell Stoyan his *rakija* is a miracle cure, when his father swings a punch at the bald man, misses, and fists the lamp instead, sending it flying against the still.

Suddenly all hell breaks loose: the glass container burst alight, with flames crawling along the floor, swallowing the still, springing at a pile of wood, leaping up to the rafters. Despite the panic and confusion, Nick can't help laughing as the men jump to their feet and begin beating the flames with whatever's at hand. Stoyan throws open the back gate as a way of escape. Nick's happy sitting here, chuckling at the spectacle, but his father grabs him by the arm and drags him out into the lane.

'What's the matter with you?' he growls.

Unable to hold back, Nick laughs in his face, spraying him with spit. His head's now spinning, the surrounding fences are titling back and forth, but the drizzle's cool on his cheeks. The men are swearing and shouting and rushing about, though he can't see the urgency of the situation. If anything, he likes the way the flames are flapping about and wants them to become stronger, to lick the men's backsides and send them running from the shed. His father appears with a garden hose, but it's useless against the fire beating wild like a flock of pigeons spooked in a cage.

'The house,' cries Stoyan, 'keep it from the house.'

'We need the fire brigade,' shouts Vangel.

'That means cops,' Stoyan shouts back.

'Better cops than a burnt house.'

As the men give up on the shed and scramble to defend the house, Vangel races out, grips Nick by the shoulders and looks him straight in the eyes.

'Stop grinning and listen.'

'I can't help it,' Nick laughs.

'You've had too much *rakija*,' he says, shaking him.

'The toothache – it's gone.'

'I'll give you a toothache.'

'Look at the shed,' Nick bursts out, 'it's burning like a beauty.'

His father shakes him again, his head loose, rocking back and forth as though about to fly off. Nick can see his father's fuming, that his laughter's really getting to him, but he can't stop – no, he doesn't want to stop because it feels good, all this laughter pouring out of him, making him pain free, happy, light.

'Look at Stoyan's face,' Nick chuckles, 'it's red as a pepper.'

'Listen to me,' Vangel shouts over the roaring inferno. 'We need the fire brigade. Understand? Run to Rowe Street, to the red alarm box on the corner. Break the glass and press the alarm. Are you listening? Wait till the fire brigade comes and bring them here. Got that? Bring them here. You'll get a ride in the truck. Now run before the house burns down.'

'But you started the fire,' Nick can't help saying.

'It was an accident.'

'You punched the lamp,' he laughs.

Vangel swings to slap the back of Nick's head, but he manages to step back, even though everything's still reeling around him. Excited by the thought of riding in a fire engine with the siren going, Nick races off down the lane, unable to keep a straight line, more staggering than running, legs going one way, head the other, like being in a dream where he's trying to get somewhere but his feet are set in concrete. He moves in slow motion, urging himself forward but making little progress, supporting himself on front fences in struggling around Alfred Crescent, passing The Haven hovering on its foundations, pricking himself on a rose bush growing between palisades, seeing the red fire alarm but unable to reach it, until he lunges desperately and wraps his arms around it, but more to keep the trees across the street from turning upside down, the houses from toppling, streetlights from lurching all over the place. He closes his eyes in the hope of steadying himself, but it has the opposite effect: his head spins like a top and he's barely able to hold back a surge of nausea. Suddenly, he's never been so sick in his life. He can hear himself moaning and groaning for his mother. He heaves and retches but nothing comes out. The fire, he thinks, Stoyan's house, his family's inside. His father's words come back through the drizzle, the swirl, the nausea. He releases the post and stumbles beneath the overhanging tree, looking for a stone to smash the glass. In reaching down for a white pebble, he loses his balance and falls into the gutter. Can this really be happening? He crawls on hands and knees over the trickle of water, unable to get to his feet, calling on his mother to help him. He straightens up on the trunk and staggers back to the alarm, just managing to embrace the post and keep from stumbling headlong in the gutter. He smashes the glass with the pebble and presses the button, and keeps pressing, while hugging the post for dear life, trying to still the world and hold back a wave of nausea. But the world suddenly lurches to one side, the nausea rises to his throat, and a torrent of spew pours out of him freely as laughter.

A siren sounds from the school-end of Alfred Crescent, and he's still retching and spewing until there is nothing left inside. The streetlights continue swaying, but at least the nausea has eased. In an instant the screaming truck arrives and a fireman in a white helmet jumps out and asks a few questions, repeating Nick's answers as if he's speaking a different language. He comments on the smell and pulls a face on seeing the vomit, telling the others the kid's suffering from smoke inhalation. He bundles Nick in the back seat and whistles to the driver, who hits the siren and speeds off around Alfred Crescent. Nick's enjoying this and before he knows it the truck's reversing into the lane and stops a few houses from Stoyan's. The fireman lifts him out and sits him on a sheltered step away from the confusion. The shed's now blazing beyond rescue, but the house appears safe, with Nick's father and the others slapping back the flames with wet hessian sacks. Despite calls to leave it, a crimson-faced Stoyan is manoeuvring a long pipe, trying to extricate the still from the inferno. A whistle sounds and one of the firemen orders the men to stand aside. Stoyan continues prodding, gold teeth flashing, until the fireman snatches the pipe from him, threatening to report him for obstructing their work. The whistle sounds again and another fireman directs a powerful hose at the shed, blasting tin sheets from the roof and fence, smashing glasses and bottles, tossing around burning crates and chairs, demolishing the still.

Nick can't keep his eyes open, while his head, suddenly feeling leaden, sinks to his knees. He can still make out voices, but they're distant, incomprehensible. And then his father's standing over him, shaking him gently, saying it's time to go home. The truck's gone, the lane's quiet, smoke's sighing, rising from the smouldering shed. He tries to stand but his legs buckle. And then, without wanting, he starts whimpering, saying sorry for getting drunk, for laughing like that, tears flowing from him as pleasantly as laughter. His father holds him firmly.

'Let's go,' he says, his breath sharp with *rakija*, 'before your mother locks us out.'

'Mum … dinner's … ready.'

His tongue's loose, floppy, unable to shape and connect the words.

'Son, you're drunk,' says Vangel, a hint of a smile breaking through.

Nick's surprised at how easily his father picks him up: he would 've been six or seven the last time he was carried like this. As the drizzle thickens, blurring McKean Street, fuzzing the streetlights, Nick feels warm, secure, his heart pounding in time with his father's.

14

Nick hasn't enjoyed the first month in grade 5. Read backwards his teacher's name describes his unpredictable state of mind. He's solid, wide-shouldered, black hair gleaming with the bottle of Californian Poppy he keeps on his table. He's always telling the class about his home town in the country and how he was a champion centre half-back in the local football team. As proof he holds up a faded newspaper cut-out of someone resembling him taking a screamer. Along with his voice, which is more sarcastic than serious, Nick also fears his hands: big, spotted with freckles, like those of a butcher or woodchopper. His strap's the most feared in school. 'Sadie the gentle lady', as he calls it, is two-feet long, a couple of inches wide, and thick as an exercise book. He grips Sadie in his left hand and smiles giving boys 'six of her best kisses'. Female teachers send troublemakers to him for punishment, and most mornings five or six line up in front of the blackboard waiting to be kissed. Before coming to the room, some toughen their palms by rubbing them with sand from the yard, while others can be heard clapping hard and loud in the corridor. Lots of kids break out in tears even before the first kiss, and a few have admitted to a trickle down below.

Last year an incident involving Sadie caused a stir that was discussed in the schoolyard for some time. Imre Gabor was a big-eared Hungarian kid who'd just arrived at the school. After a couple of days his teacher reported him for not listening in class and wrote his name in the strapping-book for the following morning. Imre was a real talker and Nick had heard him in the yard telling a group how strict life was in a communist country and how his family had fled Hungary for the freedom of Australia. When someone in the group told Imre about Sadie, he got all worked up and said straps had no place in a free country. They'd left Hungary to get away from living in fear and he wasn't going to put up with it in Australia. A whisper soon spread like scrub-fire that he planned to steal Sadie and throw her in the incinerator. A few boys tried talking him out of it, saying the teacher would go berserk if he found his strap missing and make conditions even scarier for all. But Imre didn't flinch, kept talking about his father who'd stood up to some dictator called Stalin, and how he wouldn't be silenced by a heavy-handed teacher. He said other things, too, which Nick didn't understand, like fear being used by those in power to make slaves of people. After school that afternoon, as the teacher was taking pre-season footy training across the street, Imre sneaked into his room, took the strap from its place in the second drawer, and headed for the incinerator, which the cleaners burnt every day. He didn't make it out the corridor when the teacher stopped him in his tracks, with half the footy team behind him. There was a tug-of-war over the strap, until the teacher pulled it from Imre's hands and threatened to give him a hiding. Imre met this with a daring smile, saying this was a free country, not Hungary, and as of tomorrow he'd be going to another school. And that's exactly what happened: Nick didn't see Imre again after that. Some said he was expelled for his actions, others that his father supported his stand and sent him to a private school. As for how the teacher had come to be there at that instant: Nick heard that Imre was dobbed in by Ronnie Noble, who was desperate to be full-forward in the footy team.

The strap isn't the teacher's only way of keeping the class in line. On the very first day of the year he arranged the desks in three rows of seven, with boys sitting next to girls. Maybe he figured boys are naturally shy of girls, or they want nothing to do with them, and this would keep them quiet throughout the day. His idea seems to be working. Nick sits next to Margaret, a small Maltese girl with ribboned pigtails and glasses with a pink cup over one lens. They sit on the ends of the smooth seat, as far from each other as possible, never looking at each other, or saying so much as a word. Recently, though, Margaret giggled at Nick's drawing of a kangaroo and said it looked like a rabbit. Nick leaned over and whispered she was a bloody bitch. She burst into tears and stormed off to tell the teacher. He ordered Nick to his table and asked if he'd called her a bloody bitch. Seeing his big hand reaching for the drawer where Sadie was kept, he panicked, ears ringing from a rush of blood.

'No, sir,' he said. 'She heard wrong – I called her a bloody witch.'

'A bloody witch?'

'Yes, sir.'

'Moby Dick,' he said, often calling him this instead of Nick, 'I don't care if you said bitch or witch, but good Australians never use the word bloody, especially in the company of women.'

Nick didn't understand what he meant, but his meaning became clearer when he took out Sadie and gave him four of her sharpest kisses.

Every Tuesday afternoon the teacher takes the boys from both grades for woodwork, while the girls go with the female teacher for needlecraft. They use small fretwork saws to make Australian birds from three-ply wood. Once the cut-outs are sanded and painted, the teacher chooses the best for the Gould League competition. But they're so nervous with him breathing over them, they can't keep their saws on the pencil outlines, which means no-one's job will be good enough to be entered. He's strict in these classes and won't tolerate a whisper when they gather around him to see what needs to be done. But when he wants a laugh he'll make fun of some boy's name, like calling sleepy David Nash, 'Nash, gnash your teeth' and loud Sam Ciurleo, 'Curlio the old mustachio'. If he sees anyone daydreaming, his left hand soon wakes them up with a whack to the head. Nick learns to read his moods, knowing when he's going to let fly with an indiscriminate swipe, which he avoids with a quick back step or duck. But Manuel Cassar, a snotty nose Maltese kid, wasn't so quick last week. They were lining up in the corridor to enter the room, when the teacher swung a backhander, knocking Manuel's head against the window, smashing a pane of glass. They froze. Manuel turned white and felt his head, but luckily there was no blood. The teacher was shaken, too, though only for an instant, because he then started yelling at Manuel for getting his jug-head in the way and ordered him to pick up the broken pieces. After school Nick and a few others pressed Manuel to report the teacher to his parents. He'd be kicked out of school, they said, and everyone would have a better year. They promised to back him up as his witnesses. It would be his chance to be someone, make a name for himself, gain the respect of toughies like Terry Ward and Benny Dinardio. But Manuel didn't want to go down that path. Teachers in Malta were always right, he said, and if he complained his father would belt him for being disobedient.

In the last few days Nick's fear of the teacher has been overshadowed by a darker fear – something like what he felt after seeing the film *Psycho.* This fear has gripped the neighbourhood, the entire suburb, the whole of Melbourne. It's the first week of March, still like summer, but Nick and the boys don't dare walk through the park alone, are indoors before dark, and run to the shops on Queens Parade and back, carrying knives hidden up sleeves and in socks.

It started with a Greek boy called Terry, whose father told Vangel things that were later reported in *The Sun*, and other things that never made it in the newspaper. After playing with a mate in the lanes around the Fitzroy Town Hall, Terry went home and told his parents they'd found something that looked like a person's body, only without the head, arms and legs. His father's first reaction was to curse the inventor of the television. Yes, he'd recently bought a HMV, though not for all those violent American shows, no, but because he'd been a good wrestler in his army days back in Greece and now enjoyed watching World Championship Wrestling. He scolded his son and knocked on his forehead with his knuckles, as though testing a watermelon. How many times had he told him? Stick to watching the wrestling and boxing and keep away from all that American rubbish. But no, he wouldn't listen, and now those shows had scrambled his brains and filled his head with nonsense so he couldn't tell the difference between what was real and what was in his head. His father gave him another sermon about the old days: how he'd grown up on good Greek myths and never went around making up stories about headless bodies. He then sent him to his room, saying he was tired from the factory and didn't want to hear anymore nonsense.

Next day Terry and his mate, who'd been too scared to breathe a word of what they'd seen, decided to tell their teacher. She gave them each a few jelly beans and called the police. They questioned the boys and took them to the vacant lot, where sure enough they found the body. But as the police were looking around for clues they found something which Terry swore almost made him sick, something that shocked him so much he was barely able to mention it to his father, and even then very awkwardly, unable to look him in the eyes, too shy to say its name in Greek.

The Sun's always on the teacher's table and he's now reading out to the class how the police have mounted a manhunt not only for the cold-blooded murderer but for the whereabouts of the missing body parts. He continues: a detective has said the manner in which the body was carved crude at the joints – which Nick doesn't understand – suggests the criminal was calm and calculating. At one point Nick can't help noticing the teacher's hands rustling the paper, the liveliness of his eyes, a smile tugging at the corners of his mouth, and the thought crosses his mind the killer must be someone big and strong like him. Turning the page, he reads another article, one advising people not to go out alone at night because the crime has all the signs of being the work of a serial killer, someone who might strike again at any time. As if all this isn't enough the teacher fuels their fear by saying there could be another Jack the Ripper prowling around. And just like the original Ripper, this one also seeks to operate in a poor, working-class suburb, and no suburb in Melbourne is poorer and more working-class than Fitzroy.

Nick already knows most of the details in the paper from what his father has picked up from Terry's father. But last night he heard his father telling a relative about the other thing, the one too horrible for the newspaper, which he now can't get out of his head.

After dinner Nick's with the boys at the Busy Bee, discussing what's been in the papers, on television, and the rumours their parents have brought home from work. It's been a hot day and they're sitting in the shadow of the shop, on the warm footpath, in no mood for throwing pennies against the wall or spinning Coca-Cola yo-yos. Looking down McKean Street, Nick's struck by the size and redness of the sun: it's just above the commission flats in Carlton, about to sink into the nearby cemetery. And the sky's a crimson colour, like the stains on a butcher's apron.

'They found something else in that vacant lot,' he says.

The boys become quiet as two pregnant girls from The Haven walk past in going to the shop, both in pink thongs slapping at each heavy step. Girls like these live in the big house on Alfred Crescent and come to the shop for a bag of lollies or a block of chocolate or an ice cream. They're about sixteen or seventeen, not much older than Nick, but there's already a kind of sadness about them, a look he's seen on the faces of women who've gone through hard times. The girls leave the shop looking a bit happier, maybe due to the ice creams they're unwrapping.

'What else did they find?' asks Charlie.

'You don't want to know,' Nick sighs.

'The murder weapon,' says Tony.

'Something so horrible not even *The Sun* would print it.'

'Then how do you know?' asks Frankie.

'From the person who saw it.'

'Saw bloody what?' Dom shouts.

'The dead man's dick and balls.'

The boys are speechless.

'They were hanging from a nail on the wall in that vacant lot.'

'That's worse than chopping the bloody head off,' says Dom.

'The killer's a madman,' says Charlie.

'Why'd he want to do that? asks Danny, turning pale.

'He must've hated him bad,' says Dom.

'Maybe he didn't even know him,' Nick says.

'But why do that to a stranger?' asks Danny.

'Maybe he's a serial killer.'

'What's Corn Flakes got to do with it? says Dom.

'Not that cereal,' Nick says. 'Serial – means he'll do it again and again, just for the fun of it.'

'You mean,' says Spudsy, barely able to get his words out, 'he enjoys killing and cutting off …?'

They all go quiet trying to imagine how it happened. What the killer must have been thinking at that moment? How he must have held it with one hand and cut with the other. But why hang it on the wall for everyone to see? Yes, the thought of arms and legs and head being chopped off is terrifying, but those other things being cut off strikes them with a fear they might be next. Suddenly the killer could be waiting to pounce from behind one of those maples along Grant Street, or from the shadows in a back lane, or from inside that truck parked alongside the pub. In no mood for more talk, they hurry home in four different directions. Nick sprints diagonally across the intersection, races his tall shadow on Mrs Knight's red-brick wall, turns into the back lane, startling one of her cats scurrying over the cobbles, and rams the bolt in the back gate. Catching his breath before going inside, he notices his father's butchering knife hanging from a wire in the laundry shed. His reflection is blurred in the wide blade and dry blood clings to the handle from the chook recently killed in the gully trap.

The weekend's been full of drama and by Sunday night Nick's glad to be safe at home. It started yesterday morning about eight, when Lenny's mum went out to the backyard to light the copper for the washing. They live in the end house on Grant Street, next to the ballet-shoe factory, with their side gate on Alfred Crescent. The signora is a short woman, not much bigger than Lenny, and in reaching for a log on top of the wood pile she grasped something flesh-like and cold. Terrified, she let out a shriek that woke the family and half the street. Lenny's father threw on his dressing gown and ran out barefoot to his wife pointing and screaming uncontrollably. He pushed her inside and picked up a pitchfork from the vegetable patch.

Lenny and his three sisters watched from the kitchen window, calling on him to be careful, but he told them to keep quiet and began prodding the wood as if doing bayonet practice. Nothing happened, so he slowly climbed onto a wooden crate, holding the pitchfork ready to strike. When his eyes came in line with the top of the pile, he froze for an instant, then crossed himself slowly several times.

'What is it, Pappa?' Lenny called out.

Reaching out with the pitchfork, he caught something between its prongs and raised it in the air. Lenny and the girls cried out at the sight of a naked arm. The girls ran off to their mother washing her hands at the sink, while Lenny, wanting to show more nerve than his sisters, went out into the yard. Swearing in Italian, his father kept the arm raised for some time, not knowing what to make of it or where to put it.

'Pappa, it's the killer,' Lenny managed to whisper. 'He's got someone else.'

Later Lenny told the boys it was the right arm, muscular, cut ragged at the shoulder, still bleeding, a heart tattooed on the forearm with the letters VB.

His father eased it back on the wood pile, climbed off the crate, and said they'd have to call the police.

News of the severed arm spread quickly through the neighbourhood and before long a noisy crowd had gathered around Lenny's back gate. Nick arrived just as a man in a white lab coat and gloves was coming out carrying a black plastic bag. He excused himself in passing through the knot of people, holding the arm in a strange way. It was bent at the elbow at what seemed like a right angle, and he carried it as though offering a gift. Another man with a camera followed him out.

Was it another body? Had the killer struck again? Two tall detectives with clipboards appeared at the open gate, but wouldn't answer the volley of questions, except to say forensic tests would be done to determine whether the arm belonged to the body found in Fitzroy. They then went back inside the house to ask Lenny's father a few more questions, but as his English wasn't good they used Lenny as interpreter. He told the boys later that they were the tallest men to ever set foot in his house – so tall they not only dwarfed his short, Calabrian parents, but their hats kept brushing the lights. Lenny heard his mother whisper to his sisters it was fortunate she'd done the dusting yesterday, otherwise their nice hats would've been covered in cobwebs.

Standing either side of the father seated at the kitchen table, they fired their questions at him, watching his expression, the way his Adam's apple moved in swallowing between answers, while Lenny did his best translating from English to Italian and vice-versa, sometimes struggling to find the right word. His father's head was tilted back as far as it would go, and he turned awkwardly from one detective to the other, like those clowns at the carnival, Lenny said.

Did he have any idea who the arm belonged to? No. Did he know who might be responsible for placing it there? No. Was he from Calabria? Yes. Sensing they might be on to something, the detectives took off their hats and placed them on the table. Was he aware of the feuding among Italian fruiterers at the Victoria Market? Yes, he'd read about it in the *Il Globo* newspaper. So he knew about the vendettas? Yes, just what was in the paper. Did he buy the paper every week? Yes. So he took an interest in the vendettas? By this stage, Lenny said, his father was beginning to sweat, as much from the heat as from the two big men breathing down his neck. One of the detectives suddenly put his shiny black shoe on the chair and leaned close to his father. His mother whispered to the girls the shoe was bigger than the ship that brought them to Australia. It was time to get down to brass tacks, said the detective, though Lenny didn't know what this meant or how to say it in Italian. What was he hiding? Nothing. Then why was he sweating like that? He couldn't help it – sweating ran in his family. His father turned to a small red light burning in front of a picture of Christ and a photograph of Lenny's *nonno* with a white moustache. The detectives followed his eyes, but jerked back and reached under their coats when his father raised his hand from under the table. He showed them an empty palm, turning it this way and that, then crossed himself a couple of times. The detectives relaxed. His father, God rest his soul, used to sweat all the time, Lenny translated, even in the middle of winter. The detectives nodded and allowed him to wipe his forehead before continuing. Was he aware of an Italian custom that involved body parts being sent to one's enemies? Body parts, no, never, but something of that sort happened when his father, God rest his soul, was feuding with a neighbour back in Calabria over grazing land. The detectives exchanged looks and leaned forward, their silver-nibbed fountain pens ready to strike. And then? *Allora*, Pappa? One morning his father went to the barn to find his prized ram missing. He knew who stole it but couldn't prove it, so he swore there'd be trouble if it wasn't returned by nightfall. A vendetta, one of the detectives said. The father swayed his head in a kind of yes and no. And then? *Allora*, Pappa? That evening when his father went to wash up after milking the cows, he found the ram's head at the bottom of the trough, missing its beautiful horns. Did that lead to more violence? Of course. And body parts? Bodies, yes, two, his father's and the neighbour's – parts, no, never. Were any of the neighbour's family in Melbourne? No, most of them had migrated to Uruguay. After settling on the correct spelling of that country, the detectives wrapped up with a few more questions, saying they'd be back for more information, adding that the criminal wouldn't escape the arm of the law, laughing as they went.

Swearing in Calabrian dialect, Lenny's father cursed the arm for turning his day upside down. He'd planned to work in the vegetable patch, but how could he with all those people gaping over the fence and reporters snooping around for a story? Lenny's mother sat opposite him, gave him a searching look, and asked in a whisper if he knew anything about the arm? The hand, she said, felt coarse and hard, like a concreter's. Did it have anything to do with the recent troubles involving his former concreting partner? His reaction frightened Lenny and his sisters. He blasted his wife for taking wood from the top of the pile. What devil possessed her to overlook the pieces at the bottom? If she hadn't shaken hands with that damned arm, it would've remained there unseen, and not for long, because the cats roaming the park would've carried it away and had a wonderful feast, tattoos and all.

By midday, things around Lenny's place were quieter, though the arm in the neighbourhood made Nick and the boys even edgier, because the killer had walked their streets and might still be in their midst. Not one to let an opportunity go past, Lenny had already made a few quid from the reporters. When his parents refused to speak to them, he went secretly with them across to the park and gave an account of what had happened. They took a few pictures and promised he'd be in Monday's paper. His sisters saw him from their upstairs window and threatened to tell, but he bought their silence with two bob each. He then cashed in on the curiosity of his friends. For thruppence, they were allowed into his backyard one at a time, to climb onto the box his father had stood on and see a few drops of dry blood on top of the wood pile.

The temperature has risen sharply, along with the shrill of cicadas in the park, and by mid-afternoon Nick and a few boys decide to cool off at the Fitzroy Baths. After the events at Lenny's place yesterday, they figured they'd be safer in the big, crowded pool. The blue water would take their minds off the blood, while girls in bikinis and dark tans would ease their fear of body parts. On their way they come across Vladko and Zlatko, the Serbian twins, sitting in the front of their Groome Street house, around the corner from the lower end of McKean Street. The twins have a reputation for being live-wires. They're known to ambush boys with shanghais and howl with laughter at their tears, or pick a fight if they don't like the way someone's hair is combed. Vladko is the wilder of the two, the dare-devil and thrill-seeker. They moved in a year ago not knowing a word of English, but fluent in the language of the fist. Within a week of their arrival a large audience gathered at the footbridge as word had got out that Vladko would perform a tight-rope walking stunt along the handrail, a drop of at least fifteen yards, enough to break his neck if he fell. The boys watched from below. Nick suggested they call an ambulance, just in case. Tony wanted to call his parents, their house being close to the bridge. But nobody moved. Zlakto tried to talk him out of it, even wrestled with him for a few minutes, but, being the stronger twin, Vladko shrugged him off, removed his shoes and socks, and leapt onto the handrail – a length of timber no wider than a brick. Everyone was speechless as he set off, arms wide, bare feet moving nimbly, head held high and still. At one point, about halfway along the twenty-yard distance, he faltered, swayed, pivoted on one foot. Some of the boys couldn't bear to watch and turned away. But he managed to regain his balance and continued smoothly to the other side, where he fisted the blue sky, yelled out 'Australia, Australia', and jumped to safety. The boys nicknamed him Mad Vlad after that, which he didn't seem to mind, maybe because he didn't know what mad meant, and by the time he did the name had well and truly stuck.

It was Vlad who, finding himself alone and bored one afternoon, entertained himself by peeling off the green tarpaulin of a railway wagon containing loose wheat and jumping into it from the top of the same footbridge. That day Little Chris happened to be going to the Fitzroy Baths when Vlad called him from the bridge, threatening to break his fingers if he didn't climb up. Scared to the point almost of pissing himself, Little Chris climbed to the top, knowing Vlad was capable of anything. His fears were realised at once: Vlad snatched his towel and togs, threw them down into the carriage, and ordered him to jump after them. Little Chris began crying, saying he was afraid of heights, and his father would give him a hiding if he found out. Vlad wouldn't be swayed: laughing and swearing, he pushed Little Chris into the wire running along both sides of the bridge, gave him a rabbit chop to the back of the neck, and, with a kick up the arse, forced him to climb over. Standing on the edge, Little Chris gripped the wire, refusing to let go. Vlad lost his temper and began kicking at his fingers, screaming for him to jump or he'd throw him over. Caught between being thrown off and jumping, Little Chris pissed his shorts, the trickle gleaming like a gold chain, and let go, dropping into the warm wheat and sinking in up to his chest. As Vlad laughed like a madman, saying what great fun it was, Little Chris struggled out, collected his towel and togs, and ran off home, followed by the threat of having both wrists broken if he so much as whispered a word to anyone.

Vlad's happy to go to the pool, flicking bums with his towel on the way there, but Zlatko stays home, saying he can't be bothered walking in the heat, especially the way back, when for some reason it always feels hotter than before the swim. But the boys know heat isn't the problem. Zlatko hates water, which, as Vlad has explained, goes back to their childhood in Serbia. According to their mother this hatred arose in the town church when the twins were baptised. Being older by an hour, Zlatko was first to be undressed and handed by the godmother to the priest. But the instant he was held over the water in the silver tub, the child let out a wail that drowned the priest's words and the chanter's hymn. As the priest attempted to lower him in the water, Zlatko gripped his beard, squirming and screaming. The godmother helped keep the child in the tub while the priest splashed him with water, soaped his plump body, snipped his hair in four places, and blessed his head with sunflower oil, as olive oil had been expensive that year. Finally, raising the screaming, dripping child high in the air (like a shining trout, their mother would laugh telling the story), the priest said a few more words and placed him in the godmother's towel-draped arms, who then carried the boy to his mother, in whose embrace he fell quiet. Vlad's experience had been nowhere as hellish. His mother said he couldn't wait to enter the tub, and once inside they couldn't get him out, so happy was he kicking and splashing water all over the place, including the priest's face, who cried out a curse because the soapy water hurt his eyes. When the twins were older, they'd bring up their baptism in quarrels and disputes that often led to fights.

'I was baptised first,' Zlatko would insist, 'so I've got more say.'

'But I spent more time in the tub,' Vlad would smirk, 'so I'm more blessed.'

'Mine was fresh water, so my soul's cleaner than yours.'

'Yours was half a baptism, so you're half as good as me.'

'Half as good?' Zlatko would laugh. 'Remember what Mum said? I pissed in the tub before they put you in, and because it was a drought year the water wasn't changed. Unclean water's unholy water, which means your baptism doesn't count, which means you're zero, nothing, nought.'

Shortly after arriving in Australia Zlatko nearly drowned at the Fitzroy Baths. The twins were placed in different grades so they wouldn't distract each other. It was Zlatko's first time at a swimming pool and, not having proper togs, his mother had made him a pair of baggy, white shorts that went past his knees. As the others were jumping into the deep end, he stood at the edge, afraid of the black lines wriggling at the bottom. The others laughed at his baggy shorts and gestured that he couldn't swim. He didn't understand a word but prodded by their laughter he took a deep breath and jumped. What followed was a like a blurry dream, he'd later tell Nick and the boys. He remembered going under and the sudden quiet and not being able to rise because his shorts were heavy and kept pulling him down. At one point he managed to get his mouth above water for a moment, but he didn't know the English word for help and was too embarrassed to call out in Serbian, and was pulled under again by the weight of the shorts. And then he could see bubbles rising from his mouth and lots of legs kicking in slow motion all around him. He reached up for a foot, but it slipped from his grip and he sank to the bottom. As the bubbles became fewer and the water darker, the thought flashed through his mind: Vlad, you lucky devil, you'll get all my toys. But suddenly he felt a claw hooking into his shorts and raising him up into noise and light. Was it an angel or a devil? Was he being taken to heaven or hell? And then his cheek was pressed to the ground and someone was pushing hard on his back, pushing and pushing, maybe punishing him for lying to his parents and stealing those lollies from the Busy Bee. The next instant all this water spurted from his mouth and he began coughing and spluttering. He wasn't dead and Vlad wouldn't get his toys. He looked up dumbly at the man who'd fished him and, not knowing the English word for thanks, managed a faint *hvala*.

Home alone on this hot afternoon Zlatko soon becomes bored and decides to go up to the Busy Bee for an icy pole. Leaving by the back gate – the twins always use the back because their mother's precious about the new carpet in the corridor – he trips and stumbles on what at first looks like a mannequin's leg lying across the entrance. He's about to kick it aside but notices a swarm of black flies covering the bloody knee-joint. Lenny's place flashes to mind and he jumps back in horror, fearing it might spring up and hop after him. It's a man's leg, hairy, well-shaped calf muscle, and yellowish nails in need of cutting. His first reaction is to run to the corner shop and find a few friends, but remembering everyone's at the pool, he goes back inside to tell his father taking an afternoon nap. He would've got his mother to wake him, but she's out visiting, so he tip-toes to their bedroom and presses his ear to the door, knowing how irritable his father becomes when anything interrupts his nap. He stands there for a moment, listening to his father's deep, contented snoring, wondering what to do: disturb him and cop his anger, or wait for him to wake up, by which time the leg might disappear. Recalling Lenny's takings from friends and reporters, and the fact that his picture would be in the paper, Zlatko decides to act fast, before someone carries off the leg and cashes in on what's rightfully his. Yes, he thinks, Vlad's always doing this and that better, this is his chance to outdo him and become famous. He turns the loose doorknob and enters. His father's in a white singlet and underpants, face down in the pillow, left arm hanging over the side of the bed.

'*Tato*,' he whispers, approaching the bed.

The Serbian word for father is swallowed by the snoring.

'*Tato*,' he calls, standing over him.

The father groans in the pillow.

'*Tato*, please, wake up.'

'*Tato*, *Tato*,' he grumbles, turning his head sideways and opening his left eye. 'Can't you call your mother for a change? Does a man have to lie in his grave to find peace and quiet?'

'Sorry, *Tato*, sorry, but …'

'What is it?' he snaps.

'*Tato*, there's a leg in the lane.'

As though kicked in the ribs, the father leaps up with a moan, sweeps past a stunned Zlatko, and, hobbling into his pants, makes for the yard. Zlatko follows, not to the gate though, but the garage at the back of the yard, where his father opens the door and begins counting the legs of smoked ham hanging from the rafters. Coming from a long line of pig-breeders, he has maintained the tradition of making ham, and prides himself on the quality of his product, exchanging slices with the Italian over the fence who brags about his prosciutto. When he finishes counting with his finger one way then the other, he turns and lets fly with a backhander at Zlatko, who ducks and runs to the gate.

'What's the matter with you,' he shouts, 'they're all here, seventeen of them, the best in Melbourne.'

'No, *Tato*,' says Zlatko, relieved his find hasn't run off, 'there's a real leg right here – a man's leg.'

Fumbling with the buttons on his fly, bare feet dancing on the hot concrete, his father goes to the gate. Zlatko expects a smile and a pat on the head, but on seeing the leg the father grimaces, bites his fist in anger, and curses the mother who gave birth to the owner of the leg, curses the part of her body that released him into the world. Zlatko cringes, not only at the foul language, but at the thought of his fortune and fame slipping away. The father shoves him inside and tells him to fetch the newspaper used to line the rubbish bin, while he skips off to put on a pair of thongs. And then Zlatko watches in disbelief as his father picks up the leg by the ankle, sending up a swarm of buzzing flies, and wraps it in newspaper, the way he wraps his ham selling it to friends.

'Get the hose,' he says, placing the leg inside the fence.

'But, *Tato*, shouldn't we call the police?'

'The hose, I'm telling you, and close the garage door so these damned flies don't get to the ham.'

He washes away the blood from the cobbles outside the gate and turns his attention to the leg. By the time Zlatko coils the hose around the tap and comes back to see what his father does next, the cobbles are dry again, without a sign of blood.

'Now, to get rid of that,' says the father, thinking hard.

'*Tato*, the police, they'll take it away.'

If the police came, so will reporters, Zlatko figures. He could still make a quid or two and have his picture in the paper, even though the cobbles have been washed clean.

'Police?'

His father grabs him by the ear, pulls him close, and whispers with a blast of hot breath.

'Son, we don't want the police snooping around here. Don't you know what's in the garage? They'll find the legs hanging there and all those bottles of slivovitz. You're operating a butcher's shop from home, they'll say. You're running an illegal still and selling alcohol, they'll say. And you know what that means – jail for me and a life of misery for you. So keep your mouth shut about that damned thing and let's get rid of it.'

Suddenly, filled with his father's desperation, Zlatko suggests they take the leg to Fitzroy, where the body was found, and throw it in some back lane near the Town Hall. His father likes the idea, and so, with Zlatko acting as lookout, though being so hot there's no-one about except the flies, he places the parcel in the boot of their Holden and they set off. After driving around for some time considering this place or that, they pull up in a bumpy lane between some factories, where the father throws the parcel on a pile of junk and jumps back in the car. But as he changes gears, Zlatko grabs him by the wrist.

'*Tato*,' he says, heart racing.

'What is it?' says the father, looking nervously in the rear-view mirror.

'The newspaper, it's Serbian, they might track us down.'

The father dashes out, unwraps the leg, scrunched the newspaper into a ball and tosses it on the back seat.

Cruising down George Street, feeling more at ease, his bare arm half out the window, the father turns to Zlatko and nods.

'We'll burn that paper when we got home,' he says.

'We can't, *Tato*,' says Zlatko. 'It's a total fire-ban day.'

'We'll bury it then, until the cool change. And remember, son, not a word of this to anyone, even your brother.'

When they come to the intersection of Alexandra Parade, which is noisy with laughter and screaming and bodies splashing bombs in the deep end of the Fitzroy Baths, the father turns to him again.

'You were sharp to think of the paper,' he smiles.

Zlatko feels a swell of emotion and a tickle in his nose. Those words mean more to him than the money and fame the leg would've brought. That half smile has made up for the fact that he can't swim, for not being able to enjoy the pool with his friends, for not being there right now to see all those girls with tanned bodies and bikini bottoms held together by bits of string. He promises his father he won't tell a soul, sealing the promise by placing three fingers on his heart. But he's too excitable by nature to keep a secret, and that evening, when the boys meet at the Busy Bee, he tells them everything.

'You promised *Tato* you wouldn't tell,' says Vlad.

'We won't tell anyone,' Nick's quick to say.

'You put your fingers on your heart,' Vlad continues, turning red.

'Yeah, just like this,' says Zlatko.

'You'll go to hell for breaking your promise.'

'But I haven't broken my promise,' Zlatko smiles. 'I promised *Tato* I wouldn't tell a soul, and I haven't, because you're a body and Nick's a body and Tony's a body, unless you're all dead and what looks like your body is really your soul.'

15

After a week of temperatures in the high nineties the house feels like a furnace, especially Nick's bedroom upstairs. His father's hosing the backyard, thinking to cool the concrete, but the evaporating water only makes the air hot and smelly. His mother's in the kitchen, preparing tomorrow's lunches for work and school. Last night they would've usually gone to the park, away from the sun-baked house, catching a little breeze escaping from the elms, feeling with bare feet the grass watered during the day by a stuttering sprinkler – but they remained indoors instead. The recent events have kept everyone inside, and where doors and windows would normally be wide open, they're now locked and secured. The serial killer loose in the area has made prisoners of young and old, and everyone's now sleepless and sluggish and sweating because of him.

Lethargic from a night of stifling heat and persistent mosquitoes, Nick doesn't go swimming with the boys, despite their urging. After moping around for a while, he spends the afternoon putting his stamps in order, licking the small gluey hinges and fixing his recent swaps on the appropriate page, though sometimes he isn't sure because of the strange letters. He loses himself for some time in faraway-sounding places like Travancore and Bahawalpur and Tanganyika and Sarawak. The different letters and symbols fascinate him. Why don't all countries use the same alphabet, like numbers? He knows Eire is another name for Ireland, Suomi is Finland,

Magyar is Hungary, Sverige is Sweden, and Helvetia is Switzerland. The nameless faces have become familiar, almost homely, among them the bald, broad-faced man on lots of stamps from Espana, the king and queen on the green 1956 stamp from Monaco, those motherly women poised above Nederland, the man in profile on Deutsches Reich, with parted hair and moustache and right eye gazing straight ahead as though fixed on the horizon, and the crowned head of Australia's young and pretty Queen, who appears on so many stamps and in so many countries she should be the Queen of the whole world.

By late afternoon, seeing from his window boys gathering at the Busy Bee, Nick puts away the album and joins them. Little Chris, transistor pressed to his ear, says other body parts have been found in Fitzroy and Clifton Hill. Zlatko smiles and places the first three fingers of his right hand over his heart.

'Why not Collingwood?' asks Danny.

'Could mean the killer's from Collingwood,' says Nick.

'Yeah,' says Tony, 'probably a bloody Collingwood supporter.'

The police have made no progress in solving the crime, Chris reports, listening intently, and they won't say whether the parts are from the same body. The boys turn to one another with a look of alarm, thinking they have to endure another hot night with the killer wandering around their back lanes. But then, maybe to take their minds off body parts, big Paul, who's a good leg-spinner, suggests a game of cricket before tea. This meets with a shout of approval. In ten minutes the stumps are hammered in the dry pitch, teams picked, and they're playing in the shadows of elms cast by the setting sun.

When Dom cracks the ball into the Council Yard for six, Lance bolts after it, only to stop abruptly at the edge of the long grass as though he's seen a snake. He races back to the pitch without the ball, looking shaken.

'Where's the bloody ball?' says Dom, eager to bat again.

'There's a man's head in the grass,' Lance gasps.

He is a known joker, so at first they think he's pulling their leg, trying to spook them, but when he swears on his mother's grave they pull out the stumps and follow him. On the way he keeps saying the sight isn't for the faint-hearted: the tongue's blue, hanging out of the mouth, and the eyes are white and half closed. The sight would test them, he says. Those who dared look at the face without flinching would be deemed men. Armed with pointed wickets and bats they march toward the Council Yard like soldiers marching into battle. A few yards from the spot, Lance stops and faces them with a grim look.

'If you want to pull out, do it now,' he says, 'but if you want to see it, just know one thing, you might live with nightmares the rest of your life. Grandpa fought the Germans twenty years ago and he still keeps Gran awake with nightmares of blown-up bodies and chopped-off heads.'

The group hesitates a moment, each measuring his own fear by the look in another's eyes. Sensing that some are afraid and might go back, Lance takes on the role of a platoon leader.

'Come on, boys, what are you, mice or men? Let's show the enemy a thing or two. Are you ready to follow me?'

'Yeah,' sounds a feeble chorus.

'Do you want to see it?'

'Yeah,' they reply louder.

'Then prove it.'

They put on a mock battle using wickets and bats as spears and swords.

'Come on, boys,' yells Lance, leading the charge.

They follow, sprinting toward the long grass, screaming out their fear, only to stop dead in their tracks once in the Council Yard. Some draw back in shock, others look away, a few close their eyes. Nick stands his ground, having witnessed the killing of chooks, sheep, and even pigs back in the village. Black bush flies buzz around the head nestled in the grass, face up, as though a body buried up to its neck. Nick's both curious and sickened. The hair's oily and still brushed back Elvis-style, there's a kind of sleepy look in the whites of the eyes, the mouth gapes in a silent howl, while the tongue sticks out, mocking and dark. Lance takes the bat from Dom and, against calls for them to go, pushes the head. It rolls onto its side and blood trickles from the biggish nose, making some of the boys jump back in fear.

The longer Nick stares at the face, the more the sickening feeling passes, giving way to a kind of fascination. The head was alive a few days ago, it could think and see and talk, and now it's lying there, dead. What happens to thoughts and memories when a person dies? Do they disappear suddenly, like a light going out, or do they fade, like the sunset? Of the millions of thoughts and ideas the man must have had, are a few still in there? Maybe a flickering memory of when he played cricket as a kid, or, as he was being killed, the thought that he'd forgotten to take out the bottles for tomorrow's milk. Is this what awaits him in fifty or sixty or seventy years from now? Maybe not as horrible as his, but the same in that his hopes and dreams, his feelings for his parents, his memories of these days with the boys – all this would vanish, leaving nothing, nothing, except a swarm of black flies buzzing around an empty shell.

'We gotta call the cops,' says Danny.

This alarms Lenny. Yes, he made a profit on the arm, but the head was different. His house being closest to the Council Yard means the cops will come knocking at their place first. Moving away from the biting flies, they sit on the edge of the oval.

'Yeah, it's all right for you to talk,' says Lennie, 'your old man's not the one still shaking from those flat-foot detectives. He hasn't slept a wink after the grilling from those two goons. And they'll give him another grilling for sure if they come to the Council Yard. Those goons reckon Dad's involved just because of some custom back in Italy.'

'The arm, now the bloody head,' laughs Dom, 'and only a hundred yards from your joint – you sure your old man's not the one they're after?'

Lenny grabs Dom by the singlet, but they are quickly pulled apart.

'I was only joking,' says Dom.

Hurt, Lenny turns his back and begins whimpering. They don't know what to do. Lenny's dad wouldn't hurt a fly, they all know that, and they don't want him to be grilled again, but they're caught in a real-life murder investigation, not some make-believe cop drama on television. The head will help police identify the victim and maybe lead to the killer's arrest, freeing everyone from the fear gripping the neighbourhood. They have to decide quickly. The flies are buzzing and swarming a few yards away, Lenny's sitting with head on his knees, and the sun's dipped into a reddish cloud.

'Hey, what if the head was dumped just before we got here,' says Lance.

'What if the killer's still in the Council Yard,' says Paul.

'Behind one of them mounds,' says Tony.

Spooked, they all leap to their feet, except Lenny. Just then Vlad appears at the Busy Bee. They call him over, hoping his wild, daring nature might come up with something. He's eating a bread roll with a thick pork sausage inside, another of his father's homemade products. When they tell him about the head he strolls over to where it lies and, still biting into his roll, parts the long grass with his foot. A couple of crows call from a nearby tree.

'Poor bastard,' he says, 'lost his head for …'

'For a double cross,' says Lance.

'Or maybe for love,' says Tony.

To everyone's surprise Vlad feels sorry for Lenny and his father and offers to take care of things. He instructs Lenny to run home and bring back whatever sack he can find. They boys look at each in disbelief at his daring. When Lenny returns with a spud sack, Vlad rolls the head inside using one of the bats.

'What are doing with it?' asks Lance.

'Boil it for breakfast,' laughs Vlad.

'No, serious.'

'Swear you won't tell anyone.'

'Not a soul,' says Tony.

He gets them to place the first three fingers of their right hand on their hearts. They all swear, some on God, others on the Bible, others on their mother's grave. He then gathers them around him, opens the sack, and calls on the head to haunt anyone who reveals his secret.

'Don't worry, Lenny boy,' he says, 'the cops won't grill your old man.'

'Where are you taking it?' Lenny asks, looking relieved.

'Finders keepers, losers weepers,' Vlad grins.

'We swore not to tell,' says Nick.

'All right, Nicky Boy, he smiles, 'but not a word to anyone. There's a bloke on Brunswick Street, a taxi-something-or-another, who stuffs all kinds of animal heads. I reckon he'll pay a few quid for this catch.'

Knowing Vlad's wild nature, they aren't sure whether he's joking or not. Ordering them to go home before they're spotted here, he hurries off, taking the back way along the quiet end of Alfred Crescent. Just before rounding the corner he slings the sack over one shoulder and breaks out into a jog, the head bouncing around on his back. Nick ponders Vlad's motives: has he done this from sympathy for Lenny and his father, or, envious of Zlatko's experience with the leg, is he now setting off to outdo his twin brother and regain his position as the apple of his father's eye?

The forecast said late-afternoon Tuesday, and it's here, the cool change, coming first as a breeze stirring the upper parts of the elms, next as a drift of heavy clouds, followed by a few winks of lightning and a nudge of thunder, and then the rain, big drops that vanish as soon as they splatter the bitumen, the rise of that musty smell, stronger lightning and thunder, and finally the downpour. Nick opens all the windows of the house, pushing the double-hung lower half all the way up, struggling with some because the heat's blistered the layers of gloss paint in the casement. After days of living like prisoners it's a relief to swing open the front and back door, to feel the fresh draught sweeping out the stale heat from the corridor, the living room, the kitchen, and, even more, to feel it driving out the week-long fear festering in him. Yes, they all feel better now, freer, not just for the cool change, but because the killer was arrested this morning. The killer isn't Lenny's dad, he isn't a serial killer, as they feared, or a cold-blooded murderer, as the police said, he isn't even a man – it turns out the killer's a thirty-six-year-old woman, a mother of three small children. The radio said following some sort of domestic argument the woman clobbered the man on the head with a hammer and then cut him up with a razor blade in the bath-tub of their house. She has already taken police to the places where parts were disposed. Earlier this afternoon she was brought by police to the Council Yard. An extensive search of the area didn't find the head, the last piece in the jig-saw puzzle, though there were clear signs of blood on the grass. According to the latest news update, the Inspector in charge of the case is certain she dumped the head in the disused part of the Edinburgh Gardens, but he's unable to explain its disappearance, except to say that, having been there several days, it's more than likely feral cats roaming the park have made off with it.

When the rain clears after dinner, Nick and a few boys go to the Council Yard. Walking across the oval, thongs throwing up droplets, they discuss the woman and laugh at their fear.

'Must've had bloody balls to do what she did,' says Dom.

'Yeah,' says Paul, 'and left them hanging on the wall for everyone to see.'

'What do you reckon made her do it?' asks Frankie.

'She hated him bad, that's why,' says Dom.

'Or loved him like mad,' Tony puts in.

'You don't kill someone you love,' Nick says.

'You do when they stop loving you.'

Nick's not sure what to make of his reply, but Tony, though shorter, is a bit older and maybe knows about these things.

Others are also at the spot where the head lay, curious sightseers from all over the place, pointing here and there, including Lenny's house. The boys glance at each other, thinking of Vlad and the oath they made looking into the sack. For some reason, when nobody's watching, Nick reaches down and plucks a long blade of grass with a few rain drops and spots of blood. At home, maybe as a way of keeping his oath, he places the blade in the dark-blue Bible from Sunday School.

16

The location of the annual village picnic varies from year to year – Romsey, Gisborne, Kinglake, Whittlesea. This year it's on the other side of Melbourne, Ferny Creek in the Dandenongs. Vangel's been pushing the committee to have it on Mount Macedon, saying there's no better place for a Macedonian picnic, but the majority see this as too political. With some in the community calling themselves Greek and others Macedonian, the committee has tried to please both groups by calling the association Vevi-Banitsa, using both the Greek and Macedonian name of the village. Vangel comes home from committee meetings all fired up with politics and *rakija*. He curses the *Grkomani* – the Greek-leaning members – with foul-mouthed words and sayings that make Nick cringe translating them to himself. Vevi-Banitsa! If anything it should be Banitsa-Vevi, he shouts. Menka ignores him when he's in this state, so he turns to Nick, telling him to stand up for his beliefs, and when his time comes to be on the committee to do away with Vevi altogether. Nick nods, more out of politeness than anything. Maybe the closest he'll ever come to experiencing his father's fervour is at the football – barracking for Fitzroy, cursing Collingwood.

Those with cars drive to Ferny Creek, the others, like Nick and his parents, go by buses hired for the day, catching them on Smith Street. Menka spent yesterday preparing for the picnic: baking pastries and shortbreads, frying sausages and meatballs, packing jars of pickled cabbage, tomatoes and peppers. Nothing's ever too much trouble for her in the kitchen, even baking those time-consuming pastries – pumpkin, spinach, mincemeat, fetta. She makes the dough herself, kneading the warm, fleshy mound with her strong hands, wrapping it in a blanket like a baby, then spreading it out on the laminated table sprinkled with flour. She rolls it flat with a wooden dowel, pulling at the edges, then rolls it again, until it's thin as the strips of sunburnt skin Nick peels off his shoulders. Vangel scolds her for spending all day in the kitchen and then complaining of a sore back. He says it's cheaper to go out and buy what's needed. But she continues working in silence. Women are always praising her pastries, saying no-one makes them better or lighter. She feels good hearing this, proud, maybe just like when Vangel comes home from the Club all smiles from having won at cards. And so yesterday, seeing his mother working in the hot kitchen, Nick was drawn to help her with the pastry, gently pulling the sheet from one side while she pulled from the other, making it wider and thinner, until it covered the table and he could see the swirls in the laminate through it. When his father came in and saw him smoothing the sheet, he raised his hand as though about to clip him over the ear, saying back in the old country boys never did women's work because their horse would die. Nick was about to say he didn't have a horse, or so much as a bike, but his father raised his eyebrows and ordered him to do something manly. He went into the yard and picked up the *tesla,* a funny-looking tool, part hammer, part axe, which his father had packed in his suitcase on leaving the village. Churning with anger, he sat on a stool in the backyard and struck hard at a few old palings, chopping scraps for his mother's heater on washing day.

The picnic takes place at a football ground surrounded by towering gum trees. People have set up their tables and chairs in the scrawny shade. There's always lots of food in Menka's baskets, not only for family and relatives but the fearless black flies. Vangel's esky is full of beer and ice, like the other dads, and by mid-afternoon the empty bottles are scattered all over the place. The smaller children collect the smelly brown bottles and set them up in lines and roll balls at them, pretending they're at a bowling alley. Nick helped prepare for the picnic. This morning he took the shopping trolley and went to the ice-factory behind the Fitzroy Baths. He slipped a two-bob coin in the slot and pressed the button. Nothing at first, then a faint rumbling, which soon grew to what sounded like the groan of an approaching storm, until it suddenly gathered and hardened into a great block thundering out of the depths of winter, racing down a line of steel rollers, flying through the rubber flaps and crashing into the car tyre used as a stopper. It was cold on his bare thighs as he struggled to place it in the trolley. Not wasting a minute or a drop, because the morning was already warming up, he hurried home, where his father was tearing open a carton of beer. He lifted the block into the concrete washing-trough and struck it with a screwdriver, crumbling it in pieces for the esky. Nick collected the bits that flew away, now and then slipping one into my mouth, thinking how much better water tasted than beer.

This year the committee has organised sprints for the children, tug-of-war for the men, and egg-and-spoon races for the women. When they call Nick's age-group for the hundred-yard dash, he catches a glimpse of his father standing near the fence with a group of friends whose sons are also competing. Never having his father at a footy game, Nick's now determined to impress him with his speed, show him he's got the potential to play for Fitzroy. He's nervous crouching at the starting line. The gun cracks and he takes off, but his legs feel like they are not his, his stride's cramped and jerky, and the others are getting away. It's like those dreams in which he can't run despite willing himself forward. Arms pumping in trying to catch the others, his legs suddenly give way and he stumbles and falls onto the dusty grass. He remains there a moment, knees stinging, too embarrassed to get up because his father's friends are laughing on the side. And then a shadow covers him and a hand pulls him up by the arm. His father's saying he went out too fast and lost his balance. He brushes the dust from Nick's shorts and for some reason places his hat on his head. Walking back to their table, Nick lowers the hat over his eyes and nose. His father's holding him firmly by the hand. Strange, instead of feeling embarrassed, Nick takes heart from his grip and from the smell of sweat inside his hat.

It's now late afternoon, having forgotten the stinging fall, having explored the paths through the ferns and tossed stones in the creek, Nick's tired and bored and gazing at the band and the dancers. The musicians have been playing for a few hours, driving circles of men and women round and round on the dusty field. The band – clarinet, piano-accordion, hand-held bass-drum and trumpet – is accompanied by little Pavle on the cornet, whose off-key playing the others don't seem to mind in this outdoor setting. Something in their playing tells Nick they're not a regular band, but musicians who've come together for the day.

Watching them from the table, his attention's caught by the trumpet player's right index finger: it's silver, like his instrument, and flashes in pressing the keys. The musician must be in his forties, pale-skinned, with a handkerchief spread on his bald head as protection from the sun. The finger interests Nick and when his mother returns from visiting friends he asks if she knows anything about it. She laughs at his curiosity and tells him to go off and enjoy the picnic, instead of concerning himself with how Traiko lost his finger. Sensing a story in her tone of voice, Nick pleads, saying it might be worth writing about for a school project. She shakes her head, calls him a strange boy, and sits in the chair opposite.

Traiko's from a neighbouring village, she says, swiping at black flies nibbling flakes of pastry on the tablecloth. As a young man he cut off his finger in order to save his life and the lives of others. She looks away for a moment, as though gathering the story from a clearing in the gums, the pupils of her eyes small and sharp, ringed by brown verging on green. When Nick presses her for more details she says it happened as Greece was being torn apart by the Civil War. Traiko had taken up the trumpet as a boy and by fifteen was playing at weddings and village festivals. He was eighteen when the war broke out and he feared being called up for the army. It was a terrible time, with brother turning on brother, and friend on friend. The hills were covered in bodies and blood. He didn't want to join the army because it meant using a rifle against people he knew. His hands were made for music not murder. Yes, he could've run off and joined the communists in the mountains, but even that meant using a rifle on relatives and friends. He'd always believed in the goodness of music and its power to overcome differences and bring people together. But the bombs and bullets screaming over Greece silenced his instrument, and death now crouched in village squares where dancers had once skipped. When the authorities called him for the army, he anguished over what to do, until he remembered something his grandfather had told him. When the Ottomans ruled Macedonia mothers would chop off the right forefinger of their infant sons so they wouldn't be taken as Yanissaries – Christians drafted in the Turkish Army – because the Pasha rejected young men who couldn't pull a trigger. So Traiko went into the barn and ran his finger over the *tesla*'s blade. He anguished again, this time between not killing and not being able to play the trumpet. Finally, he tightened his heart and struck. He lost half a finger but saved his entire life, and the lives of many others, because the army didn't want soldiers with anything less than ten fingers. After the war Traiko had a silversmith make him a false finger, complete with a nail, an oversized thimble as he still calls it, which allowed him to play his trumpet, and with more feeling than before, because of a twinge of pain in pressing the key.

As his mother tells the story Nick's eyes are fixed on the shining finger. Could he ever do such a thing? If he were called to fight for the Australian army, to kill soldiers in some faraway country, would he chop off part of his finger to avoid going? He can't say, maybe not, because there's no way he'd have the confidence to fly for a high mark missing half a finger, and that would mean never playing for Fitzroy.

Moved by the story, Nick takes a piece of pumpkin pie and goes closer to the band, to hear the click of the silver finger pressing the keys. Vangel and his friends are red-faced, as much from the sun and dancing as from all the beer they've drunk, but there's no sign of them slowing down. The outdoor setting, Nick thinks. These trees, the hills, that nearby creek – reminds them of a village festival. Strange, these Macedonian tunes: he's been to functions where people have spilt blood for them, shed heart-felt tears in singing them, sweated out their soul in dancing to them, and forgotten their hardships in just listening to them. What is it about music that moves people so much? At times it seems to have the kind of power he reads about in science fiction novels – a power that's able to turn flesh into something like spirit-energy. These old tunes raise people above the here and now, above who and what they are, releasing them into a kind of timelessness, expanding them so they become something more than human. His thoughts are vague, unformed, but he can see it in the dancers, in their black shoes kicking up clouds of dust. It seems to be more of a man thing than a woman, and yet he doesn't feel what these men are feeling. Is it because he's twelve, still a boy, and those feelings don't happen until you become a man? Or is it because he has already spent half his life in Australia, and those tunes have no sway over those who leave Macedonia as a child?

About thirty men are dancing in a circle, their steps slow and measured, arms spread wide, dark sweat stains on white shirts, hands gripping each other's shoulders. This dance is called the *gaida* – the bagpipe – and it features the clarinet, which, Nick has learnt, replaced the sheepskin bagpipe when his father was a child. The dancers are led by a thick-necked man who often comes to the Club. He's easy-going with his money, throwing Nick tips when he wins at cards, always happy to shout the old-timers drinks and coffees. Once, as Nick was dumping a pile of butts in the outside bin, the man came in quickly from the back lane as though being chased. Surprised to see Nick in the yard, he didn't say a word, even though he was always teasing him about his niece, saying he'd act as match-maker when the time came. But he seemed different at that moment, looked all flushed, sort of embarrassed, and smelt not of after-shave but perfume. It was only after he went inside that Nick realised: he must have been in the brothel next door, visiting one of those women who struggle up the stairs in their high-heel shoes.

Knowing his carefree attitude to money, the musicians move into the centre of the dancers and follow him around, hoping to make something on top of their set payment. They're not disappointed. An instant later he pulls out a roll of notes from his shirt pocket and, peeling off and spitting on fivers, slaps one on the forehead of each musician, including Pavle, shouting there's plenty more if they do as he says.

'*Le-le, le-le*', shrieks a woman in a white sun-hat running out from the side and trying to snatch the money from his raised fist.

'Don't shame me, woman', says the man in a low voice.

'Stop him, stop him,' she cries above the music.

'Don't listen to her,' he tells the musicians.

'He's throwing away his holiday pay,' she cries, 'a month's wages.'

'She's lying, boys, keep playing.'

'Lying, may the earth swallow me if I'm lying.'

'She doesn't want me to have good time.'

'A good time – we'll have nothing to see us through January, nothing.'

'Keep playing, boys,' he says, plastering them with another note.

'Stop him,' she shrieks. 'He's drunk. Our hard earned money. He doesn't know what he's doing.'

'Hard earned,' he laughs. 'Yes, earned with sweat and blood. Keep playing, boys, keep playing. Kire, beat that drum louder, bring down all the factories so we never set foot in them again. Hard earned, yes, won at manilla last night. Keep sounding your trumpet, Traiko, bring down the heavens so we can have it out with grandfather God. Two hundred quid, boys, won at cards, and it's all yours. Come on, Donche, put that clarinet to my ear and fill me with lightness. What's a hundred quid if it can't buy an hour of happiness? Dimko, squeeze that plump girlfriend of yours, caress and tickle her, fill the air with her sweet sighs. It's yours, boys, a hundred quid. Long live manilla. Where's Pavle? Here's another fiver. Play your lungs out, my friend, and may all my enemies go to hell.'

He peels off several notes and throws them to his wife, who snatches them up from the ground. She's about to get stuck into him again, but two women appear from the circle of spectators and pull her away, though unable to stop her from shouting: A month's wages, a month's wages.

Breaking off from the head of the circle, though still keeping his step, the leader draws other men into the dance, including old timers who can barely walk but somehow manage to find a spring in their heel once they join in. A few fathers wave to their teenage sons, who, uncertain at first, run into the space created for them. Vangel signals to Nick, who shakes his head and points to his knees grazed from the fall. The next instant the leader, red-faced as on that day in the Club's backyard, grabs Nick by the hand and almost drags him beside Vangel. A roar of approval sounds from the dancers. Gripping Nick's shoulder, Vangel smiles and throws back his head. The steps are slow: one, two, three, followed by a kick, kick. His mother has taught him this dance at home. The men add to these basic steps, doing turns and squats and sometimes going in the opposite direction. Nick's a bit stiff-legged at first, shy being here among these grown-ups, but after a few minutes he loosens up, feeling bouncy and light.

By the time he completes a full turn, he forgets himself in the whirlwind of music and dancing. The men are now shouting and whistling and breaking off to clap hands and perform unusual gestures. Five minutes ago he couldn't have imagined enjoying himself like this, waving his arms with the men, copying their actions, feeling part of something bigger than himself, something old as these gum trees, yet new as the small white cloud drifting overhead. Vangel's happy too, as are the other fathers, all proud of their sons dancing next to them. And then, in the flash of Traiko's silver finger, in the squawk of Pavle's cornet, Nick sees this as a kind of initiation. Yes, he's being drawn from childhood into the world of men. He's being entrusted with the ancient secrets of music and dance. Here, in Ferny Creek, on a dusty footy ground thousands of miles from Macedonia, he's being made a member of the tribe, just as his father was made a member by *Dedo* Risto in the village square.

Suddenly the leader strips off his shirt and singlet, tosses them aside, and gestures for all to do the same. Nick's never seen this before, nor have most of the men, because they're looking at each other in surprise, not knowing what to do, until one, then another, follows his example, including Nick and the other boys, when the ground's soon covered in white.

'Like January's snow in the village,' Vangel laughs in Nick's ear.

Bare-chested, the leader throws his arms in the air, performs a few turns, and plasters the musicians' sunburnt foreheads with another note. Then, hopping on one leg, then the other, though still keeping step to the music, he pulls off his shoes and socks and tosses them in the centre of the dance circle. He cries out that everyone should do the same, and the next instant shoes are flying through the air like crows. Caught in a kind of frenzy, whistling and shouting, they do a full turn barefooted, clapped by the women and children surrounding them. The leader slips a note in each instrument, orders the band to follow him, and leads over the shirts and singlets, past the pile of shoes and socks, into the scrub surrounding the ground. As they dance on a dirt track leading to the creek, Nick's shocked to see the leader taking off his trousers, spinning them over his head, and throwing them into the bushes. This is greeted by a wild chorus that all should do the same. A few of the dancers, including Nick, break off and watch as trousers fly through the air, some falling on scrub, others catching on branches. Soon a line of men in nothing but white underpants winds among the trees and ferns, shouting for the band to play louder. One of those who broke off comes back with a big, clear bottle of *rakija,* which is passed from hand to hand, bubbling from mouth to mouth. As the men sing wildly something about a red apple, black and white cockatoos screech, kookaburras laugh, while a few magpies back up the clarinet player with their warbling notes. Away from the women and children, the dancers are now gripped by a kind of madness, so when the leader makes another offering to the band, one of the men cries goes out: underpants!

'*Gushti*!' shouts the leader and kisses the man on the head.

'*Gushti*,' echo the others.

He slips his off, waves them like a flag, and puts them on his head, followed by the others, some wearing shop-bought underwear, others homemade boxer shorts. Embarrassed, unable to watch when his father's turn comes, Nick runs back to the edge of the clearing, from where he glances back over his shoulder at a tribe of thirty men, stark naked, all with white underpants on their heads, dancing and singing in the Australian bush.

Ten minutes later, emerging from the scrub with trousers on, the men spend some time sorting through identical white shirts and singlets, black shoes and socks. Quarrels arise over ownership. A shirt's ripped in a tug-of-war. What could turn into a brawl is stopped by a few women who sort out the confusion and drive their husbands back to the tables.

As Menka brushes a footprint from the back of Vangel's shirt and scolds him for acting like a fool, Nick tries to make sense of what's just happened. Yes, he felt the strange power of music – it moved him in a way he couldn't have imagined, but only to a certain point. What drove the men to dance naked without shame or so much as a hint of embarrassment? Is it a Macedonian thing? He's seen pictures of ancient Greek pottery with naked men running and jumping and dancing. Is what he's just witnessed somehow related to that? Or were the men driven by drunkenness, first by beer, then by that bottle of *rakija*? Whatever the cause of that wild scene, Nick knows he'll never see anything like it again. Yes, the leader might try to repeat it next year, but it won't happen, no, because outbreaks like that can't be planned – they occur unexpectedly, from forces beyond anyone's control.

17

Nick measures his height almost daily on the red-brick wall in their backyard. For months the piece of timber he places on his head aligns with the mark on the mortar-line, leaving him despondent, fearful of remaining short like his father and, from what he's told, his *Dedo* back in the village. But then, at the start of grade 6, a sudden growth spurt sees the mark move up a course and a half. This shows in the way his bony wrists protrude from his sleeves and ankles from his trousers. His strength and confidence grow accordingly, increasing his appetite for football. Being short isn't a problem playing soccer, but it's a major set-back for footy, especially someone dreaming of playing full-forward, taking screamers, kicking the winning goal in a grand final. But the round-ball game has never interested Nick, even though some of his relatives play for the Greek-leaning Alexander Soccer Club and others for Preston Makedonia. Knowing he's fast, with sharp reflexes, his father tried to steer him away from football, saying the Australian game's dangerous and will leave him a cripple at thirty, but Nick stands his ground and his father doesn't bring it up again.

At school the footy coach uses Sadie on anyone who dares bring a soccer ball to school. In Australia it's Aussie Rules, he says, spinning a football in one hand. He calls soccer a sissy's game, pointing out how those players fall to the ground at the slightest bump, writhing in agony in a way unbecoming of real men, only to spring to their feet a minute later. Real men don't show their pain, he says, no matter how bad. And so when big Bruno comes to school straight off the boat, with a round ball under one arm and a half-loaf of bread under the other, Nick knows his toothy grin won't last long. He entertains Nick and a few others at morning recess with his foot and knee and head skills, until the teacher storms into the yard and confiscates his ball, threatening him with six of the best. Not speaking a word of English, a startled Bruno looks around for an explanation, finally settling on his cousin Mario. Despite itching to enlighten him, Mario remains tight lipped, knowing the teacher also punishes the use of foreign languages, saying it holds children back from learning English. Giving up on an explanation, though sensing he's done something wrong, Bruno somewhat morosely picks up a gum-nut from the ground and gives it a mighty kick, sending it flying over Alfred Crescent, over the footy ground across from the school, and through the goal posts. Hanging his head, he's about to walk away when the teacher orders him to stand still. He examines Bruno up and down, feels his biceps, feels one thigh then the other, and places the football in his hands, saying he's being recruited as a ruckman. Bruno shrugs his shoulder in bewilderment and turns to Mario who keeps back his Italian by biting his lips. Nick and the others watch in disbelief from the fence as the teacher takes Bruno across the street, to the centre of the football ground, where he acts out in pantomime the action of kicking a football, finally gesturing for Bruno to follow his example with the real ball. Bruno turns it this way and that, holds it vertically, at an angle, horizontally, and then thumps a mongrel punt that flies over a line of rail carriages loaded with briquettes just then clattering through the Edinburgh Gardens. A month after that fifty-yard kick, with daily practice at lunch time and after school, Bruno becomes the team's new ruckman.

The extra inches have boosted Nick's hopes of some day playing football at senior level. He's stopped helping his father at the Macedonian Club on Saturday afternoons because he's now a keen Fitzroy supporter. Living close to the Brunswick Street Oval, he watches the team train on Tuesdays and Thursdays, mixing with the players afterwards in the changing rooms. Football has begun to draw him away from his Macedonian heritage.

Where the very mention of Alexander would fire his imagination and his legend serve as inspiration, he now finds his boyhood hero waning, giving way to another, the great Haydn Bunton, who played for Fitzroy in the thirties, which to Nick feels like centuries ago. He questions some of the old timers in the changing rooms about him, envious they saw him in action, felt the sweat in tapping him on the back after the game. He was poetry in motion, they say, which Nick doesn't fully understand. He had the ball on a string, read the play better than anyone, ran like the wind, and side-stepped opponents with the grace of a matador avoiding a charging bull. Nick finds himself staring at a framed photo of him caught in full flight, the ball tucked under his arm, as though overcoming gravity. Yes, the Fitzroy great's beginning to replace Alexander in Nick's imagination. He wants to wear his number, win three Brownlow medals, lead Fitzroy to a premiership. And when the old timers mention his tragic death in a car accident, Nick immediately recalls Alexander's death at a young age. He ponders this for some time: whether greatness comes at the price of dying young. Would he accept greatness under this condition? Yes, he thinks, better to burn in a blaze, to be a short-lived comet sweeping across the night sky, than be a nameless star, one amongst millions, fixed in one spot for eternity.

The growth spurt has come at a price: a painful swelling below both knees that keeps Nick from playing football. At times it's so bad he can barely walk. He tries the green coolness of Penetrine, the pungency of Dencorub, the unbearable burning of Capsolin. When these fail, he turns to home-grown measures suggested by relatives, including a kerosene rub that leaves both knees red raw, without improving his condition. The specialist at the Epworth Hospital calls it Osgood Schlatter disease, but even this hasn't eased his frustration or lessened the soreness. Growing pain, he says. Nothing can be done. The condition will pass with time, maybe six months, maybe a year. As a last resort Menka takes him to see *Baba* Magda, who lives around the corner on Rowe Street. She's old and thin, her skin slightly yellow, and dressed in black from head to foot. People come to her for all sorts of conditions: sore backs from working in factories, migraines, insomnia, reading coffee-cups, interpreting dreams, even making and breaking spells. Menka says she learnt these things in the village, where she also acted as midwife. One time Nick overheard his mother telling a friend *Baba* Magda's helped women with unwanted pregnancies. After the harrowing experience with his unborn brother, Nick finds this hard to comprehend, uncertain of what exactly she does with the babies, though he shudders at what his imagination conjures.

She feels the lumps under his knees with her shrivelled fingers, twists his legs this way and that, then suggests a poultice made of olive oil and chopped onion. At home Menka carries out her instructions, wrapping his knees and helping him into bed. He remains still all night, praying for a miracle, only to find in the morning he's still unable to walk freely.

Accepting his condition, he spends hours on the balcony overlooking McKean Street, the corner shop with its tingling doorbell, the bare elms in the Edinburgh Gardens, the winter sun setting in the Carlton cemetery. He watches men and women going home from work, familiar faces tired from a day in the factory or the assembly line or the construction site. Tony's father walking with hands behind his back, the silver heels of his Italian shoes scraping the footpath. Andoni, the Greek, clicking his worry-beads, father of four sons all under six, husband of Maria who's said to have stabbed him with scissors when he lost his wages at cards. The Ryan couple, Mr and Mrs, no children, both tipsy from stopping at the pub after work. A pregnant girl from The Haven, walking heavily from the shop, with an ice cream in her hand. Nick's seen her many times during the winter months, her stomach getting bigger, wearing the same green cardigan. How did she become pregnant? What will she do with the child? The boys call these girls no-good sluts, but he can't help feeling sorry for them, especially this one, who looks as if she's going to give birth any day. He observes and daydreams on the balcony until it becomes dark and mist gathers around the streetlights and his mother calls him for dinner, when he walks painfully down the stairs, to the warmth of their small kitchen.

With his son's painful knees preventing him selling papers and helping at the Macedonian Club, Vangel's determined to keep him active, saying idleness is a curse, so he comes up with a resourceful plan to occupy the boy. After having his tax return done by a Macedonian-speaking Albanian up the street, and picking his brains on this and that, Vangel goes through the tax form with Nick, showing him where earnings and deductions go, how to work out taxable income, and then how to use the table of figures on the back to calculate tax payable or refund. He then brings home a pile of forms from the post-office and sets Nick to practice, giving him different examples, stressing the importance of beefing up deductions: an extra ten pounds to medical expenses, the cost of five new knives instead of two for an abattoir-worker, three dust-coats instead of one for a woman working as a packer in a warehouse.

'But isn't that cheating?' Nick asks, mindful of God's watchful eye.

'Cheating,' he scoffs, 'God helps those who help themselves.'

Satisfied with the speed and accuracy of Nick's work, Vangel tells people his son can do tax returns at half the Albanian's price. In order for clients not to walk through the house, he sets up an office in the front room, with a makeshift desk and packing cases for chairs. Soon relatives, friends, even complete strangers come through, especially on weekends, when there's no letting up from morning to night. Vangel sets the fee and collects the money – three shillings a form, five for more involved work – and they split the takings. Word spreads that Nick's better than the Albanian, much quicker, delivering refunds the likes of which people have never seen. So, all through wet and chilly July and August, Nick sits in the warmth of the front room, feeling pretty good about himself, as people who can't read or write English, and a few even their own language, wait nervously for their name to be called, fidgeting envelopes bulging with receipts. But he barely glances at what they've brought, even though some hold shoe boxes full of papers. It's enough for him to know their occupation, see their certificate of earnings and tax paid, and in a flash he completes their form and announces a refund that lights up their grey face. And when he points to where they must sign, some struggling to make even a cross, he suddenly understands the power of the pen. Men who've fought in wars and seen all kinds of terrible things, who slaughter sheep and operate heavy machines – these men stand in front of him, a twelve-year-old boy, as though before their superior.

He's sitting on a park bench, aching knees at right angles, enviously watching friends playing kick-to-kick on the oval across Alfred Crescent, his heart kicking at each thump of the leather. An old Greek everyone calls Geros appears on a path skirting the oval. Speaking Macedonian at home and with relatives, Nick's lost most of his Greek. His mother uses it from time to time so he won't forget it all together. She says he spoke it so fluently in the village he could've passed for a little Greek boy. The more languages you speak, she often says, the better off you'll be in life. And a person who speaks three languages is worth three people. A year ago she insisted Nick attend Greek School on Saturday morning, which he hated because it took him away from playing with the boys. He was pleased when his father saw his unhappiness and intervened. Greeks gave us hell back in the old country, he said, and he wasn't going to see his son being tortured by Greek teachers here in Australia. Better for the boy to explore the back lanes of Collingwood and learn something about the ways of this country, he said, than be forced to learn what Greeks did thousands of years ago.

Nick knows *geros* means old man in Greek, but he's not sure how this nick-name came about, unless Geros used it in referring to himself. The name's now so widespread even Danny, who's taught Nick words like 'strewth' and sayings like 'I wouldn't be dead for quids', has learnt to pronounce the first letter with that soft Greek 'g' verging on 'y'. A wisp of a man, Geros moves with mincing steps and a walking stick. Nick first noticed him in the park last summer, shuffling along on a path, each step no more than half a shoe-length. He always sat on the same bench, watching for hours the boys playing cricket, chin resting on the crook of the upright walking stick between his legs. From the occasions the ball rolled in his direction, Nick noticed his white moustache twisted to a point, a dark blue cap like those worn by Greek fishermen, and a string of amber beads in his restless fingers. Once when the ball stopped at his feet, he pushed it toward Nick with his stick and chuckled in Greek what sounded to Nick like: What a nice red ball, what a nice red ball. Nick stopped and said *Efharisto*. His thanks seemed to excite him: his small wrinkled face, like those lively monkeys at the zoo, lit up in delight, and he twisted the rubber end of the walking stick into the grass.

Today Nick's uneasy at seeing Geros. Last week Paul told the boys the old man made an indecent gesture to a kid from another neighbourhood and tried to lure him into the row of bushes near the wood stacks behind the National Can factory.

'To kill him?' asked Chris.

'Worser,' said Paul.

'What's worser than that?' said Danny.

'Being bummed off by an old poof,' said Paul.

Nick was shocked, but dismissed this as mischief-making, even though Paul swore on his mother's eyes it was true.

As Geros shuffles to his usual bench, Nick can't imagine how such a frail old man could possibly want to do what Paul said, let alone have the strength to do it. He's been brought up to respect the elderly, remembering, even though very vaguely, the kindness of his grandfather and other old people back in the village.

When the ball tumbles and stop near the old man's extended legs, Paul and Dom begin taunting him with obscene Greek words and teasing him with rude gestures. His reaction surprises Nick: instead of telling them to stop, he appears to be enjoying their attention. Clapping and prodding the ground with the stick, he accepts the vilest of names with a toothless grin, as though a compliment. Is it the madness of old age? Is he lonely and playing the fool simply to have some company? Or is Paul right after all? Is Geros trying to win them over, waiting for the moment to strike?

The following afternoon, returning home from school on a short-cut along the pebbled path, Nick see Geros scraping around a circular flower-bed, taking small, quick steps toward him. His first reaction is to run but the pain in his knees holds him back.

'*Yiasou, Papou,*' says Nick, putting on show of confidence, referring to him as granddad rather than old man.

Geros chuckles and rubs the crook of the walking stick with both hands. The buttons of his fly are undone, his dark trousers stained around the crutch. The forgetfulness of old age, thinks Nick, feeling sorry for him. He says something in Greek and giggles. Nick shrugs his shoulders.

'*Ela etho,*' he says, a shrivelled hand gesturing for Nick to come closer.

'*Yiasou, Papou,* Nick repeats, feeling afraid, backing away from his reach.

'*Ela mazi mou,*' he grins, poking Nick in the groin with the rubber end of the walking stick.

Alarmed, Nick brushes away the stick and takes a few painful steps. The next instant Geros places the end of the walking stick in his fly, holds it upright in the middle with both hands and performs half-a-dozen quick thrusts with his hips in a way Nick would not have believed possible by a person his age. When Geros takes a step toward him and reaches out with the crook of the stick, Nick hurries off, limping in pain, not daring to look back, pursued by the old man's high-pitched *ela etho, ela etho* all the way home.

Nick's thankful Geros hasn't been around since that incident a few weeks ago. He can't seem to get him out his head, especially that horrible grin and the way he moved with the stick. Shocked and embarrassed, he hasn't told anyone. His parents are in the backyard, preparing the vegetable patch for spring planting. He's throwing darts at a board, when he hears his father say an old Greek man was found in the park early this morning, bashed to death with his own walking stick. Nick's dart strikes the wall. His father straightens up, sighs *Bog da go prosti* – God forgive him – and complains of the violence in this country, saying people were much safer in the village. A shudder goes through Nick at the thought of the shiny walking stick bashing in the old man's head. He has his suspicions about what must have happened but says nothing. He didn't deserve to be clubbed to death, not for a few Greek words and a gesture that now seems more ridiculous than dangerous.

In the course of the week everyone speculates about what might have led to such a shocking death. His recent encounter with him still vivid, Nick listens eagerly to what grown-ups are saying, curious to know more about the strange old man. From a conversation at their front gate between his father and a Bulgarian neighbour, he learns that Geros lived as a boarder in a house on Brunswick Street. He was from Athens, served in the Greek merchant navy, worked as an opal miner in Coober Pedy, and settled in Melbourne about ten years ago. He kept to himself and, from what the owner of the house could tell, had no next of kin and few belongings, the most stand-out being a shimmering, green, Italian piano-accordion. It was an expensive instrument, bought during the old man's navy days when he travelled the world. He'd embrace it in his room every night and play all the old Greek favourites, played them very nicely, too, the owner told the Bulgarian, especially the ones by Kazantzidis, whose crooning voice makes Nick's mother all thoughtful and misty-eyed, and his father all angry and grim-faced. The Bulgarian said Geros died penniless and the owner's been given permission to sell the accordion to pay for the old man's debts, including his funeral expenses.

The thought of starting High School begins to cast a shadow over the last days of the summer holidays. Nick's parents have wasted no time getting his uniform, which he already hates: the dark blue blazer's thick, the grey trousers coarse and prickly, the striped tie feels like a noose. They make him wear it whenever visitors come, so he's already put it on about a hundred times. It's a Sunday evening: twilight's blazing above the leafy elms in the park, a light breeze carries the scent of the fenced-off flower beds, three pregnant girls are strolling arm-in-arm around Alfred Crescent on their way to the Busy Bee. School's not mentioned as they gather in the park for Bull. Nick's knees began improving before the holidays and now the pain's completely gone and he's back playing with the boys. They've learnt the game Bull from Carlo, a thick-set boy who arrived recently from Sicily. He wears shorts made of velvety material and sings in Italian walking up and down the street. The boys begin by splitting into two groups of six. After the toss of a coin, a member of the losing team leans forward and embraces the trunk of a tree, others join him, bracing themselves head to hip, forming a long, continuous back – the Bull. Members of the other team take a running jump onto the Bull. If the Bull's back breaks at any stage, the jumpers have another turn, but if it supports all the jumpers, the roles are reversed. It's a rough game, with some jumpers taking a flying leap and coming down with their knees on the arched spines, causing the sounding of cries and curses. Other times the Bull breaks under its own internal pressure, when bean-driven farts rip out of backsides, gassing close-pressing faces. The boys are playing this bruising game, when Archie, at the end of the jumpers' line, speaks up.

'Jeez, he's taken her in the Council Yard,' he says, pointing.

'Who?' asks Tony, next in line to jump.

'This bloke and some sheila.'

'You need specs,' says Tony, itching to jump.

'God's honour,' says Archie, crossing himself with four fingers. 'He had her by the hand.'

'You mean he was forcing her?' asks Dom, turning from the head of the Bull.

'Forcing her, alright.'

'Hey, what if he's a rapist?' says Chris.

'What's a rapist?' asks Lenny.

'Rapist, my arse,' says Lance. 'They're going to have a root.'

They abandon the game and race off to the entrance of the National Can Company, Tony complaining on the way he missed out on his jump. It's closed on Sundays so they scramble under the gate and come behind the tall picket fence running along the back of the Council Yard. The couple's in the long grass between two mounds. The boys watch, trying to subdue their breathing after the run. The man seems to be playing his own game of Bull with the woman. She's on hands and knees, dress raised back, and he's on top of her, pushing in and out.

'See,' Lance whispers, 'he's rooting her silly.'

Nick's shocked and confused: he imagined it was done face to face, because love's supposed to be caring and tender, not like this, the way stray dogs do it. The man's expression alternates from the pleasure of a smoker drawing deep on a cigarette, to the anger of a man who's had his smokes stolen. But it's the woman who takes him aback: her pretty face, turned sideways in their direction, is twisted in pain, her mouth's gaping, eyes closed, all from the force with which the man's pushing into her body. Suddenly his actions became more vigorous and the woman begins groaning, calling in a raspy voice for him to stop, but he doesn't, becoming instead angrier, now heaving, his thrusting violent. Alarmed at the way she's moaning and moving under him, as though struggling to escape his hold, some of the boys whisper he's hurting her and will strangle her if they don't act.

'He'll kill her?' Nick whispers.

In an instant the woman has a dozen helpers who rush to the fence, shouting at the top of their voices, beating the pickets with whatever they can find. Startled, the couple scramble up, arrange their clothes and, hand-in-hand, ran off through the grass, followed by raucous cries. They climb over the fence and gather around where the couple lay. The long grass crushed by their bodies is straightening up and the woman's perfume hovers in the air. They're all a little puzzled: if the man wanted to kill the woman why did they run off together, hand-in-hand?

'What's this?' says Frankie.

He pokes in the grass with a branch and holds up something looking like a longish balloon with a bit of milky liquid inside.

'A franger,' says Lance. 'Told ya they were rooting.'

As the branch is passed around, Lance's telling them the milky fluid contains millions of sperm, just like the Milky Way contains millions of stars, and that each tiny sperm can produce a child if it enters a woman's egg. Nick's little brother comes to mind, filling him with confusion and sorrow. He reaches for the *dekara* around his neck. Millions of babies left behind to die in the grass, he thinks. It's just as cruel, in some ways even more so, than the murder of millions of people in those concentration camps. Frankie twirls the branch above his head and flicks the franger away. Nick watches it fly through the air, arc across the crimson sun, and fall into a pile of household rubbish – millions of babies gone without trace. They return to their game of Bull, Tony insisting on his jump, but Nick can't get the franger out of his head, knowing it will remain with him for the rest of his life.

18

Why has Nick taken such an interest in this pregnant girl? Curiosity – how could she have allowed such a shameful thing to happen? Sympathy – where other girls visit the Busy Bee in pairs or in threes, she's always alone, sad-looking. Or is it from lingering guilt – something to do with what happened to his unborn brother? This interest having grown the last couple of evenings, he decides to be in the shop at the same time. The instant she appears crossing Grant Street, he leaves his lookout on the balcony and races downstairs, telling his mother he'll be back for dinner at six.

She's inside with a few other customers. Nick's about to enter but realises he has no money. He remains outside, pretending to be looking at something in the window, watching her placing a few coins on the counter. She's sixteen, seventeen, sharp-featured, with short dark hair held to one side by a clip. Her cardigan's unbuttoned and her striped dress appears too thin to keep the baby warm. The bell above the door strikes sharp and cold as she leaves with an ice cream. Nick watches her reflection as she removes the wrapper, drops it in a bin, and bites into the crisp chocolate coating. A large piece breaks away, but she managed to catch it. Nick wants to speak to her, ask why she's always alone and so sad-looking, but can't find the courage. She walks off slowly, heavily, her white thongs sounding on the bitumen. When she crosses the street, he follows, keeping his distance, imagining he's her protector, though unable to say from what. He turns into Alfred

Crescent, staying about twenty yards behind her. Evening light clings to chimneys, crowns the elms in the park. A few boys are kicking a football on the oval. A man in a shabby brown suit hurries past, swaying a little, a paper bag with bottles tucked under his arm. Instead of continuing around the Crescent to the Haven, the girl crosses the street and goes to a bench on the side of the oval, beside a tree twittering with birds. Nick crosses a little before the bench and pretends he's walking the perimeter of the oval.

'Are you all right?' he asks, standing on the chalk boundary-line.

She studies him a moment, biting the ice-cream stick.

'Do you need any help?'

'What are you after?' she says.

Her abrupt manner throws him off guard.

'Nothing,' he says, struggling. 'I was just ...'

She fixes him with a sharp look while gnawing the splintered end of the stick.

'How long before you ...?'

'Before I give birth?'

He takes a few steps, close enough now to see the blue rings under her eyes, the small red pimples on her forehead.

'The little bastard in here,' she says, prodding her stomach with the stick, 'will never see the light of day.'

She snaps the stick and throws it away. Nick's speechless, overwhelmed again by a feeling of remorse for his dead brother.

'But you're ... it's sacred,' he finally manages to say.

'Sacred! There's nothing but a bastard in here,' she says, fisting her stomach.

'Don't,' he says, restraining her by the wrist.

She pulls away, scowling at him.

'What's your name?' he asks.

'What do you care? What does anyone care?'

'My name's Nick. I live around the corner.'

'And I live in there,' she indicates with a turn of the head. 'The Haven – run like a prison by the God-fearing matrons of the Salvation Army. Been there two months, but won't be there much longer – a few more days and I'll be free of that place and free of this bastard.'

Nick sits on the end of the bench, arms crossed against the cooling air. The light's now slipped away from the top of the elms, but the boys are still kicking the ball in wide arcs against the darkening sky. Next year, he thinks, he'll be bigger and stronger and kicking the ball fifty yards. But suddenly his football aspirations seem boyish, trivial compared to what this girl's going through.

'What's upset you?' he asks.

'Better you don't know, kid.'

'I'm twelve,' he says.

'Some things are best unsaid.'

'I help my father in the Macedonian Club. I've heard lots of stories about the terrible things that happened in the war.'

'Go home, kid, before you regret it.'

Nick's now determined to be her protector, but perhaps more than that – the protector of her unborn child. What he didn't do for his little brother he'll now do for her child, despite her attitude toward it.

'I won't regret anything,' he says. 'I want to help you.'

'Nobody can help me,' she says, flaring up. 'The bastard's due any day now, but I'm not sticking around to have it. No, soon as I feel it coming, I'm sneaking out of that prison and having it on my own in this park, in that long grass over there. I'll cut the cord myself and leave it the bushes to die.'

Nick shudders at the thought of the baby left to the dogs and feral cats wandering about in the Council Yard.

'You can't do that,' he says, now sitting close to her. 'It's wrong, it's a crime, a sin before God.'

'There's no God, kid, only the devil disguised as God, only Satan passing himself off as the Father.'

Her talk unsettles him: he's never come across such ideas. He feels himself being drawn into dangerous territory – a place where everything he's known to be sacred and true is suddenly turned upside down.

'If only those Salvation Army matrons new the truth! But they don't, kid, and I'll never tell them, not in a thousand years. They keep on preaching to me about how I've done wrong to get knocked up and how the child will be born pure in God's eyes, without the stain of my sin. My sin! I could scream when I hear that. And I've been going along with them, kid, you understand? Playing their game – what else can I do, where else can I go in this condition? Letting them think I was knocked up by a good-for-nothing who shot through to Sydney when he found out. Yeah, kid, they reckon when the time comes I'm going to drop the bastard, give it up for adoption, and return to my old life. But they don't know half of it, nobody does. A couple of days and I'll have my revenge on all of them, on the entire stinking world.'

Sitting close to her now, Nick's struck by her grey eyes steeled in hatred, thin lips set in determination, while noticing the smell of Velvet soap – the big yellow block they use in the bathroom.

'You'll go to jail,' he says, 'maybe for life.'

'It's my flesh and blood – I can do what I like with it.'

Nick doesn't understand where these terrible words are coming from. Are they due to anger and resentment at having been left pregnant after some one-night stand? Or is there something else, darker, that's turned her against God. Suddenly he sees himself caught in a life and death struggle: it's up to him to save the baby boy – for some reason he's certain it's a boy – to make sure it's delivered safely and kept from harm.

She stands, saying her jailers will impose extra kitchen duties if she's late.

'The little bastard's kicking to get out,' she says.

'Can we meet again tomorrow?'

'Go home, kid,' she says and walks away.

'I'll be waiting here,' he calls after her, 'at the same time.'

The image of the helpless baby left to die in the long grass of the Council Yard fills his mind. He has no appetite for dinner. His mother asks if he's alright, saying he looks pale. His father tells them about an accident at work: a man was running across the tracks at the rail yard, trying to beat a coming goods train, when he tripped on the gravel and fell across the tracks. The train let out a mighty screech that filled the air with burning breaks, but it was already too close and there was nothing the driver could do. The man was killed on the spot, a shocking mess, blood everywhere. Menka crosses herself and scolds him, saying the table's no place for such talk, adding *Bog da go prosti* – God forgive him. But even this fails to draw Nick's thoughts and emotions from the girl.

Vangel's in the living room watching his favourite TV show – the police drama *Homicide* – never failing to exclaim how much the old inspector resembles an uncle in the village who disappeared over the border during the Civil War and was never seen again. Nick's hovering around Menka in the kitchen, helping her put away the dishes. He wants to ask how babies are born, whether a woman can deliver one on her own, and what they do when it first comes out, but he's embarrassed, uncertain what to say without arousing her suspicion. He has a vague idea of what takes place when a man and woman come together, and that only from what he's heard from the older boys in the neighbourhood. Yet he knows almost nothing about the process of birth. When he was smaller he once asked his mother where he came from. Her armpit, she replied, turning away with a funny smile. This baffled him for some time. He'd seen her armpit in the summer months when she wore sleeveless dresses: it was hairy, a bit smelly, and probably sweaty as his. He couldn't grasp how he came from such a place. How could something the size of a watermelon possibly fit through an armpit? Having seen baby chicks snuggling under a hen's wings, he thought maybe something unusual happened at such a time, a kind of miracle that opened the armpit to allow a baby to slip into the world.

Recalling the suffering his mother went through losing his little brother, he's determined to find out what takes place at birth, to help the girl in the event of an emergency.

'Is giving birth hard?' he asks.

She turns in surprise from wiping the new, white stove. They got rid of the old fat-yellow Metters that came with the house a few weeks ago – it took three men to carry it out of the kitchen and onto the back of a truck bound for the tip.

'Yes,' she says. 'Why?'

'We're learning about it in school.'

'They teach such things here?'

'Can a woman give birth on her own?'

'What are these questions?'

'Please, I have to know.'

Menka closes the door between the kitchen and living room as a police siren screams on the television. She turns the crochet doily on the table this way and that. Nick looks down at the green swirls and clouds on the laminated top, seeing the girl's features, long grass, babies in twisted positions. In the village, she begins, awkwardly, women gave birth in fields and vineyards, sometimes with no one around. Women had lots of children in the old days – six, seven, as many as ten – but not all survived, some died at birth, others in infancy. Necessity can be a cruel teacher, she sighs, without feeling for women. His *Baba* Tonka was heavy with her first when she set out for the grape harvest. Her father-in-law was a strict, tight-fisted man, who treated his four daughters-in-law like slaves. No malingering in his household, he'd say. A woman must do her chores up to the hour of birth.

'Your *Baba* felt it coming picking grapes.'

'How did she know? What were the signs?'

'Women know – first the contractions begin, then the waters break. Well, your *Baba* lay in the dusty shadow of the vines and pushed and pushed until the little one slipped out. But it was stillborn and …'

'What's stillborn?'

'It was born dead.'

'Like … my little brother?'

She nods and picks at the doily.

'And what did *Baba* do?'

'What could she do? Pulled out the afterbirth and …'

'What's that?'

'The sack that holds the baby.'

Nick tries to imagine how a baby could live in a sack without suffocating.

'Your *Baba* cut the cord with the knife, dug a hole, and buried her first-born under a rock, as though burying a dead pup.'

Nick's shocked as much by the details as his mother's matter-of-fact tone. It's as if back in those days death was somehow more part of everyday life. As if people, especially women, were stronger, not afraid to bury death under a rock and continue harvesting black grapes.

'Was there no service?' he asks.

She shakes her head.

'No priest to say a prayer for its soul?'

'The sky's dome was the church,' she smiles faintly, 'and the jackdaws were priests.'

Nick's caught in a whirlwind of thoughts and emotions. What should he do? How can he best help the desperate girl? Should he tell his mother who might suggest something? *Baba* Magda springs to mind: she delivered babies in the village and will help the girl in an emergency. He'll see the girl tomorrow, talk her out of her crazy idea, persuade her to go to *Baba* Magda's if things start.

He can't concentrate on a thing at school: his mood swings from excitement at being the baby's protector, to panic at the thought she's already done something desperate. He hurries home, throws off his uniform, and goes to the bench. She's not there, but it's still early. For some reason he's certain she'll come, maybe from the way she fiddled with the button of her cardigan walking away yesterday. The Serbian twins are squabbling at the far end of the oval. Not wanting to be seen by them, Nick waits behind the trunk of a nearby elm. Vlad's insisting Zlatko's last kick wasn't a goal. Voices rise, tempers flare, and they begin karate-kicking each other. Zlatko stashes the ball under his jumper and runs away, followed by Vlad, calling on him to stop and fight. He catches Zlatko by the jumper in front of Imbesi and Sons, the small upstairs factory that makes pink ballerina shoes. They grapple under the shelter covering the footpath, until Zlatko breaks free and races off, past the Busy Bee and around the corner. Left alone, Vlad turns this way and that, like a caged tiger. Suddenly, he lets loose with five or six kicks at a wire gate, tucks in his shirt, and walks off calmly, limping slightly on the kicking leg.

Relieved the twins have gone, Nick returns to the bench, concerned the girl mightn't show. Having observed her from the balcony, he knows when she goes to the shop for her evening ice cream. Has she gone another way? But what if she's already in the Council Yard carrying out her crazy idea? What if she's already done it and left the baby dead in the long grass? He's about to race off when the slap of thongs sounds from behind. She's walking gingerly, grimacing, holding the lower part of her stomach with both hands.

'Help me, kid,' she says, struggling for breath.

Nick springs up, takes her plump arm and eases her onto the bench. She holds her big stomach and moans, her solid legs straight out and wide apart.

'Is it coming?' Nick asks, heart pounding, scattering his thoughts.

'Ah, the bastard,' she groans, 'it's on the way.'

'I'll call the fire brigade,' he says, desperate to do something. 'Look, the red alarm box at the end of Rowe Street. They'll be here in minutes.'

'No, kid, you want to help, get me over there, quick.'

She indicates the Council Yard.

'No, I won't help you do that.'

'Ah, kid, if only you knew …'

'Knew what?' he asks, at the same time wanting not to know.

'Get me over there, kid, before ...'

Nick watches her a moment, flustered, not knowing what to do, as she moves awkwardly getting to her feet.'

'Please,' she cries, extending a hand.

And without thinking, Nick helps her up, surprised by the softness of her hand. She grimaces and lets out a groan. He considers the red fire-alarm. But she's now on her feet, unsteady, and he's afraid she'll collapse if released. Besides, he's not sure he could break free of her strong grip without a struggle. He's got himself into a terrible mess. What will his parents say? He should've told his mother. It feels like a bad dream from which he'll wake and find himself safely in bed. But she pulls him onto the oval pock-marked by boots from a recent school match. He has sprinted the length of this ground, jogged its perimeter, practised kicking for goal at both ends. He has played matches here with the neighbourhood boys until the ball couldn't be seen in the winter-dark. And no matter how upsetting his father's heavy drinking, no matter how dispirited he sometimes feels, just stepping onto this oval has the effect of dispersing his sadness, sweeping away the heaviness of thinking, making him feel light and free. But this now seems remote, nothing more than child's play in the face of life and death.

She wraps her arm around his forearm and pulls him across the oval. Nick feels as though caught in a powerful current, heading toward a waterfall, over there, in that gloomy Council Yard with its small bare mounds, its hollows and dips covered in long grass, the dishevelled willows along the back. He tells himself to stop. Stand his ground, tell her he won't go any further. It's his duty to help bring the baby into the world alive and well. His little brother comes to mind and *Baba* Magda – she'll use her ways to reason with this girl and deliver the child.

'We're not going there,' he says, surprised at the firmness in his voice.

As she tightens her grip on his arm, the back of Nick's hand presses against something hard in the pocket of her cardigan. He pulls out a small knife with a serrated blade and black handle.

'What's this for?'

She lunges at it, almost taking them both down, but he manages to avoid her grasp and remain upright. His scalp tingles at the thought of her intention.

'We're not going in there,' he says. 'Let's go to *Baba* Magda's – she knows what to do.'

'I'll drop it here if we don't hurry.'

'We're going to *Baba* Magda's,' he says, pulling her away.

'Then give me my knife, kid, and piss off,' she says, releasing his arm. 'You don't know what you're doing.'

'I'm killing the bastard, that's what.'

'Don't say those awful things. Look, I know something happened and you got pregnant and now you're angry with whoever it was that got you this way. But you can't take it out on the baby, you can't. Let's go to *Baba* Magda's – she lives right there, on Rowe Street, across from the fire-alarm. She'll make the cross on your forehead and drive away those awful thoughts and help deliver the baby.'

'You know nothing, kid, nothing,' she says painfully, eyes filling with tears.

'Tell me,' Nick says, bracing himself.

'If you knew,' she moans, supporting her stomach, 'you'd help me do it.'

'Knew what?'

And again he feels he's about to be swept away by some dark current, this time one coming from the rings haunting her eyes. If only he were kicking the footy, not thinking or questioning or deciding, but connecting with that red leather in just the right way, with that sweet thump that transfers his being into the ball, sending it and his essence spiralling in a happy arc across the evening-sky. But no, he's here instead, standing on the wing with this pregnant girl who's about to tell him why she wants to kill her unborn baby. Does he really want to hear something likely to change him forever, something never to be unknown?

'This bastard's … my father's.'

Jolted by the clash of 'bastard' and 'father' Nick struggle to put them together, make sense of their combined meaning. She wipes her eyes on the folded sleeve of the cardigan.

'He'd come to my room at night and whisper he loves me.'

The dark current catches Nick and loosens the surroundings.

'Said his love's the purest kind.'

The dark elms swirl around the oval.

'Said it had to be our secret.'

The houses across the street sway from side to side.

'Everyone thinks it was a one-night stand with a boy gone to Vietnam.'

The Council Yard is spilling toward him.

'You're the only one that knows.'

Horror and disgust rise from the depths of his being and catch in his throat.

'I'm sorry,' he manages to say. 'I'm so, so sorry.'

'Let's just hurry before …,' she grimaces, taking his arm.

As they continue across the oval toward the Council Yard, Nick's feeling of revulsion begins to subside and he finds himself yielding to what she intends. Suddenly the child's something unnatural and doesn't belong in this world. In his sympathy for her, he wonders whether what she plans is any more horrible than what she's experienced. But then he'd be a partner in her crime. The matrons in The Haven would ask questions, the police would be called, they'd be interrogated, the truth would come out, and they'd spend years in jail. His little brother comes to mind again, as though countering his willingness to assist her. No, he can't have another death on his conscience. The boy in her stomach is meant to make up for his little brother. Surely life of whatever form, no matter how awful and deformed, is better than death. With life there's always a chance that some good might arise from evil. With death there's only darkness, like that now descending on the Council Yard. Surely the baby has a right to live. It's not to blame for the horrible way it came into being. And what would happen if it were born? The Salvation Army would give it out for adoption, the father's role would never be known, and the girl, seeing neither again, would be spared further suffering. He's pleased with his clear-headedness: under the impact of that shock he could so easily have been drawn into a dark and dangerous place.

A plan suddenly springs to mind, a gamble, a long shot, yes, but one which might overcome this hopeless situation. And if it doesn't, if …? But this isn't the time for questioning – better to act decisively with a glimmer of hope, than be hamstrung by ifs and buts. The evening has deepened, blackening the still elms, quickening the steps of a small boy shuffling leaves on a path flanked by oaks. Homely light shines in some of the front windows along Alfred Crescent. The smoke of fires warming living rooms rises straight from red-brick chimneys. Following their own call, four crows beat strongly overhead. In the Council Yard the mounds crouch like humped beasts of prey, the willows look like hooded figures.

They make their way there slowly, stopping for breath every ten or so steps, her moans and groans now more frequent, stronger, his heart dropping at each sound. Finally he steps on a length of sagging barbed wire and helps her through a break in the hedge. Firming his hold on her arm, they plod through the long grass between mounds, skirting dumped furniture, building rubble, parts of cars, and pushing deeper into the Yard, toward the back corner.

'Here,' she heaves, surprising Nick with her certainty.

They stop before the overhanging branches of a willow somewhat hidden from the oval by one of the bigger mounds. She directs Nick to a nearby shrub from where he pulls out a large paper bag containing a blanket, some towels, a cushion and torch. Following her instructions, he spreads the blanket beneath the tree, places the cushion against the lumpy trunk, and eases her down. She's now breathing hard, sitting with knees up and apart, dress down around her full, pale thighs, with nothing on underneath, her wedge of hair black and fully exposed. Stunned, Nick looks away, heart pounding like a fist.

'Give me the bag, kid, quick. The bastard's coming.'

As she places the towels beside her, Nick knows it's now or never.

'I'll be back in a minute,' he says.

'Where are you going?' she screams.

'I'll be back.'

'Where's my knife?'

He sets off, swishing through the grass, sprinting crossing the oval, past the many staring windows of The Haven, stopping for a second at the fire-alarm box, then continuing across Rowe Street, to *Baba* Magda's white, double-fronted house. He twists the loose bell. Footsteps race down the hallway and a girl of nine or ten swings open the door. The large family's seated around a small table in the kitchen, steam rising from plates of potatoes and meat. He can barely explain the situation, pleading with *Baba* Magda to come at once, saying the girl's not right in the head and sure to kill the child if they don't help her. The thin little woman springs to her feet, instructs her daughter to bring a few things, disappears into a room off the hallway, and emerges a minute later with a black carry-bag. They hurry off into the gathering dark, the women discussing what needs to be done, their slippers slapping at each step, and Nick urging them to be quicker, hoping the girl hasn't carried out her threat.

It's now dark in the Council Yard, the nearest light fifty yards away on the path running beside the hedge. Not wanting to startle the girl, Nick tells the women to wait behind a mound while he assesses the situation. The silence in the back corner worries him. His heart races as he picks his way through the grass.

'I'm back,' he says, a few steps from the tree.

She groans. Nick pushes through the willow branches. He can just make out she's in the same position as before – no sign of a baby.

'Help me,' she moans.

'You'll be all right now.'

'The bastard,' she moans and strains, 'it's killing me.'

Searching for the torch around the base of the trunk, he feels wetness on the blanket. He shines the torch on her exhausted face, her fringe fallen from its clip, her closed eyes, on a dark patch spreading out from under her.

'I've brought help,' he says, keeping the torch away from her legs.

Her eyes open in alarm.

'No, not from The Haven – *Baba* Magda and her daughter.'

'I don't want them,' she heaves.

Nick returns to the women and leads them to the tree. The daughter takes the torch and gives Nick a large plastic bottle with a finger-hold at the base of the neck, instructing him to fill it with water right away. He knows the tap at the junction of several paths, but hesitates, watching as they push through the branches, only to be met by abuse. And then *Baba* Magda begins speaking in Macedonian, her voice high-pitched and playful, telling the girl to lie back, saying words Nick's never heard before, making strange sounds, until the girl's groaning eases and she settles.

'What are you waiting for?' says the daughter, seeing him standing there.

Nick feels less anxious knowing the girl's in good hands, though still uncertain how the women will handle her when the child comes. He hurries to the tap and fills the bottle with a thin trickle catching the overhead light. Here and there through the vault of overlapping elms a star twinkles brightly in the clear sky.

The daughter pushes through the curtain of branches and asks what took him so long, snatching the bottle from him.

'Has it come out yet?' Nick asks.

'Slipped out like a fish,' she laughs.

'What is it?'

'A boy, with a full crop of black hair.'

Nick tries sneaking a glance through the leafy branches into the lighted space, but the daughter blocks his view with her ample size.

'They need cleaning up,' she says, 'before they can accept visitors.'

It must be past seven, he thinks. Looking across the oval, he can make out the outline of their chimney, and further on, the steeple of St John's Church. His parents must be worried he's not home for dinner, but he can't leave now, not until he helps the women take the girl and her baby to The Haven.

'Alright,' the daughter calls from behind the branches.

She's pouring water from the bottle onto *Baba* Magda's bloody hands. The torch shines down from a fork in a branch. The women are smiling, chatting in Macedonian, saying they've never seen such a healthy boy. A bundle of bloody towels and sheets lies beside the trunk. Next to this, wrapped in what looks like a pillow-case, Nick can see a reddish-brown, crumpled little face with a cap of black hair. The girl's leaning against the trunk, heavy-eyed, washed-out, legs flat on a different blanket, her fringe brushed aside and held in place by the clip. The daughter picks up the baby and shows him to Nick. He runs a finger lightly over the sticky hair. She then lowers him to the girl.

'Is goot baby, goot,' says the daughter.

'Goot, goot,' says *Baba* Magda, wiping her hands.

'You lucky girl for this baby,' says the daughter.

'This baby from *Gospo*,' says, *Baba* Magda, pointing up with a bony finger.

The girl's eyes open wider, but they're white and vacant. *Baba* Magda draws Nick closer and uses him as her interpreter. He tells the girl *Baba* Magda read her baby's future from the lines on the soles of his feet. He'll become a great man, someone who'll save many lives, maybe a doctor. Nick's unsure how much the girl takes in, but he detects what appears a faint smiles pulling at the corners of her colourless lips.

Saying it's time to go, the daughter passes the baby to *Baba* Magda, who presses it close with one arm, while reaching for the torch with the other. The daughter gathers up a few things, throws the blood-stained items behind the tree, and calls for Nick's help getting the girl to her feet. Groggy and weak, she offers no resistance as they pull her up. He holds her propped against the tree as the daughter folds the blanket. Supporting her on each side, they follow *Baba* Magda leading the way with the torch. The women chatter softly in Macedonian as they cross the now dewy oval, over Alfred Crescent, and up the steps of The Haven. A tall woman in a starchy uniform and blue cap opens the impressive front door.

'Linda,' she cries out, 'are you alright, my girl?'

She calls over her shoulder for help and two women come running down the wide staircase, their uniforms rustling like paper. They take the sleepy girl and walk her to the back of the residence. The first woman takes the baby from *Baba* Magda, thanking God for the miracle.

'We were about to call the police,' she says. 'What happened?'

As Nick gives a brief account of events, highlighting the role of *Baba* Magda and her daughter, she examines the baby, putting her ear to its face, feeling its pulse.

'Thank you,' she says to the women, 'thank you.'

'Tenk you,' they reply, 'tenk you.'

'Linda's been quite a difficult girl,' she says. 'Very high-strung, makes up all sorts of wild stories about the child's father, but her parents will be pleased she's come through this alright.'

She asks *Baba* Magda to come back in the morning and help her complete a proper report for the register of births, adding it's such a human-interest story she'll arrange for a reporter from *The Sun* newspaper to be present. Nick translates this for *Baba* Magda, who shakes her thin finger and clicks her tongue. No, she says, no pictures in the paper, adding she prefers the shade to the sun. At the front gate Nick thanks the women for leaving their dinner to help the girl. The daughter hurries away, to make sure the children have eaten, while *Baba* Magda arranges her black shawl, tying it at the back.

'The poor baby,' she says, in a low voice.

A streetlight catching the glint in her eyes sends a shiver down Nick's spine. He's about to ask what she means but wishes her good-night instead and runs off around Alfred Crescent, wondering what to tell his parents.

19

Out of football season Nick continues helping his father in the Macedonian Club, but this will soon come to end: the row of buildings is scheduled for demolition in a few weeks. Slum reclamation – that's what the notice taped to the front window says. In protest one of the older patrons has drawn a big black cross on the back. Plans for what will go up have been shuffling around the Club for some time: high-rise flats, with sketches of figures in open space, children in a playground, a row of wintery trees where the Club now stands. The word 'slum' surprises Nick. He thought places like that existed only in Bombay or Calcutta, yet the notice refers to this part of Fitzroy as slum, which means people living and working here are slum dwellers, which makes him a kind of slum kid. A cloud heavier than cigarette smoke hangs over the Club. The card players are quieter, thumping the tables with less force, the dice aren't as lively on backgammon boards, and Vic looks as if he's in mourning. Patrons tap him on the shoulder in sympathy, shake his hand slowly as if not wanting to let go, tell him how much the place has meant to them, especially when they first arrived in Australia. He's already started taking down the prints and photographs from the walls. He assures patrons with a show of forced enthusiasm that he's looking to open a bigger and better place just down the road, on the corner of Gore Street. But his eyes moisten, because he knows the new place might be bigger but it won't be the same. Vangel's also taking it badly as the Club's been like a second home. Apart from the extra income, he's been in his element here – joking, singing, sometimes leading a few patrons in a dance around the tables. For Menka the demolition can't come soon enough. The place has been a bad influence on the boy, she says. It's kept him from attending Greek School, or learning a musical instrument like the accordion or bouzouki. Nick hates change, like going from primary to high school, and migrating from the village to Australia. Working at the Club for almost three years, he's come to know many of the patrons well. He'll miss their jokes and stories about Macedonia and what Australia was like years ago. Vic's planned a farewell party, maybe more of wake, in the coming week.

Nick's keeping tabs on the tables, when Danny's head bobs up above the opaque lower half of the front window. He signals for his friend to go around the back lane. Having drifted apart from Charlie since the theft of his pigeons, Nick's now best friends with Danny. As his first real Australian friend, Nick's learnt a lot about the country from listening to him, visiting his house, taking in its smell, its furniture, the state of the kitchen, seeing how he relates to his parents and sisters. He's heard about an ancestor who came out not long after The First Fleet, another who struck gold in Ballarat, his grandad at Gallipoli, and his father, who was sick with malaria on the Kokoda Trail and almost died. He's seen a photo of him from that time: skin and bones in baggy army shorts and a dark singlet. For his part Nick's told Danny things about Macedonia, taught him to say *sho praish* and *ka te vikat* – how are you and what's your name – and shared with him his mother's mincemeat pies. But he also wants to show him the Club before it disappears.

He opens the back gate and takes him to the kitchen. Danny sips a bottle of lemonade as Nick explains his work, rattling the coins in his pocket. As they walk around the tables, Nick shows off a little, strutting about confidently, joking with patrons, teasing and being teased. They sit down at an empty table to a game of chess. Danny was born in McKean

Street but has never walked along Gertrude Street, having being warned by his father it's a dangerous place. Nick tells him of his adventures here, the story of Horny Thorny, his encounter with the King brothers. In no mood for chess they return to the kitchen. Nick notices Danny's looking a little bored. As his friend has walked all the way from McKean Street to see the Club, Nick feels obliged to make his visit worthwhile and memorable. Still trying to impress him with how street-wise he is in this tough neighbourhood, he asks if Danny wants a real adventure.

'What sort?' he asks, brushing aside the fringe of his Beatles-style haircut.

Nick's father would never allow him to have his cut like that, not that he would want one, anyway. The boys at school are divided in two groups: the Europeans fancy Elvis and his hair-style, while the Australians prefer the Beatles. They go out to the backyard where Nick indicates the adjacent building, saying the wooden stairs lead up to a brothel and the man leaning on the railing is a pimp. Danny is wide-eyed with curiosity as Nick explains the sorts of men and women he's seen going up and down the stairs. They both turn away as the pimp straightens up and gestures to someone down in the back lane. As Danny takes a nervous piss in the toilet, Nick watches furtively a man climbing the stairs, hat low over his eyes, newspaper concealing his face, wearing a dark-brown suit and matching two-toned shoes. He slips the pimp some money and goes inside.

'Follow me,' says Nick, when Danny comes out.

They go back to the kitchen and sneak up a flight of stairs to the left. The rooms up here are used for storage. One contains cartons with supplies, tools, brushes, cans of paint, a ladder. In another, old furniture and broken chairs meant to be repaired. In the third, a couple of single beds which Vic offers to men until they find a room to rent. In the bedroom, Nick positions the ladder beneath the man-hole in the corner of the ceiling and closes the door. He climbs up, pushes aside the cover and raises himself into the spacious roof cavity.

'Step on the rafters,' Nick whispers, 'or you'll fall through the ceiling into deep shit.'

The row of buildings has a common roof space. Light squeezes in from gaps and cracks in the slate. A shared brick chimney rises from each pair of properties. It's dusty, but the rafters are visible, and they set off toward the brothel, holding onto the overhead beams. Having been up here a few times, Nick's positioned a plank over the place of interest. A pigeon scatters and swoops over their heads in flying out through a small opening in the roof. Chicks squeak at the far end. As a tram rumbles past outside, Nick turns to Danny and asks in a whisper if he's ready for an unforgettable show. He kneels on the plank and looks through the small opening around a brown electricity cable running down into the room below. The shadow of a figure moves on the white sheets of a double-bed. And then a woman appears in a crimson petticoat and matching bra. She's full, puffy-faced, flabby around the hips. Sitting on the bed, she raises the petticoat to her milky-white thighs and begins peeling off her stockings. Nick straightens up and allows Danny to look, whispering thirty seconds each. Danny bows close to the cable, head slightly turned, peering through one eye.

'Jeez, her tits, they're, and now she's …'

When Nick looks the woman's naked, sitting against the bed-head, arms wrapped around her knees. A studded belt flies through the air and falls at her feet. A man steps in view, head covered in a khaki-green balaclava with holes for the eyes and mouth, wearing only a white singlet tucked into white underpants. He gets on the bed and approaches the woman on all fours. Danny pulls Nick away and presses his cheek on the dusty ceiling slats.

'What's he doing?' he whispers.

'What's he doing?' Nick says.

'She's putting a belt around his neck like he's a dog.'

'Come on,' says Nick, 'my turn.'

Danny moves aside reluctantly, head shaking in shock and disbelief. Pulling on the belt, the woman draws the man toward her until his head's between her full thighs.

'What's he doing?' Nick says.

'My turn,' says Danny, pulling at Nick's jumper.

'Not so loud.'

Trembling, he presses his cheek to the slats.

'Jeez, she's riding him like a horse.'

'First a dog, then a horse – what next?'

When Nick looks the woman's straddling the man, bouncing vigorously up and down, his upper body concealed by her ample size, thin legs kicking and thrashing.

'She's crushing him,' says Nick.

'Come on, my look.'

Danny's head knocks against Nick's in his excitement not to miss a second's viewing.

'She's riding him harder,' he says. 'And now she's pulling off ...'

Suddenly Danny straightens up, eyes closed, trembling all over. Nick's first thought is he's having an emission. It happens in dreams why not in reality? When he opens his eyes, Nick asks if he is alright.

'Let's go,' says Danny, looking dazed.

Nick's curious to see what's upset him so much, but Danny grabs his jumper and says he wants to go. Nick replaces the man-hole cover and climbs down the ladder. Danny's still shaking, as though having seen a ghost instead of all that flesh. His eyes and cheeks are smudged with dust. They go downstairs to the kitchen, where he washes his face and brushes his hair. At the back gate he looks up at the landing – the pimp's no longer there.

'Are you alright?' Nick asks.

He turns abruptly and sets off down the smelly lane, its uneven bluestones wet and greasy from restaurants and hamburger shops and backyards. Watching him tuck in his shirt and tighten his belt, Nick's convinced it was an emission, maybe his first, and Danny was too confused and embarrassed to say anything.

A few days later, their game of kick-to-kick stopped by the hated dark, Nick's sprinting his shadow on Mrs Knight's red-brick wall when he sees

Danny's father approaching from The Recreation hotel, where he stops for a few beers every day after work. Their paths cross under the streetlight at the entrance to Nick's lane. Mrs Knight's cats are prowling around the row of smelly rubbish tins. A newspaper tucked under his arm, the brim of his hat low over his eyes, cigarette glowing between fingers, he would've walked on had Nick not said hello. He glances up without saying a word. Nick's father wears his only suit on special days, whereas Danny's works in a clothing store and has lots of suits, summer and winter, all with matching hats. Nick's suddenly struck by the fact he's never seen Danny's parents out and about as a couple: they don't shop together, visit friends in the street, or just sit in the park on summer nights. Being such a smart dresser, maybe he doesn't want to be seen out with a wife wearing old-fashioned clothes. But he's more casual indoors, often in shorts, sitting in the living room, saying nothing to anyone, staring through cigarette smoke at nothing in particular. Danny has excused his father's silence, saying it's because of the war and his mates killed on the Kokoda Trail.

Now, barely acknowledging Nick, he makes a psst sound at the cats and marches on, steps crisp from heels silvered with half-moons. Nick's struck by his shoes – brown, two-toned, shining in the overhead light – and suddenly everything makes sense: they're the shoes he saw on the stairs to the brothel. Danny must've seen the woman taking off the balaclava. Nick watches him striding beside Mrs Knight's house, his shadow on the wall larger-than-life, heels glinting at each sharp step. What made him visit the brothel? Something to do with the Kokoda Trail? Nick wonders about Danny. Will he ever get over it? Yes, he must hate him now, and probably for a long time, but maybe one day, when he grows up and has the feelings of a man, he might see things in a different light. He might accept that wars wound people inside as much as out, leaving scars that can't be seen, even by family members. And then Nick thinks of his own father and his three years in Australia before he and his mother arrived. Did he ever visit a brothel? And how would he feel if he did? Would he despise him? But those years were like being in a war: conditions were hard, the locals saw him as an enemy, and he fought to survive. And if in that war he visited a brothel from time to time, it was a way of enduring the hardship until re-united with his wife and son.

Making his way down the dead-end lane, the breeze scraping sagging barbed wire on a corrugated fence, Nick vows never to say a word of this to anyone, never to mention that day to Danny.

No cards this afternoon, no chalk boards, no backgammon, no thick Turkish coffee. (Nick's always thought it strange that many of the elderly patrons discuss with bitter resentment the centuries of Ottoman rule in Macedonia, while, with the same breath, cooling their cup of Turkish coffee before sipping it with a satisfying slurp.) The tables and chairs have been pushed against the walls, opening a space in the middle for guests. The atmosphere's more like a funeral than a farewell party. People are dressed in their Sunday-best. Vic's wife and two daughters are serving drinks and food. Some of the patrons have brought their families along. A few kids are grabbing meatballs and pieces of cabana from the table and running around. Wives who've never been here before, but have no doubt cursed the place for its hold on their husbands, are looking around and wondering what it is about this grimy place that gripped their husbands and led to those terrible domestic arguments. The walls are dull yellow from years of cigarette smoke, but the once lighter colour is still visible in the rectangles where the prints and photographs hung. Menka's talking to a couple of women in the corner. Vangel's filling small glasses with *rakija*, helping himself between serving others. Pavle was one of the first to arrive, placing his cornet case on a chair in the corner. Kocho *Kokoshkaro* is also there, though not as loud as usual. Horny Thorny has come out of uniform, a good head taller than everyone else. He winks at Nick and flicks a shilling his way. He likes Nick, not just because of his win at the races that time, but because he follows Fitzroy, his team, and because he plays football, not that round-ball game. He encourages Nick not to give up on the Lions, never to follow those umpire-bribing Magpies, and to avoid walking on the Collingwood-side of Smith Street. Yes, the maroon-and-blues are on the bottom of the ladder now, but their fortunes will change when the great Kevin Murray comes back from Western Australia. He's the gutsiest player going round, a dead-set certainty for a Brownlow Medal. He'll lift Fitzroy up the ladder and see to it they make the final four, carrying the team and all the supporters in his tattooed arms. Nick gives him a glass of *rakija* and he ruffles his hair.

Vangel waves his feathered hat and calls for attention. Vic climbs on a chair. Colourful in floral dresses, his wife and daughters stand beside him. He hooks his thumbs around the elastic suspenders holding up his trousers with creases like a knife's edge. Nick observes little Pavle as he backs away to the corner, opens the case, and takes out the silver instrument. After a few silent finger exercises on the valves, he lets out a flurry of notes. A few men turn and abuse him. Vic settles them down, saying back in the village a band would often lead the coffin to the cemetery, and as they're here to pay their respects to the dead Club, a tune or two is very appropriate. Pavle flutters about, falters, and finds the slow melody he played in the Town Hall that night. Accompanied by the cornet, Vic reminisces about the Club's beginnings and how it was a kind of home-away-from-home for men who came to Australia on their own. How his wife worked the kitchen, providing breakfast and dinner to men going and coming from work. He's always run a good and proper place, he says with a note of pride. He refused big-money manilla games upstairs, not so much because it's illegal, but because that game breaks long-standing friendships, destroys marriages, and makes men forget their obligations to family-members left behind in the village. No, he's never gone the way of the Greek and Italian Clubs. He relates a story about the Italian shoe shop down the street. How males asking for a size 42 would be directed to the back for a fitting by a woman who took off more than their shoes. Yes, he's served a little *rakija* from time to time, but nothing too much, nothing his good friend the Sergeant wouldn't mind. Standing beside Horny Thorny, Nick translates Vic's heartfelt words. The Sergeant raises his glass, saying he's dealt with them all – Greeks, Italians, Spaniards, Albanians, Yugoslavs – but the Macedonians, and his old mate Vic, have been the most law-abiding of the lot. As he proposes a toast to Vic's health, Pavle continues playing, slowly, sadly, seldom pressing a false note.

Two scruffy Aboriginal men open the door and stand in the entrance. One's carrying a didgeridoo decorated with white snakes. Nick's seen him playing for coins on Gertrude Street. Aborigines come into the Club from time to time, most a bit tipsy, asking for hand-outs. Vic's always kind to them, offering a nip of *rakija* or a slice of pie. Putting on a serious look, Vangel strides to the front and tells the men this is a private function. But Vic calls him back and invites them inside, saying they're more than welcome to a little hospitality. After all, this is their land, even though the government treats them like third-rate citizens. He reminds people that Macedonians have much in common with these people. Past Greek governments have Hellenised Macedonian names and forbidden the language.

A fellow of about sixty goes to the front and expresses his gratitude to Vic. He came out to Australia years ago, leaving a wife and child back in the village. Feeling lonely and in need of company, he shacked up with an Australian woman, and might have married her, but for Vic, who advised him to bring out his family at once, or his life would be miserable, torn between two worlds and two families. Well, he took the advice, brought out his family and was saved from certain ruin, maybe from drowning himself in the Yarra in Abbotsford.

The man with the didgeridoo stands beside Vic and, scratching his matted hair, thanks him with broken words for his kindness to Kooris over the years. And on behalf of his people, he falters, he'd like to play a traditional piece for him. Vic signals to Pavle, who stops playing and shakes spit from the cornet. The Aboriginal sits cross-legged on the floor and blows a few deep sounds that send a shiver down Nick's spine. The other man sits beside him and strikes two painted sticks together. Nick can see some of the guests are moved: heads nod, feet tap, fingers click. Pavle closes his eyes and presses the cornet valves, without making a sound, as though trying to pick up the tune. The didgeridoo's hum grows stronger, filling the room, causing a slight tremor in the glasses on the table. Pavle sits between the men and begins playing softly, as though holding back from respect, until the didgeridoo player signals his approval. His notes become louder, without being too pushy, in a way that adds to the didgeridoo, while allowing it to continue leading the way. People draw closer to the players, children stop to listen, Vic wipes his eyes. As Pavle's feeling for the tune grows, his playing's surer, until a subtle change takes place: he slips in and out of a Macedonian melody, nothing too forceful, a few notes at first, then more up-front, finally taking the lead, with the didgeridoo and sticks gradually retreating, as though happy to follow. The instant they recognise the melody, a few men start a slow arm-on-arm dance around the musicians. Vangel throws his hat to Nick and joins in. After a few turns, he calls on Vic to lead the circle, who accepts, followed by his wife and daughters. Vangel gestures for Nick to come next to him, but he shakes his head and backs away. Strange, in the past he'd dismiss an invitation to dance without a second thought, now, maybe because of the sad occasion, or the unusual music, he holds back with less reluctance, and when Vangel signals again he joins in, feeling as he did at the picnic that day. Soon all the guests are dancing in farewell to the Club, stepping lightly on the melody, carried by the cornet and didgeridoo, the strong blend of Macedonian and Aboriginal, the warmth of human breath.

20

'Yah!'

Startled, Nick almost falls off from riding the metal box. Having crept up behind him, Zlatko's laughing at catching him by surprise.

'You shit yourself,' he says, poking Nick in the ribs.

'I didn't see you coming.'

'Don't turn your back on the play?' he grins.

It's the start of the two-week school holiday and Nick's been on the dark green metal box at the corner of McKean and Grant Street for some time, waiting for someone to show up. A meeting place, the box also serves as a drum, when the boy sitting on it will bang away with his heels, signalling to others to come out and play. Nick would've preferred Danny or Tony, but with no-one around he resigns himself to the less unpredictable of the twins. Pigeon-toed Zlatko's eating salty pumpkin seeds and spitting out the husks. He reaches into his pocket and extends a generous handful to Nick. They chat for some time, throwing up ideas of what to do, covering the area around the box in husks. Eventually Zlatko suggests they raid an overhanging quince tree in the back lane behind Queens Parade. Nick knows the lane: one of the longest in the area, with right angle turns, a couple of dog-legs, and smaller lanes branching off it, some with opening so narrow you almost have to squeeze through. Apart from the variety of fruit trees in both summer and autumn, there's always the sense of adventure, junk worth going through, peeping into backyards.

They enter the lane just after Delbridge Street, continue to Michael Street, pick it up again on the other side, and follow the twists and turns all the way to Rushall Crescent, stopping here and there to pick not only sharp-tasting quince but crack open pomegranates for their bright, juicy seeds. From there, red-tongued and red-fingered, they turn into Queens Parade and head toward the shops. Approaching the bike shop, Nick's attention is caught by the penny-farthing leaning against the tree at the front. The old-fashioned bike has always fascinated him, and now, more in jest than serious, he says to Zlatko how he wouldn't mind trying it out.

'Do it,' says Zlatko, with a steely look.

Nick suddenly realises his mistake.

'You scared or what?'

'We'll get in trouble.'

'Don't be gutless.'

He continues badgering, saying he'll go inside and distract the old owner to make things easy. Nick squirms, until Zlatko calls him a sissy, when he plucks up the courage to nod. He waits as Zlatko talks the white-haired owner from behind the counter, pretending to be interested in a racing bike. Using a rubbish bin and the tree, Nick climbs onto the seat above the big wheel and pushes off, his feet just reaching the pedals. The owner must have sensed something, because suddenly he swings around and limps to the door, calling on Nick to stop. Zlatko bolts out, promising to catch the bloody thief and return the bike. Nick's cycling erratically, swaying, jerking the small handle bars to keep from falling, startling pedestrians shouting for him to get off the footpath. At one point he braces for a crash with a veranda post, but manages to swerve, regain his balance, and wobble toward Michael Street. Zlatko races after him but is soon left behind as the bike speeds up and Nick's control improves. With the traffic lights at the intersection green, Nick turns hard left, then right onto Queens Parade, heading toward the city. He now manages to keep a straight line, but cars are honking and drivers shouting for him to get off the road. Feeling confident, he replies with a thrust of his thumb while pedalling furiously. Zlatko's calling on him to stop and take the bike back before they get into trouble, when he realises the bike has no brakes and he's travelling too fast to jump off. Terrified, he shouts back for Zlatko to catch up and grab the frame. He's now approaching the intersection of Delbridge and Wellington Street, where again the lights are green. Zlatko's running like mad and making up ground, but Nick's now in front of the Clifton Hill Cinema, staring at a downhill that sends a shudder through him. With the bike now accelerating, Nick yells for Zlatko to run faster, but he's out of breath and slows to a walk. Nick grips the handle bars for dear life, legs out wide to the sides, the pedals spinning on their own, careering down Queens Parade toward Smith Street, where there are no traffic lights. A tram rumbling in the opposite direction sounds its bell, passengers point and gape, cars driving past honk loud and long. In flying past the bluestone St John's Church, Nick quickly makes the three-fingered sign of the cross. With north-bound traffic from Smith Street turning into Queens Parade, Nick braces himself for disaster. As luck would have it, a truck driver who honked further back has parked across the bend of Smith Street, stopping the traffic, giving Nick a clearway through the danger. In the intersection he sees the opportunity and veers into the service road, but still accelerating, heading toward busy Brunswick Street. Suddenly the truck appears beside him, the driver shouting for him to grab onto the lengths of timber protruding from the tray. A splintery four-by-two in one hand, the small handlebars in the other, he just manages to manoeuvre the bike until it slows, stopping in front of the Council Depot.

When Zlatko arrives Nick's shaking, barely able to tell the ginger-haired driver what happened. The man lifts the bike onto the truck and takes them back to the bike shop. Quick to distance himself from Nick, Zlatko reminds the owner of his promise to catch the thief and return the bike. Nick apologises, he meant only to sit on it, nothing more, but somehow it just took off and he couldn't stop. The old owner checks the bike, sees it hasn't been damaged, and warns Nick about touching other people's property. Outside, Nick thanks the driver for saving his life and pulls out a pomegranate from his pocket intended for his mother. The man accepts it with a laugh, saying he'll share it with his children tonight.

Back at McKean Street Zlatko drifts off with Dom, saying his feet are killing him from all that running, while Nick joins a few boys on their way to explore the neighbourhood's underground drains. Yes, thinks Nick, this is why school holidays are the best: with parents at work, he and his friends are free all day to do as they please, go wherever they want, follow whims to unexpected adventure. Limping from a broken ankle last summer, Billy leads the way to the Groome Street corner of the Council Yard. Using an iron rod hooked at one end, he and Charlie pull up the round grate and roll it away. He then shines his torch at the water flowing along the bottom. The boys follow him down the metal rungs and gather around him in the vaulted drain the height of a room. It smells like rain on bitumen at the end of a hot day. Billy shines the torch in both directions, explaining if they go left far enough they'll eventually come to the Yarra River. He speaks slowly, with a serious expression, pointing out how a storm can swell the flow to a river. Alarmed, Lenny says he's seen enough and wants to climb out. But there isn't a cloud in the sky, Billy says, pointing the torch at the curved ceiling made of bricks. They follow his torchlight, which really needs new batteries, as it struggles to push more than a few yards into the thick darkness. Turning right and left, stopping here and there, Billy looks up at a circle of blue and explains exactly where they are. Nick's excited being down here, not only because of the remote danger of sudden rain, but because of films set in underground caves and mines, and this is the closest he'll ever get to that kind of adventure. Yes, he thinks, they're in a world of their own down here, a place that deepens their voices and draws them closer together, where the darkness smells of fear and fun, and where a candle would've felt safer than Billy's feeble torch.

'Where are we now?' Billy asks.

The boys look up through the grate at the sky crossed by a few black cables.

'Queens Parade,' says Nick, still thinking of his narrow escape.

'Nope.'

'Brunswick Street,' says Lance.

'Nope.'

'Richmond,' says Lenny.

Lance laughs and calls him stupid, adding it's impossible to get that far in five minutes. Hurt, Lenny replies everything's possible, especially in a place like this where you lose your sense of direction and time.

'Intersection of McKean and Grant Street,' Billy announces.

The boys look up in disbelief.

'Hey,' says Lance, 'we might see a sheila walking over.'

'We'd get a good look,' says Chris.

'We see black,' snorts Bruno.

But then Billy's torch goes off. He tries the switch a few times – nothing.

'How we getting back?' Lenny panics.

'We'll never get out,' says Lance, playing on his fear.

Billy assures them he knows these drains with eyes closed.

'Well keep them open,' says Lenny.

They follow him through the darkness, at times hands on each other's shoulder, swearing when stepping in the water. Nick thinks about being at the Busy Bee corner almost daily yet knowing nothing about the world below his feet. He finds this strange, almost uncanny, but is unable to give it thought. Maybe something like what Lenny said about place and time, he thinks. Maybe there are places in the universe like this dark drain, where time stands still, where fifty years is a twinkle of a star, where a person can travel the distance from Melbourne to Macedonia in the interval between heartbeats.

In the afternoon, just before his mother returns from work, Nick and Danny are walking down Rowe Street from exploring the Merri Creek. Danny has been quiet lately, sometimes drifting off with a vacant gaze, but

Nick hasn't said a word about the brothel. Walking past The Haven, Danny spits at the roses along the front fence.

'Reckon they're all sluts in there?' he asks.

'Some, maybe,' says Nick, wondering what became of the girl and her baby.

'They're all sluts,' he says, spitting again.

They continue in silence to Danny's front gate on Alfred Crescent.

'See ya tomorrow,' says Nick.

Danny brushes aside his fringe, is about to say something, but lowers his head and goes inside. Nick continues around the Crescent, trying to make sense of his friend's reaction, when he notices an old man, Aboriginal, sitting on the edge of the park, legs extended over the gutter, a pair of walking sticks beside him. He's turning from side to side and pushing with his arms as though trying to stand. Looking like the derelicts he sees on Gertrude Street, Nick's first thought is: he's had too much grog at The Recreation. But getting closer, he's alarmed by a gash on his forehead.

'Need help, mister?' Nick asks, keeping his distance.

The man moans something about not being able to move his legs. Nick offers to call the police, pointing to the police station across the road from the primary school.

'No, no cops,' he says. 'I need me White Lady.'

'You mean a nurse?'

'Yeah, she'll warm up these stiff legs.'

'I'll call an ambulance.'

Struggling, he reaches into his pocket, pulls out a few coins, and extends a light-skinned palm, asking Nick to count it.

'Not enough,' he winces.

'Enough for what?'

'Metho and lemonade.'

Maybe the metho's for his legs, Nick thinks, having seen his father use it as a rub for his sore back. He asks Nick to help him up, saying he needs to push on into the garden, away from the street.

'Where do you live?'

'Lost me room a few days ago,' he says.

Nick's shocked to think he's spent nights sleeping in a back lane or in a doorway like a dog. He places a walking stick in each hand and helps him to his feet. He's unsteady at first, but then manages a few steps by dragging one foot forward, then the other. Nick supports him by the arm, holding his breath against the stink of piss.

'Where are you going?' Nick asks.

'Anywhere, just away from the street.'

'Your head's bleeding,' says Nick. 'You need a doctor.'

'Me White Lady, she'll fix me up.'

'Let's go to the Council Yard.'

'I'm in your hands, sonny.'

Nick helps him to the corner of the Council Yard near where the girl had the baby. The man thanks Nick and asks his name, adding he's a good boy to be helping old Harry. He offers Nick the coins to buy himself an ice cream. Nick thanks him through a lump in his throat and pushes back his hand. Watching him position his legs with the walking stick, Nick's suddenly taken by an idea. He's nursed pigeons mauled by cats and puppies left to die here in the Council Yard, but this is his chance to nurse a human being. He recalls the story his father's often told about how, as a fourteen-year old in the Civil War, he helped a wounded partisan cross into Yugoslavia. Imagining the night, the bullets whistling overhead, the danger of mines underfoot, Nick would lament having experienced nothing to compare with his father's life-and-death story. Yet now, here he is, with this old man's life in his hands.

'I have to go,' he says, itching to put a plan in action, 'but I'll be back soon, with metho and lemonade.'

Despite starving from wandering the lanes and drains, and facing a tongue-lashing from his father for being late for dinner, Nick dashes around to half-a-dozen houses and musters the boys to bring material for a shelter, old blankets, food and whatever else they think might be useful. They agree to meet at the Busy Bee in thirty minutes.

His father scolds him for being late, calling him *miskin*, which Nick takes to means something like rascal. They've finished eating. He's finished one bottle of beer and going through a second. With several rounds at The Recreation after work, he's now glassy eyed, in a state Nick knows not to annoy. His mother's at the sink, looking tired even though it's only Monday. Nick fears it's more than the factory: he's been with her to doctors, specialists, but they can't explain why she's unwell. Nick wishes she'd stop working in that factory. The unbearable smell of glue can't be doing her any good. But the house isn't paid off yet, they need new furniture to replace the table and chairs his father bought second-hand from Gertrude Street, and the carpet in the corridor and stairs is old and worn. With his mother's silence and his father's drinking, there's little conversation between them these days, none of the happiness Nick saw in the first few years after their arrival. Would they be like this in the village? Is he somehow to blame? Is there anything he can do to improve things between them? Next summer holidays, he thinks. Yes, he'll get a job somewhere, in a factory or warehouse, and help pay off this house, so his mother can stop working and start feeling better.

Nick eats quickly, almost burning his mouth on the steaming lentil soup, which is doubly hot from a sprinkling of chilli seeds. He takes the bowl to the sink, almost whispering to his mother he's going out for a while.

'Out, again?' Vangel growls, froth on his lips.

'I won't be late.'

'Where are you off to?'

'The park.'

'Say something, woman,' he shouts at Menka. 'Tell him he can't go.'

'What's he going to do at home?'

'There you go, spoiling him, letting him run wild.'

With Harry on his mind and wanting to avoid an argument, Nick promises to be home before dark and slips away. The coldness between his parents saddens him. He wonders whether Danny's parents are the same. His father hasn't kissed his mother in ages, hasn't bought her anything, or shown her so much as a smile. Maybe it started with the death of his little brother. Or maybe it goes even further back, to when his father was in Australia without them. Three years is a long time – people forget, feelings change, families break apart. Once in the laundry he shakes off these thoughts and fills a shopping bag with a bottle of methylated spirits, a candle and matches, a bottle of lemonade, a few apples and pears, a hammer, saw and a can of nails.

The word's gone out and a working party gathers at the Busy Bee. They march through the park on a mission of mercy, excited by the idea of caring for a helpless human being.

'Hey, he's an Abo,' says Lenny.

'And you're a Dago,' says Chris.

'So what?' says Nick.

'He's black,' Lenny replies.

'Yeah, but his hair's white,' Chris laughs.

Harry's dark, weathered face lights up on seeing the group shuffling through the grass. He's pressing the gash on his forehead with a broad dark-green leaf. Having found the injured man, Nick assumes the lead in the operation, giving orders in erecting a shelter from a couple of old corrugated sheets and lengths of timber. As the sun sets behind the elms, a few boys start a crackling fire with branches and scraps from a pile of building rubble. They sit around Harry on rocks positioned in a semi-circle, his face now alive in the firelight. He pours metho into a jar, adds lemonade, and drinks. The boys are stunned as the bottle says poison, avoid swallowing. But they soon realise he's done this before and it hasn't killed him, so they say nothing as he sips with a look of satisfaction. He's no longer aching, Nick thinks, so maybe mixing metho with lemonade removes the poison, making a kind of medicine. Chris runs off with a towel to the nearby tap and brings it back wet for Harry's face and hands. Danny hands him a chipped plate with a few slices of bread and corned beef. The fire pushes back the encroaching dark. Feeling better after the food and drink, he sits more upright and begins telling stories. He is half-Aboriginal, originally from Queensland, his father was a German cane cutter. He tried enlisting in the Army at the beginning of the First World War but was rejected because of his colour. After a few years the law changed and people like him were allowed to join if they could show one parent was European. And so he cocked his hat to one side and sailed to Gallipoli thinking to become a hero, only to return hatless and a cripple. The boys cringe as he raises his cuff, exposing a shin mangled by shrapnel. He couldn't work anymore, apart from pushing a broom, and never married because no sheila wanted a man with a bad leg. He came to Fitzroy at the start of the Depression, sweeping from factory to factory, dragging himself from boarding house to boarding house.

'I gave me leg for the gov'men,' he says, eyes opening to the whites, 'but the gov'men give me nothin'. You think you seein' Harry but what you really seein' is nobody.'

'See,' Lenny whispers. 'Abos are spooky.'

'Not as spooky as your Mafia,' says Danny.

'Got no voice, don't count for nothin', can't even vote.'

Nick swallows back a swell of emotion. Harry was once a boy like him, with parents who loved him, and dreams of coming back a war-hero, but has ended up like this instead. Suddenly, he's alarmed by the thought he might end up like Harry sixty years from now. The time will come when his parents are gone and he's left on his own. Yes, he dreams of playing for Fitzroy and being another Haydn Bunton, but life has its own plans. He might end up like Harry, wandering the streets of Fitzroy, looking for somewhere to spend the night.

The sky now bristles with stars. Light shines in the windows along Alfred Crescent. The three-quarter moon above the steeple of St John's sheens rooftops, silvers the grass on the oval. After gazing at the spritely flames as though seeing something familiar, Harry reaches into his coat pocket and takes out a black leather pouch tied with a yellow ribbon. Nick expects to see a pipe and tobacco, but he slips out a red harmonica.

'Lightens the heart as much as me White Lady,' he says.

He finishes the drink and begins playing Waltzing Matilda, slowly, stretching notes, imbuing each with a tremor. He asks if they know the song, explaining the meaning of words Nick has sung but never understood. They hold back at first, until Nick takes the lead, when the others follow, singing in tune to his playing. Danny asks for the Beatles' song Rain, Chris for Elvis' Return to Sender, but Harry taps the harmonica on his yellowish palm and says he hasn't got an ear for the modern stuff. He then plays some Christmas carols, which they sing full-voiced, ending each with a cheer and clap.

Nearing nine o'clock some of the boys stand to go, which reminds Nick of his promise to be home early. They settle-in Harry for the night, gathering a supply of firewood, spreading another blanket over him, pointing out the store of food. As the boys move off, Nick remains a moment, making sure things are within his reach.

'Thanks, son,' he says, 'you're a real trooper.'

'See you in the morning,' says Nick.

'You set me up real good here. I'll fix you up come pension day.'

He slips the harmonica in the pouch and leans back against the fence. Nick places a candle and matches next to him, in case he needs light if the fire dies out.

The following day's overcast and sultry. The boys take turns checking to see Harry's alright. At dusk they gather around him again, listening to stories of his ancestors: how stars came to be, which song-lines they followed, why kangaroos stand upright. And then he plays the harmonica, an unfamiliar tune this time, with long notes in the lower register broken by short high-pitched sounds, reminding Nick of the didgeridoo at the Club's farewell party. He continues like this for some time, eyes closed, hollow cheeks working, shadows dancing on his gashed forehead. He stops abruptly, shoulders falling, as though his strength has played itself out. A moment later he starts again, this time sounding each football club's theme song, harmonica gleaming in the firelight, the boys singing with heart, saving 'We are the boys from old Fitzroy' for last.

It's pouring and Nick can't sleep thinking of Harry. In the morning, straight after his mother leaves for work, he races out to check on him, only to see a police van parked on the oval side of Alfred Crescent. He sprints to the Council Yard, stopping as two policemen escort Harry from the shelter.

'What are you doing here?' one of them asks.

'The kid's me mate, officer' says Harry.

'Where's all this stuff from?' asks the other.

'From home,' Nick says.

'Pick up his walking sticks and follow us.'

Supporting Harry by each arm, they take him to the van, where one of them unlocks the back door.

'In you get, old timer,' says the stern one.

Nick places the walking sticks beside his outstretched legs.

'Thanks, matey,' he says in a raspy voice.

Nick checks a swell of emotion, suddenly resenting the policemen, the callous way they've taken the poor man from his protection. Harry takes out the pouch and extends it to him.

'Looks like I won't be round on pension day.'

'No,' says Nick, choking up, refusing to take it.

'Want ya to have it.'

'No,' says Nick, 'you need it.'

'What's in there?' asks the stern policeman.

Harry replies with yesterday's tune, only much slower, with deeper feeling, each note a protracted cry of pain. As the van pulls away Nick can see him through the small back window, eyes closed, harmonica shaking in his hands, a nobody in his own country, a shadow of a man, though perhaps at this moment one in spirit with his ancestors.

21

A silver-jawed monster is tearing through the row of two-storey shops containing the Macedonian Club. The day's cool, patched with white clouds, and Nick's wagged school for the occasion. If the opening of a new building is celebrated with festivities, the demolition of a century-old landmark needs witnesses, a gathering of mourners. Nick's both fearful and fascinated watching the jaws devouring sections of walls and floors and disgorging rubble. As the machine groans toward the Club, he feels as though it's coming to rip out his memories of the place. Yes, he's enjoyed working here, felt proud going home with pockets full of coins he'd count to his mother on the kitchen table. But more than money and pride, there was also the sense of belonging to a bigger family. He'd call the regulars uncle and granddad, and they in turn were affectionate toward him. As their English was limited they'd come to him with letters from government departments and forms for pensions and unemployment benefits and taxation returns, thanking him by calling on God to grant him good health and fortune. He valued these sentiments more than the shilling or two they pushed his way. Yes, he's enjoyed the Club because it's been both a second home and a school. He's learnt lots of Macedonian words and sayings from the customers, some practical, others humorous, and others again too shameful to repeat. He's noticed how Australian men seldom swear around women and children, even at the footy a bloke who's downed six cans will abuse the umpire by calling him a white maggot, holding back from using stronger language. Macedonians are more relaxed about swearing. The customers would swear freely in his presence, as they did at home around their wives and children. Expressions vented in picking up a bad card or playing a losing hand would shock him with their crudeness when he translated them to himself into English. Despite this, he's enjoyed listening to old-timers reminiscing about their youth and village-life, detailing acts of bravery and betrayal during the Greek Civil War, and becoming heated on the topic never far from their hearts and minds – Balkan politics – and why people some from their region chose to call themselves Macedonian, others Bulgarian, and others Greek.

Vic's here, too, along with a few elderly regulars. Nick's with them, watching from across the street, just down from the Champion. Timber hoarding has been set up along the footpath in front of the shops. The buildings on Gertrude Street between Brunswick Street and the Club have already been demolished and cleared. Nick's seen kids running around and kicking a footy in the open space. The jaws bite into a side wall and half of what used to be a fruit shop collapses in a cloud of dust, exposing glossy paintwork in empty rooms, a kitchen stripped of appliances, a bathroom with the outline of where the tub once stood, an internal stairway leading nowhere. A few more bites and the shop's nothing more than a pile of bricks with timber beams sticking out. The brothel's next. The jaws open and tear out a hole, exposing the inside of the room Nick and Danny looked into that day. In a few minutes the brothel's reduced to rubble, and Nick's struck by the thought: the building is there in the broken bricks and beams, and all that's needed to make it rise again is imagination and will.

When the machine squeals into position to start on the Club, Nick turns to Vic, as though looking for support to face the terrible moment. Eyes glistening, the owner crosses himself the way people do at funerals: three times, very slowly, pausing to touch his forehead, his navel, his right side, his left, finishing with an open hand placed on his chest. The others follow his example as the jaws open to devour the Club. A massive chomp brings down part of the roof, scattering a flock of pigeons.

'It's only brick and mortar,' says a man in a grey trench-coat.

He taps Vic on the shoulder, the way people comfort mourners. Appearing from behind a fluffy cloud, the sun shines on the grinning jaws, streams through the swirling dust. Large chunks of render crash down from the ceilings on the top floor.

'The Club will live in our heart,' says another.

The jaws bite through the side wall, collapsing the slate roof.

'You've lived through wars,' says a third. 'You'll survive this.'

The top section of the front wall crashes inward, smashing through the floor, shattering the window with Macedonian Social Club on it. Vic sighs and rubs the back of his head as though struck by something. Nick can barely contain his emotion. As the jaws prepare for another attack, he notices a patch of sunlight on the still-standing side wall, its brightness on the glossy nicotine-yellow paint, as if claiming this space after being kept out for over a hundred years.

'It was old and rundown,' Vic sighs.

'Of course it was,' adds the man in the trench-coat.

'I'll open another Club,' says Vic, sniffing.

'We can't live in the past,' says the man.

'You're right,' says Vic, 'Australia's changing.'

'Sure is,' says the man, 'and by the time young Nick grows up there'll be no need for a Macedonian Club.'

'Not only that,' says another, 'he'll forget his mother-tongue.'

The thought of growing up in a world without a Macedonian Club and forgetting the language he speaks with his parents alarms Nick.

'No, I won't forget our language,' he says, annoyed at how the man's shirt is buttoned around his fleshy neck. 'I'll always use it with my parents because they'll never speak English. I'll never forget how to say *zhimi mama* because it comes easier than 'I swear on my mother's grave'. I'll never forget *vodichka* and *lepche* because I'd die without water and bread. I'll never forget *le-le* because it lessens the pain when something bad happens. No, I'll never forget Macedonian, because it would be like forgetting my own name, and that'll never happen, not in a thousand years.'

'Don't listen to him,' says Vic, pulling Nick close. 'Of course you won't forget your mother-tongue. A language doesn't wilt and die like a flower in autumn. Ours is a tough, earthy language. It survived for generations without writing and books, just by word of mouth, from father to son, from mother to daughter, and it will survive in you and in your children and in their children.'

'You'll open a new Club, granddad Vic,' Nick says, getting worked up. 'And I'll be there on weekends, marking time on new chalkboards, serving coffees in new cups, keeping your new place clean and tidy.'

'You will, you will,' he says, removing his glasses and rubbing the red dimples on either side of his nose.

'And that's not all, granddad,' Nick continues, unable to hold back his tears. 'When I grow up I'll buy the Club from you and run it myself.'

'I'll give it to you, my boy,' he says, wiping his eyes.

'Is that a promise, granddad?'

'*Zhimi Gospo* – may God by my witness.'

They all turn to the machine as its jaws snarl at the sun, driving it behind a drifting cloud. The next instant they gleam open and rip out the bottom of the side wall, dropping the entire Club in an upsurge of dust. Nick's momentarily stunned, but then, through his tears and dust swirling in the suddenly empty space, a vision of the new Macedonian Club rises from the debris. He's grown-up and running the place, but it's not for people of his age, no, it's for granddad Vic and for the man in the trench-coat and for his father and his friends – all those men who left mothers and fathers behind to make a better life for Nick's generation in Australia. It's clean and quiet, with polished floorboards, comfortable chairs, and a big front window with the name of the Club painted in gold. A tape-recorder plays old Macedonian songs in the background. Photos of heroes and villages and houses hang on the walls. There are no time-keeping chalkboards here, no price-lists for drinks: patrons are welcome to stay as along as they want, to play cards or reminisce or just to sit and daydream. Yes, by then he'll have learned from Stoyan how to brew the best *rakija* in Melbourne – a drop that draws and teases drinkers with its mellowness, making them close their eyes and smile in following the taste back to their youth. Yes, he'll offer all his patrons a free glass of *rakija*, together with a plate of pickled cabbage, in gratitude for their sacrifice.

Later that day, the machine's jaws still tearing at him, Nick enters the Clifton Hill Post Office to stamp his father's letter to his grandparents. Last night he stood at the table as his father lick-sealed the envelope and wrote the address, his little finger protruding as he wrote.

'Christos Mangos,' he said, shaking his head. 'I'll never get used to it, writing my father's name in Greek, it's like a thorn in my side.'

He filled his glass from the beer bottle and downed half at once.

'Risto Mangoff, that's his name, that's what I should be writing.'

'Why don't you?'

'The letter would never get to him.'

'Everyone in the village knows *Dedo* Risto.'

'Yes, but Risto Mangoff doesn't exist in Greece.'

Nick thought about Harry and how he doesn't exist in his own country.

'Ah, Kolche, promise me when you grow up you'll respect your ancestors, promise you'll throw off Mangos and call yourself Mangoff.'

Nick nodded half-heartedly. Yes, he felt at home in the Macedonian Club, spoke Macedonian rather than Greek, yet he sided with his mother when it came to maintaining their Greek surname and attending the Greek Church. He has no problem with the name and wears it like his own skin. It isn't long and unsayable like lots of Greek names, but short and easy to say and spell. He was Mangos in his mother's passport, in his schoolbooks, even engraved in fancy writing on his football trophies. He can't understand his father's hostility to the name, and, growing up in Australia, perhaps he never will.

Leaving the Post Office, he comes across the Serbian twins quarrelling in front of the funeral parlour. From what he can make of their angry outbursts, they're arguing over the year of a Serbian battle. Vlad calls his brother an idiot, screaming it took place in 1389. Zlatko calls Vlad a stupid idiot, screaming back it was June 1388. Nick tries to come between them, saying what happened more than five hundred years ago in some remote corner of Serbia doesn't matter in Melbourne. They turn on him, threatening to bash his head in for dismissing their history. Knowing their volatile tempers, Nick apologises and backs away. The next instant they're at each other again, spitting abuse like Nick's never heard, not even in brawls on Gertrude Street. Their language shocks pedestrians, causing a few older women to hurry off, their shopping trolleys squealing in protest, while a mother covers her child's ears. A man packed tight in a pair of mud-stained overalls steps sharply toward them.

'Cut it out, you wogs,' he yells. 'Where's your respect for women?'

They ignore him at first, but when he pulls Zlatko by the jumper, they turn their fury on him. He jumps back as though from two Alsatians in a panel beater's yard.

'Wogs,' he shouts, from a safe distance, addressing the spectators gathered around the twins. 'Ship 'em back to wogland.'

After another volley of abuse at each other, Vlad begins bouncing around and shaping up with his fists, calling on his brother to have a go. He lets fly with several karate-style kicks which Zlatko deflects, retaliating with his own side-on jabs. A man in white shirt and tie comes out from the funeral parlour and, pointing a fountain pen as though a dart, chastises the twins, demanding they take their argument to the nearby gardens, where they can scream till the crows fly backwards. The couple in his office have lost a son in Vietnam, he says, and it's impossible to make funeral arrangements with all this swearing and shouting. Dancing around and kicking at each other, they ignore him, until he raises his voice and threatens to call the police, when they let loose with a sewer of abuse that sends him scurrying inside.

Their argument moves from the footpath to the service road, where they take short run-ups at each other and let go with mid-air kicks like two bucking stags. Cars stop, horns blare, drivers blast them to get off the road. But they're caught up in their own world, on a distant Kosovo Field, the years 1388 and 1389 flying between them like blackbirds. They end up on the wide median strip where a ring of spectators opens and closes around them, some enjoying the show, others waging bets on who'll win, a few eating fish-and-chips wrapped in newspaper.

Maybe tiring from all the running and kicking, they begin wrestling, grappling and letting go, catching each other in a headlock and breaking free, spilling from the median strip onto the main road busy with the five-o'clock rush. City-bound traffic stops as they fall to the ground locked like Siamese twins, squirming and thrashing on the tram tracks. A truckie with tattooed arms jumps out, swears he's running late for his last delivery, and threatens to drive over the little bastards if they don't clear off. The twins hear nothing but their own heaving and grunting in each other's ear. The outbound 88 tram strikes its bell aggressively at the build up of traffic. Faces are hard-pressed with curiosity against the windows, tempers flare, fists thump on doors to open before the next stop a hundred yards away. When the driver succumbs and the doors slide open, passengers disembark among the idling traffic, some cursing the congestion, others joining the crowd around the knotted wrestlers. An elderly woman demands the boys be pulled apart, as much for their own safety as for getting home to put the roast in the oven. But the two men nearby, possibly Public Servants judging by the pens gleaming in their top pocket, appear excited by the show after another boring day at the office. And then, as though exhausted from the furious struggle, the twins become dead still, caught in each other's headlock, with Vlad's occasional 89 countered by Zlatko's 88. Those near the front speculate on the meaning of the numbers.

'1788 or 1789,' says one of the Public Servants. 'The First Fleet's landing in Botany Bay.'

'Kids aren't interested in history,' says the other. 'It's about how many runs Lawry made in the Second Test last summer.'

'Nah,' says a sharp-nosed man, whacking a newspaper against his thigh. 'They're fighting over Collingwood's losing score last week.'

'Well, they're both wrong', chuckles another, 'it was 90 points.'

At the sound of an approaching police siren Nick whispers 'cops' in Vlad's ear. They disengage at once and spring to their feet. A few spectators clap, others mutter under their breath. At first the twins look dazed, confused, as if coming from another time and place, but then, pricked by the siren, they barge through the bewildered crowd and bolt down Queens Parade, urging each other to run faster. At one point Zlatko trips on the edge of the median strip and would've stumbled head first into the gutter if not for his brother's quick reflexes. Hobbling in pain, Zlatko yells he can't run any faster, but Vlad urges him on, pulling him along, saying the cops will get them if they slow down. Nick follows as they scurry toward Delbridge Street, Vlad now almost dragging his injured brother. At the corner fruit shop, seeing the owner on the footpath and straining to make out what's happening, Vlad swipes two red apples from a front stand. They were irresistible, he'd latter explain, because apples were tied to Serbian spears that pointed toward the Battle of Kosovo in 1389.

Making his way down McKean Street, Nick wonders why history and wars and losing battles move people to outbursts of the kind he's just witnessed from the twins. Does it stem from their fanatical father, who sees everything through Serbian eyes, and has, over the years, drummed this into his excitable sons? He thinks of his own situation: his father's single-minded view on Macedonia. But he's maintained a certain detachment from his father's sentiments, thereby avoiding impulsive arguments and feuds. In fact, these days he's more likely to get worked up over a rare Fitzroy victory, especially over Collingwood, than argue over whether Alexander was Macedonian or Greek.

22

The second-last Saturday of August and both sides of McKean Street are packed with cars, including a row along the middle all the way to Rushall Crescent. After several days of constant rain the afternoon's clear, breezy, an occasional cloud drifting past, its shadow gliding over the neighbourhood. With only one win for the season the Lions face the three-coloured Saints many are tipping to win the flag. But the ground will be heavy, the ball slippery, adding a touch of unpredictably to what would otherwise be a certain loss. Yes, Fitzroy fans are hoping against hope for an upset, like the one a few years ago when the Lions had one win for the entire season, and that against Geelong, the eventual premiers. Yet more than the perennial hope of a win, today's match has stirred supporters at a deeper level: it's Fitzroy's last game at the Brunswick Street Oval.

Nick and his friends meet at the Busy Bee. The milk bar's doorbell doesn't stop tingling with customers buying snacks and cigarettes for the game. The Boss is being run off his feet, but his hard work will pay off when he counts the day's takings this evening. The boys join the crowd marching down to the footbridge. Nick's usual excitement is subdued by the sadness of the occasion. He recalls the closure and demolition of the Macedonian Club, and now it's the Fitzroy Football Club, forced to leave its home ground of eighty years. Change, he muses, looking at his friends. They are growing, their voices are breaking and the down on their cheeks is darkening. Nothing stays the same, not that fluffy white cloud hovering over the gasometers, not old Mrs Brown's small milk bar which has a For Sale board, not even the sun, which, according to his Science teacher, will run out of light and die away in darkness.

By the time they get to the end of McKean Street the boys have shaken off moving to Princess Park next year and concentrate instead on today's game. The Lions will rise to the occasion and give their loyal supporters a memorable win. Yes, they say, their excitement returning, each match has its surprises, and there's always the chance of an unexpected win. Such is footy, no telling what will happen, especially on days like this, when mud levels out sides and makes the game more of a slog than a contest of skill. As they climb the stairs of the footbridge, they sense again the spring in their step, the bounce in their heart. Yes, such is footy, a dose of weekly hope that sustains them through the bleak winter months. The bridge affords a good view of the ground and people, mainly local pensioners, watch the entire game from here. As the ground's almost their backyard, the boys know the gaps under fences and the places not patrolled by officials in white lab coats. They hurry along between the ground's eastern wall and the timber yard.

Bertie Ryan from school is leaning against the yard's picket fence, eating a meat pie. He turns his back on the boys as they pass, pretending to wipe his mouth dripping with filling. But they know he's here as a retriever, waiting for the ball to spiral over the posts and the crowd and the wall, when he goes after it like a skinny greyhound and returns it to an official. He makes fifty cents a ball, which amounts to a nice sum in a high-scoring game. Bertie's poor, one of ten kids, the family crammed in a tiny two-bedroom house. He's learnt to survive and made good money scalping tickets at last year's finals, even selling Nick one to the grand final. Nick saw him in action that day. Dressed in patched trousers and a dirty jacket, with green snot showing from his nose, he'd approach a Salvation Army person for a ticket, knowing they had tickets donated by companies and businesses. He did this five or six times, mainly with women Salvoes who felt sorry for the skinny, snotty kid, and proceeded to sell their kindness for a good price. On the morning of the same grand final, Danny saw him on the Collingwood-side of Smith Street, basking outside the Post Office, singing 'When the Saints Come Marching In'. When Danny asked why he chose to sing St Kilda's club song, he explained Collingwood supporters wanted the Saints to win, otherwise Essendon would have twelve premierships, closing in on the Magpies' thirteen. Not too long ago Nick was also like Bertie, going to the footy to collect bottles and later, armed with an opener from home, offering to open cans of beer, hoping for a tip. But that was before the game's hold on him.

The boys try a couple of ways in, but they're patrolled today in expectation of a large crowd. They go around to the tennis courts, having previously used the hole under the high, rusty-wired fence behind the Haydn Bunton Pavilion. At the gate flanked by smelly agapanthuses, Dom becomes edgy and says he'll try the entrance opposite the Bowling Club. His mother ironed his jeans this morning and the old man would kill him if they got dirty crawling under fences. Tony runs a finger along the crease and laughs it's sharper than a blade. Dom's scared of his father, but they all know why he won't enter the tennis courts. Desperate for his first pair of Levi jeans, and having argued with his father who wouldn't give him a cent, Dom sneaked into the tennis courts one Sunday night, ripped out the lead line-markers and filled a hessian sack. Too heavy to carry, he dragged it through the Edinburgh Gardens, across the oval and Alfred Crescent, to Lenny's place. He swore Lenny to secrecy, promised him an ice cream, and hid it behind the chook house. The following day he loaded it on Lenny's billycart and took it to the scrap metal dealer on Queens Parade.

Once in the ground they first try the Visiting Members' grandstand, on the off-chance the attendant lets them stand at the very back, which they sometimes do when it rains, but the man at the top of the stairs waves them off. Nick looks around at the people sitting close to each other on the long benches, well-dressed men and women, with bags of food and steam rising from thermos of tea and coffee, and blankets wrapped around their legs, watching the reserves in action before the main game. Families are here, too, children in nice clothes and warm duffle-coats. They must be rich, he thinks, to be able to afford seats, away from the wind and rain. This is one thing he'll never experience: being at the footy with his parents. Seeing a lady biting into a spongy lamington, he's suddenly struck by how different his mother is from the Australian women in here. His father's a regular at the Recreation Hotel after work and on Saturdays at the new Macedonian Club on the corner of Gertrude and Gore Streets – but where's his mother's enjoyment, her afternoon of happiness? He's never really thought much about her sighs and complaints, but now, listening to this woman barracking in a high-pitched voice, those complaints echo in his ears: the *pusta bossitsa*, as she calls the heartless forelady at the shoe factory, the sickening smell of glue, her sore back from standing at the work-bench all day, the constant cooking – they've never been to a restaurant or had fish-and-chips on a Friday night – the weekend washing and cleaning, the pain in her hands and knees from waxing the lino to a slippery shine, the yearning for the village and her mother and in-laws, the sighs for those winter months when work would ease off and she could spend time on the loom and the embroidery hoop, the evenings with neighbours, telling stories and reading coffee cups. Today, maybe because he's growing and sees things differently, all this touches him with sadness, like the shadow of that stray cloud drifting over the crowd.

They watch the last quarter of the reserves match from this part of the ground, but once the siren sounds they jump the fence and make their way around the boundary line lost in mud to the section with the grandstand for Fitzroy Members. Knocked back here as well, they head for the old scoreboard, which should have been pulled down when the new one went up. As many as thirty kids are on the wooden decking with the black-tinned backing board. Only a few seasons ago the scorekeeper would be up here, exposed to fierce winds and driving rain, changing the numbered shingles that hung from hooked nails. FITZROY is still painted white, and below this the opposing team, VISITORS, though both teams are now deadlocked in black. The boys have a good view of the ground from up here, and it's cosy sitting next to friends, sharing whatever's in their pockets.

A loud boo from around the ground greets the umpires: the field umpire in white shorts and shirt rolled to his elbows, flanked by lab-coated goal umpires with flags folded under their arms. They thump the decking and backboard as the Fitzroy players run out from the changing rooms beneath the grandstand, arms and legs gleaming with oil, the smell of liniment reaching as far as the scoreboard. The field umpire raises the shining red ball, the siren sounds, together with a roar from the crowd. Their barracking ebbs and flows during the game, rising to a pitch at each goal, when they pound the backboard, shaking the entire structure, so people below look up fearing it will collapse on them. Yes, this game's all about heart: the flutter of hope during the week, the throb of happiness when a goal's kicked, the swell of joy at a win, the flatness of disappointment at a loss. And the very shape and colour of the ball resembles the heart. Where the soccer ball always rolls in a straight line, this ball can be spinning along the ground toward a certain goal, only to break suddenly left or right for a miserable behind. Yes, life's like that, too, Nick thinks, unpredictable, sometimes you're cruising along like a sixty-yard drop kick, other times spiralling like a torpedo caught by the wind, and then wobbling about like a mongrel punt whose bounce is impossible to read.

The ball's in the forward pocket right in front of the boys, slipping and sliding like a greasy piglet, chased by Fitzroy's full-forward who's a bit stiff-legged from a polio condition as a child, but who can still take a strong mark in a pack and kick a good goal from fifty out. It's only the first quarter and he's already covered in mud. He paddles the ball close to the boundary line, picks it up, twists and turns, then snaps a high one over his left shoulder. The boys follow the heavy ball tumbling through the air, lean to one side as though steering it toward goal, spring to their feet, feel their heart rising to their mouth, clench their fists ready to thunder the backboard – only for it to hit the goal post for a behind. As Nick slumps down on the decking he thinks about his feelings and the game's scoring system. A goal now would've had him jumping for joy, whereas a behind, one-sixth of a goal, doesn't bring one-sixth of that joy. Would six quick behinds amount to the same emotion as a goal? Or do emotions have their own rules, an arithmetic different from what's taught at school?

The boys are one with the players slogging it out in the mud, diving headlong into packs, fearless of being taken out by a shirtfront. In watching them, they're living out their dreams of someday playing in those maroon and blue jumpers. But there are moments when the spell breaks, like when the ball's kicked over the back wall, maybe into Bertie's arms, when Nick looks down on the crowd and thinks: what will become of all these people fifty years from now? What will become of that kid with the snack-tray strapped around his neck? Nick knows him from school, Petros, a recent arrival from Greece. He can't speak English, but has learnt parrot-fashion to sing out 'Drinks-peanuts-lollies-chocolates-pararachips' without a trace of accent. And what about the man with the hessian sack slung over his shoulder, selling peanuts in brown paper bags? He's here every home game, crying out 'Peanuts, shillin-a-bag' even though the shilling has been replaced by the ten-cent coin. And where will Bertie's little sister be fifty years from now? There she is, scavenging soft-drink bottles, swooping on them like a seagull, netting them in a shopping bag. The radio commentators and sports writers are in the narrow brick building right next to the old scoreboard, together with the timekeepers, who sit with their clocks in a separate room. Nick can see Jack Dyer, his huge hands in front of the microphone. He was known as Captain Blood because of the biffs and backhanders dished out by those hands. Bloodbaths were common in the good-old days before television, when players often got away with murder. Will Jack be remembered fifty years from now? Maybe football needs its heroes and legends as much as war. Who knows, Nick thinks, with the game changing each year, becoming cleaner, faster, less violent, people will look back on those rough-and-tumble days as the age of real football, and they'll speak of Captain Blood in the same breath as Gallipoli and Ned Kelly.

In watching the game, Nick loses sight of the fact he's Nick Mangos, a kid born overseas and who still speaks Macedonian with his parents. On this windy Saturday afternoon, sitting on the old scoreboard at the Brunswick Street Oval, he feels Australian as Danny or Lance. More than reciting 'I love God and my country' on a Monday morning at school, more than learning English and reading about the First Fleet and the Eureka Stockade and the disaster at Gallipoli, more than his name on the citizenship certificate, it's this game and barracking for Fitzroy that makes him feel at home in this country. When the full-forward kicks a goal and he shouts 'Carna Roys', he's caught up by the roar that echoes his shout, drawn into the sporting heart of Australia, feels a sense of belonging maybe like his parents must have felt being part of a village community. And watching these toothless heroes slogging through mud and slush, scrambling on hands and knees, winning the hard ball from a crush of bodies and thumping it forward, he cheers their courage and wants to be like them when he grows up.

At the start of the last quarter the Lions are down by fifty points and not even a miracle from the boot of full-forward Lazarus can raise them from the dead. Another flogging, thinks Nick. Why endure this weekly heartache? Why not give up on Fitzroy and barrack for Collingwood? After all, he hasn't signed a lifetime contract to be a Lions supporter, his parents don't care who he follows, and Victoria Park's a fifteen-minute walk down Hoddle Street. As a Magpie supporter he'd taste the sweetness of victory almost every week, watch them play finals year after year, and live in the hope that a premiership's within reach. But he knows in the depths of his heart he could never follow another team. It would be like a soldier deserting his country because they're losing the war, or abandoning his family because they're poor. And there's something else, too: the sense of belonging evoked by club colours, the tingle of excitement on hearing the club song, the burgeoning of hope for next season after what seems like an endless winter of defeat.

In the dying minutes of the game, the margin now 84 points, Nick ponders things he wouldn't have considered last year, maybe another sign he's growing up and leaving childhood behind. It occurs to him that maybe people come to the footy in order to forget. When his emotions are running high, he forgets for a whole quarter the fact his mother hasn't been feeling well lately, forgets his father's drinking more, especially *rakija*, and becoming touchy as a snake. That man down there with the crew-cut and lined face might be here to forget the hardship of working in an iron foundry. That other bloke, the one abusing the umpire, calling him a white maggot, might be here to forget he's unemployed and has nothing to his name. The three Aboriginal men near the players' race might be here to forget their anger at not having a home of their own. And that old woman in the fur-collared overcoat, the one pushing her way through to the front fence, might be here to forget that her past's longer than her future. Yes, he thinks, maybe the game has a way of raising emotions to the point where they blur in forgetfulness life's suffering and pain.

When the siren sounds the game's end they climb down from the scoreboard. Nick's hands are cold from having clapped one miserable point for the entire last quarter. As the boys make their way to the changing rooms beneath the Fitzroy Members' grandstand, supporters are leaving, dejected, swearing they've had enough of defeat, saying Fitzroy should go back to calling themselves the Gorillas, or even the Monkeys, because they can't play for peanuts. Victory and defeat, Nick thinks, two sides of the same coin. You can't have one without the other. The joy of that kid in a number six Saints jumper comes on the back of Nick's disappointment. The bounce in his step contrasts with Nick dragging his heels. His eyes shine at his team making the final four while Nick's face is shadowed by thoughts of yet another wooden spoon for the Lions. The fullness in his heart comes at the expense of Nick's heart being crushed like an empty beer can. Who knows, maybe there's only so much joy going around at any one time, never enough for all, just like money and gold. Or maybe there's some law in nature, like gravity, that precludes everyone from being a winner. And maybe this law says: for each rich and happy and successful person there must be ten thousand poor, sad losers. Yes, his thoughts and feelings are a bit confused, but he senses a basic truth in what he's trying to grasp. It might be there's very little of the very best – like there is only one premiership cup at the end of the season – and it's this that leads to struggle, that makes winners and losers, filling some with joy, others with sorrow.

They push their way into the crowded changing room and stand behind the committee-men. The grey, grizzly-haired coach is tongue-lashing the players: their last quarter was a bloody disgrace, they let down the Club's proud tradition, their loyal sponsors deserve better, their faithful supporters would remember the last game at Brunswick Street as a humiliating loss. The players are sitting on benches in front of lockers with the numbered names of past owners. They're covered in mud, heads hanging almost between knees, copping in silence the coach's spray. When he finishes, they unlace their boots and throw them to the boot cleaner, strip off their heavy gear and toss it to the property steward, step out of their jock straps and head for the showers. They're casual being naked in front of all these people, their dicks hanging, bums quivering, almost showing off. Nick looks away as they stroll past. Is this what Australians do at home? Maybe they're more at ease about their bodies than shy Macedonians. And then he's struck by the thought: what will he do when he grows up and plays for Fitzroy? He could never walk around like that. The players come out of the showers smiling and cracking jokes. Red from the scrubbing and steam, they're like new men, ready for next week's game. The shame of defeat has been washed down with the mud, bruises will be rubbed away with liniment by the masseurs in white, pride restored when they slip into their Fitzroy blazers.

It's twilight when the boys leave the changing room. Several girls about their age are waiting for players to sign their autograph books. A blonde girl with a ponytail looks Nick straight in the eyes and smiles. Her lively blue look lasts no more than a second, and was perhaps meant for a player she expected to come out, and maybe would've made no impression had it occurred last month, but for some reason it sets Nick's heart racing. Paul notices the look, reckons she likes Nick, and encourages him to go back and chat her up. But he's shy around girls and can't believe that one so good-looking and smartly dressed and Australian would be interested in him. No, she probably saw something funny in his appearance, maybe his brown checked trousers or this olive-green overcoat his father bought at the Victoria Market from a vendor with a number tattooed on his forearm, or these suede shoes given to his father by a cousin who repairs shoes on Gertrude Street.

Litter's swirling in the walkway behind both grandstands, the smell of piss is strong from the men's toilets, bottles clink being sorted into hessian sacks. An old committee-man in a grey gabardine overcoat stops at the turnstile to light a black pipe, his wrinkles deep from the match flaring in his face. He breathes in a few times and lets out a cloud of fragrant smoke as they pass.

'That's it, boys,' he says, 'last game at Brunswick Street. Next season it's Princess Park, poor tenants of Carlton.'

Speeches were made in the rooms just now, some angry at the Fitzroy Council for not doing more to keep the club here, others excited by the prospects of the move, a few, like this committee-man, shook their heads and wiped their eyes.

'Been coming here since I was your age,' he says, words dispersing with smoke. 'Seen them all, I have – the premierships, the Brownlow medallists, the champions.'

At a quick calculation Nick figures he must be over seventy, which means he was born in the eighteen-nineties, a time so distant it seems almost mythical. He voted against the move, he says, but the younger blokes, those accountants and lawyers, pulled out facts and figures to show the Club would fold up if it remained here. They managed to frighten the others and got what they wanted. But their plan won't work, just like two families living in the same house never works.

'Don't get me wrong, lads,' he says, 'it's not for me I want them to stay.'

He raises his glasses and rubs his eyes with the back of his thumb.

'I've seen the good times and the great players and there's not much seeing left in these eyes. No, I want them to stay here for your sake. The sight of you lads in the changing room nearly broke my heart. Will those lads see Fitzroy win eight premierships? I asked myself. Will they see the likes of Haydn Bunton in their lifetime? Will they follow the Lions for the next sixty-five years? No, I told myself. Once the team's uprooted from this old ground it will wither and die, and these lads will have nothing at my age, neither a team nor premierships.'

'Let's go,' says Dom, 'the old codger's talking shit.'

The idea of Fitzroy dying as a club is as far-fetched as this grandstand disappearing in fog or Australia sinking in the ocean. Sir Kenneth Luke, President of the Victorian Football League, wouldn't let it happen. He'd support Fitzroy no matter what because his metal-work factory backs onto Mc Kean Street, a few doors up from Bruno's place.

'You're right, young fella,' he says, 'an old codger like me doesn't know what he's talking about.'

He draws thoughtfully on the pipe for a moment, puffs the smoke over their heads, and strolls away, though not to the wide gate pushed open for the rush, but to the entrance with the turnstiles, where he steps on the pedal of one of those clunky contraptions, turns its rotating part backward and squeezes out. Nick's puzzled by his action, until Dom says it just goes to show the old codger's lost his marbles.

They take a drink from the tap set in a monument just outside the ground and head off through the park, bodies drained of excitement, in no hurry to get home. The girl's still on Nick's mind as they follow the bitumen path past the empty tennis courts, past the women's bowling club with yellow light spilling from the windows onto the smooth green, over the single-track railway line. It's almost six o'clock, but the day's grown and the colours in the well-tended flowerbeds are still visible. A leafy tree twitters with what sounds like hundreds of birds. The mild breeze stirs the elms whose bare branches are starting to bud. Those blue eyes have unsettled Nick. He should've listened to Paul and gone back and said something to her. Will he see her again? Next week's game is away and the season will be over? No, he's missed his chance for all time. And then a kind of sadness comes over him thinking how that moment will never come again, thinking they'll never again watch Fitzroy at this ground, thinking he'll carry this regret for the rest of his life. He doesn't remember much of the village anymore, but what he felt the day they left comes over him from time to time, and what he's feeling now, this evening sadness, is the same. He glances at his friends – Danny living with his father's secret, Dom in his razor-sharp jeans, freckle-face Spudsy with the sprained wrist, big Paul whose voice has already broken, little Tony who punches above his size on the handball court. Yes, they are all growing and changing and the day will come when they'll go their separate ways. And suddenly, maybe because of this sadness, he wants to hug each one of them and thank them for sharing these childhood years, this afternoon at the footy, the park on the verge of spring. Yes, he knows this sadness will arise throughout his life, and when it does he'll remember this evening, these boys, Fitzroy's last game at Brunswick Street, and the fact he didn't answer the look in that girl's blue eyes.

23

Having left school at lunch time to pay an insurance bill in town, Nick's walking home along Napier Street when Vlad surprises him from the steps of the Fitzroy Library. In no mood for his pranks, Nick walks on, head lowered, but Vlad's calling is so insistent he looks up, embarrassed in front of several pedestrians. He wonders why he isn't at school and what he's doing at the library of all places. At Fitzroy North Primary those with fairly good grades went up the street to Fitzroy High School, the others, like Vlad and Zlatko, were sent down to Collingwood Technical School to learn a trade. At primary school Vlad wanted to be a dentist, boasting his uncle in Serbia was making a fortune pulling out teeth that hadn't seen the light of day in ages. This uncle had promised to send Vlad the text books he'd used in his own studies – all covered in plastic, not a single underline, hardly read. But managing a bare pass in grade 6, Vlad soon gave up the idea of dentistry and decided to become a boilermaker instead, saying better the light of a singing blow-torch than the darkness of a stinking mouth. More level-headed, though no more academic, Zlatko settled on becoming a bricklayer, saying he liked working outdoors and following straight lines.

Vlad made a name for himself at Collingwood Tech from day one. As he would later tell the boys, when his turn for the dreaded initiation came – head-dunking in the toilet bowl – he pretended he was afraid, asked if he could take a leak, then turned and projected a stream of piss that arced more than three yards, sending the bullies scrambling for cover. Because of this bravery he was made a lance-corporal in the cadets, only to be expelled shortly after for punching an officer in the face. The officer, a student a few years older than Vlad, had stopped him during bivouac and ordered him to salute. Brought up in a proud Serbian household, Vlad couldn't bring himself to salute an officer of Croatian background. Name-calling quickly led to pushing, tempers flared, and Vlad gave him one in the eye.

'Serbian, Croatian – what's the difference?' Nick asked. 'Tito has made Yugoslavs of you all, hasn't he?'

'The old man came here to get away from being called a Yugoslav,' Vlad snapped back. 'We're Serbs and we'll die Serbs, just like our brave ancestors died in Kosovo fighting the Turk. As for them Croats,' he snorted, and spat a greenie in the gutter, 'mate, they'll pay for stealing grandad's prized pigs in the war.'

At the hearing, a real army captain castigated Vlad, saying ethnic violence had no place in Melbourne, that his loyalty must now be to Australia not Serbia, and if he couldn't behave like a true-blue Aussie he should go back to the old country, because true-blue Aussies honour the Australian flag and cheerfully obey their parents, teachers and the law, including officers in the cadets. Here the captain pointed to the Croat sitting smug in his uniform, but wearing the mark of Serbian courage around his left eye. Vlad had to be silenced several times during the captain's address, until he could no longer hold back his sense of injustice.

'Yeah,' he burst out, 'but that Croats stole grandad's pigs.'

Vlad's first job as a boilermaker was to weld together two three-foot lengths of pipe in making what he called a blow-gun. A dart made from a paper-cone and a six-inch piece of bike spoke sharpened at one end was slipped into the pipe and shot out by blowing hard. Nick was amazed by his first demonstration: the dart flew almost the entire length of the footy oval in the park. In the second, he fired the spoke through a corrugated tin sheet. When Nick tried, the dart went no more than thirty yards and barely dinted the sheet.

'How do you get so much power?' Nick asked.

'Euphonium,' he grinned.

'Eu-what-ium?'

'My secret source of power.'

'A Serbian drink like slivovitz?'

'Mate, better than slivovitz.'

'Your dad's pork sausages?'

'Better than them.'

After teasing Nick for a while, he explained the euphonium was what he played in the Collingwood Tech school band. It was a big, brass instrument, and hard to play, but practice had strengthened the muscles around his lips and the power of his lungs. Nick was surprised, never imagining Vlad the musical type.

'What made you take it up?'

'It was the only instrument that was free.'

'So what?'

'The music teacher said it needed a man's strength to play it.'

'So what?'

'The old man threatened to rip off my ears if I didn't take it up.'

'Why?'

'Because grandad played the big tuba back in Serbia.'

And he went on to tell Nick he didn't give a stuff about the school band. No, he was taking lessons from a Serbian musician and learning to play the old folk songs. He wasn't interested in rock-and-roll, Elvis, the Beatles? That type of music was here today, gone tomorrow, like a fart in the wind. The Serbian songs were hundreds of years old, rooted in the heart, and when he played them on the euphonium people cried and danced at the same time. It started with his old man making him stand on a chair at a *slava* – a big family party with lots of food and drink and usually a suckling pig on a spit. He refused to play at first, but when the old man gave him that one-eyed look, he didn't want to be slapped in front of relatives so he brought out the instrument. The first few melodies were shaky, though recognisable, but when he saw their effect on people, when he realised the hold he had over the gathering, his confidence grew and his playing became stronger. Soon men were slipping money into his pockets, encouraging him to open his lungs and pour out the struggles of the Serbian people. He made almost twenty quid that night, more than his old man's weekly wage at the abattoirs. And there was no stopping him after that: the euphonium always shone happily by his side at festivities, ever ready to tickle a spine and squeeze a tear from a misty eye, to transport the tipsy gathering back to Serbia, to join in a slow dance the living and the dead.

Vlad's leaning against one of the columns along the front of the Town Hall, jingling coins in the pocket of his jeans.

'You wagging school, too?' he laughs, eyes restless as sparrows.

Nick nods, eager to be on his way.

'Where you been, anyway? The city? Seen anythin' good?'

'The new Adidas footy boots.'

'Yeah, thirty bucks a pair'

'More than Mum earns in a week.'

'Want a pair for fifteen?'

'Where from?'

'What's it to you? Want them or not?'

Nick knows Vlad's doing a brisk trade in the neighbourhood selling Levi jeans, footy gear, records, smokes, or anything else in demand. When asked about the source of his goods, he laughs sheepishly they fell off the back of an invisible truck – invisible to everyone except him. At the Busy Bee recently Lenny was telling the boys how Vlad talked him into going on a shopping trip to Buckley and Nunn's on an order for a navy-blue duffle-coat. He promised Lenny a cut from the sale if he helped him with the job. When they got there Lenny followed Vlad's instructions and fell down in front of the counter, rolling and moaning on the floor, pretending to be having a fit. As the shocked assistant went to his aid, Vlad slipped into the duffle-coat and calmly made his way to the lift. But as luck would have it, an assistant coming out of the lift noticed the coat, maybe because the tags were still on it, blocked Vlad's exit, and called 'shoplifter' to his colleague. Lenny leapt to his feet and bolted to the back stairs, stopping for a moment to watch from behind the big, dark banisters. To his amazement, Vlad kept his nerve and stood up to both assistants, insisting he was just trying on the coat and looking for a mirror to see how it fitted him. When they demanded to see his money, he took off the coat and threw it at them, saying it was cheaply made and Myer had a better one for half the price. Seeing the assistants gob-smacked, Vlad went on the attack, shouting at the top of his voice he'd never again set foot in a store run by such rude people. Not only this, he'd also make sure no Greek ever came here because his father, Con Karamanolopoulos, was president of Melbourne's Greek community. He repeated the name, adding they'd be getting a call from him as soon as he got back from his meeting with the Prime Minister in Canberra. Did they know how many Greeks lived in Melbourne? The assistants blinked at each other. More than a hundred thousand, he announced, drawing the attention of a few other customers. The size of a grand final crowd! Had they ever been to a grand final at the MCG? Did they have any idea what it would do to their business? And then, suddenly full of daring, he demanded to see the manager, saying he'd report them for having no respect for an honest customer. When the assistants didn't reply, he snapped his question again, swore at them in Serbian and entered the lift, leaving them holding the duffle-coat.

'Ever been in there?' Vlad asks with a nod to the library.

Nick would often walk past the library in coming and going from the Macedonian Club though he never thought to go inside. He'd rather play in the Park and on the streets and explore back lanes than read fiction. At school quiet, pimply-faced Fiona White goes through a novel a day. Her head's always buried in a Mills and Boon love story – recess, lunch time, even in class, hiding the novel behind a textbook. The Maths teacher has given up on her, maybe reckoning she's better off reading in silence about romance than complaining out loud about the uselessness of algebra.

And then there's Steven Cornwell, first it was nothing but science fiction, now he's obsessed with the adventures of some character called Biggles. Adventure! He should come with Nick when they go exploring the Merri Creek, starting from the northern end of McKean Street and following it all the way to where it flows into the Yarra. Who'd want to be stuck inside, turning clean pages, when you could be out and about getting your hands dirty discovering things? Maybe reading's all right for old people, Nick thinks, or those who can't mix it with the world, but for those with energy and curiosity, there's more adventure in the rough and tumble of the neighbourhood than in some far off place in a book. Yes, he'd rather spend an afternoon scrounging in the Collingwood tip, picking through mounds of rubbish, finding a bit of lead worth a bob or a ball-bearing for a billycart's wheel, than read made-up adventures in places that mightn't even exist. And even if in the future one of the boys were to write about their experiences, it would mean nothing to readers, or at least not what it would mean to Nick. It would be like trying to feel a flame having only its shadow on concrete.

How can anyone describe their adventure last week? It was a cold, overcast Sunday, around four in the afternoon, the time when the thought of homework yet to be done dampens the week-end spirit. Alexandra Parade was quiet, hardly a car in sight, especially the end going down toward the Yarra. The boys left their bikes in the back lane and climbed over the brick wall strung with barbed wire. The metal door to the shot-tower chimney was chained, but they came prepared with a hacksaw. A metal stairway spiralled all the way to the small circle of sky at the top. Nick pulled on the handrail and the stairs rattled, filling some with misgivings. Spudsy was scared just looking up, so he was left behind to keep watch. The others set off, Charlie leading the way, going round and round, stopping for a breather to look out from the small window-like openings onto rooftops and backyards becoming smaller and smaller. After a few more stops and some unease about the safety of the stairs, they were suddenly standing on the metal grate at the very top, breathing hard in trying to overcome their fear, the grey sky above, wind blowing fresh in their faces, and Melbourne spread all around below. They held onto the brickwork, felt more at ease, and began laughing and looking over the edge and shouting and spitting down. They pointed to landmarks, located their houses, schools, football grounds, parks, and the Yarra snaking out from the trees in the east and spilling out in the bay. Tony said this was taller than the ICI building on Nicholson Street, where he'd sneaked up in the lift. Charlie pointed to the brick flue from which smoke would have once come out. It was built inside the chimney and went up several yards above where they now stood. He went to the flue and gripped one of the metal rungs fixed into the brickwork. They tried to talk him out of it, saying there was no telling the condition of the rungs further up, but his mind was set on the top and off he went, as though climbing the monkey-bars in the playground. Once up there, he punched the sky in victory and shouted out his name. They called on him to come down, but he reached into the flue instead, raised his sooty hand, and drew a black cross on his forehead. He climbed down and looked each boy straight in the eyes. The brotherhood of the black cross, he said, pointing to his forehead. Who was next? His dare silenced them for a moment, but then his black cross got the better of Nick, who set off, despite his uneasiness about heights. Not daring to look down, he also punched the air, shouted his name, and blackened his forehead. Soon, all marked with the black cross, they felt like a secret society, the privileged few to have climbed so high, the keepers of Melbourne, because they stood above it as no politician had stood, and took it all in as few others had ever done. Yes, Steven Cornwell could have his adventures of Biggles, at that moment, their hearts racing, the boys were living an adventure that authors would struggle to grasp and readers could barely imagine.

'Come on, let's go in,' says Vlad.

Nick's wary of going anywhere with him.

'Want a pair of them Adidas for nothing?'

Having shot up over the past year, Nick feels a little more confident standing up to Vlad and dealing with his erratic behaviour.

'I'll buy a pair when I'm ready,' he says.

'You can have them for nothing – niente, nishto, nada.'

'I don't want stolen goods.'

'Since when have you been a goody-goody?

'See you later, Vlad,' Nick says, taking a few steps.

To his surprise and relief Vlad doesn't grab him by the arm or threaten to bash him. Maybe knowing the Fitzroy police station is around the corner keeps him in check. As Nick makes his way down, a little woman in a green overcoat struggles up the steps with a bag full of books in each hand. A knitted cap pulled over her ears and a matching scarf knotted big around her neck make her look older than she probably is. Nick notices a kind of childish happiness about her as she says hello in a high-pitched voice. He offers to help her with the bags.

'Thanks, sonny,' she grins, nose curving down, chin pointing out.

Vlad's quick to take the other bag.

'Oh, two helpers,' she chuckles, her clapping muted by woollen gloves.

Following the quick-stepping little woman inside, Nick's struck at once by the solid, old-world look of the place. Dark bookcases carved with flowers and scrolls rise up to the ceiling's wide cornices, so that a tall ladder's needed to reach the upper shelves. The biggest mirror he's ever seen, and that's ever seen him, hangs above an empty fireplace with a marble surround. And the number of books! The school library has nothing compared to what's in here. Not only the number, but their look and size as well: big, hardbound in brown and black, with gold letters on the spines, and stacked tight in volumes and sets. They remind Nick of how Alexander the Great arranged his troops: soldiers with shields and spears pressed together in a phalanx formation, withstanding the might of the Persian army. Unlike the paperbacks in the school library which seem to be made for delicate hands, these are manly books, larger than life, as though from a mythical age of giants, each heavy as Sisyphus's rock, thick-spined as those ancient Macedonian soldiers, all standing firm in defending a truth greater than Alexander's – silence – and all shoulder to shoulder against an enemy stronger than the Persians – time. There's a warm, cosy, secure atmosphere in this place. Since the Club's demolition Nick's been thinking more about change and the passing of things, and that someday his body and bones will also crumble, just like those bricks. Strange, those disturbing thoughts and feelings seem to lose their grip in here. The books, their order, the calm mirror, the shining old furniture – all this raises his spirit, strengthens his sense of hope. Suddenly, he feels the concentration of energy in these books: a creative force able to withstand those silver jaws and give lasting meaning to life. Looking around, he sees proof of this in the readers sitting at the sturdy tables: yes, they're mainly pensioners, a few almost derelict-looking, but there's a certain light in their eyes which can only be coming from the open book before them, an energy that fills their old bodies and carries them off to places beyond flesh and bone, beyond change, to a place of permanence.

Stopping at the front counter, the little woman removes her gloves and claps with her fingertips. Vlad winks mischievously at Nick. She bounces on the balls of her feet, turning this way and that, whispering to herself. The counter's piled with books, unused borrowing cards, and several newspapers, one with the headlines: GORTON CALLS URGENT F-111 TALKS. A mass of borrowers' slips arranged in rows covers the entire length of the counter's lower section. They hold open the bags as she takes a book at a time and places it on the counter, addressing its author by name, saying how much she enjoyed their work. A name-plate on the far end of the counter says: Ernest Harridence, Librarian. And then, as Nick's reading the name, he appears from behind a free-standing bookshelf in the middle of the room: an ancient man in a black suit, with snow-white hair ruffled as though just up from bed, smelling of pipe-tobacco. He walks with a shuffle behind the counter and places a hand on the returned books.

'They were terrific, Mr Harridence,' says the woman, her hands fluttering about excitedly. 'There's nothing better than cuddling up to a good book, is there? Who wants a crabby husband when you can have a quiet book, and a different one each night?'

She giggles in a girlish way, but Mr Harridence is concentrating on his work. He flicks through a row of slips, locates the ones belonging to the woman, pens a line across the due date, and returns each slip to the envelope stuck on the inside of the book's back cover. Vlad cocks his head for Nick to follow him. Nick's curious about his reason for being here, but right now he's fascinated by the old librarian. There must be thousands of return slips in front of him, yet he located the woman's in a few seconds, his fingers moving quickly, his eyes sharp, taking in everything at a glance, without glasses. How old is he – at least seventy, maybe eighty? Why hasn't he retired? He's so spritely and alert. Is it because of the books in here? Does he draw on their power every time he touches one? Is this why he's still going, still so full of life, when others his age can barely move? Suddenly, Nick wants to talk to Mr Harridence, ask about his long life, how he got to be a librarian, and whether these old books have a secret power. But what's come over him? He sensed it the moment they entered: a mysterious force drawing him inside, opening his mind to these books, giving rise to a feeling of belonging, even though it's his first time here. Is it because of the void left in him by the demolition of the Macedonian Club? Who knows, maybe he was drawn to walk past the library this afternoon from a need to sense something permanent in the building's large foundation stones and massive columns. But being inside he senses a deeper permanence in Mr Harridence's old-fashioned suit, in the books ordered on the shelves like troops, in the grained and knotted catalogue with its rows of lettered drawers, in the mirror that takes him in without asking a thing. And in the flutter of the moth in the overhead light-bowl he knows with certainty that this library will provide the homeliness he felt in the Club, and these books will tell their stories in a language just as moving as Macedonian.

Vlad grips Nick's arm. The woman thanks them, saying it's heartening to see young people visiting the library, considering the distractions and temptations out there. Mr Harridence glances at them from under white eyebrows needing a trim.

'Some come only for mischief,' he says in a firm, clear voice. 'They talk and laugh and return books in the wrong place, making them impossible to find.'

Nick wants to ask him a question or two, but Vlad pulls him away to a long table behind the free-standing bookcase. They sit close to each other at one end. A man's reading at the other, holding up a newspaper fitted with a wooden spine. Vlad looks around.

'What's on your mind?' Nick asks sharply, determined not to be drawn into whatever he's scheming.

'Books,' he says, leaning over and breathing in Nick's ear.

'What do you mean?'

'There's good money in old books.'

'You want to knock off books?'

'Yeah, just talk to the old codger – I'll do the rest.'

'No.'

'It's shit-easy, mate. I've done it plenty of times.'

'Why do you need me then?'

'I think he's woken up to me.'

'Stop doing it.'

'You want them Adidas boots or not?'

'No.'

'See this,' he says, clenching his fist.

For some reason Nick's now unafraid of his threat. Maybe he's drawing courage from these books. But he also feels for Mr Harridence, who's devoted his life to looking after these books and giving happiness to people like that little woman. Nick's determined to stop Vlad upsetting the librarian's ordered world. But it's no use reasoning with him. There must be another way of getting the better of him. Yes, he thinks, Vlad's obsession with things Serbian.

'Vlad,' Nick says, containing his excitement. 'You ever opened any of them books you knocked off?'

'What for, mate?'

'They're full of stuff about Serbia.'

He's taken the bait: Nick can tell from the sudden focus in his restless eyes.

'Show me,' he says, gripping Nick's forearm.

'Alright, but you got to prepare yourself first, get in the right frame of mind.'

'You bullshittin' me or what?'

'Forget it, if that's how you feel.'

‘Okay, okay, I’m listening, but no bullshit, or see this.’

He raises a fist with bruised knuckles.

‘These old books have got magic power,’ Nick whispers.

‘You trying to spook me?’

Nick attempts to stand as if to go, but Vlad’s grip tightens.

‘What sort of magic power?’

He swallows so hard Nick can hear his throat crackling.

‘The power of … the world … the word,’ Nick says, thinking fast, making things up. ‘These old books are like boxes … coffins … yeah, they’re like coffins … and the dead things in them come back to life through … the power of the word … and the warmth of breath … but only when you’re in the right frame of mind … only when you’ve prepared yourself.’

‘How?’

Not knowing where this is going, Nick instructs him to spread his hands flat on the table in a way that will draw his Serbian ancestors. Vlad’s left hand releases Nick’s arm and slides on the smooth surface, followed by his right, which opens reluctantly from a fist to five fingers uncertain in their singleness. Nick positions his hands so the tips of his thumbs and forefingers touch to form a triangle. He then tells him to look into the triangle while breathing in the numbers 1,3,8,9, holding them for five seconds, and breathing them out.

‘The Battle of Kosovo,’ Vlad smiles.

To Nick’s surprise he carries this out without question, looking very intense, like the time in the park he played the euphonium for the boys. Leaving him breathing in and out, Nick goes to the catalogue cards, but decides it might be quicker to ask Mr Harridence. He’s processing a pile of books someone’s just left on the counter, stamping with a thump the date of their return on the back.

‘Excuse me,’ Nick says, somewhat nervously, thinking he must be the oldest person he’s ever spoken to.

The librarian thumps again and fixes Nick with a sharp look.

‘I need something on Serbia,’ he says.

‘Do you mean Yugoslavia?’ he asks and smooths his white moustache.

Vlad's often spat at the mention of that name.

'No, just Serbia, its history – something in a really old book.'

'You may not understand the words in the old books.'

'Please, Mr Harridence, I'm a good reader.'

Nick's often been told by his father that a person's name is like a key to their heart, and he's right: the librarian turns to a wire screen on his left and directs Nick to a bookcase on the back wall, beside the mirror, where he'll find information on the Kingdom of Serbia in the encyclopaedias located on the third shelf, volume seventeen.

'Do you know the Latin for seventeen?' he asks, writing it on a slip of paper.

Nick's curious about his age, his knowledge of books, but he's also mindful that Vlad's still preparing, so he thanks him and hurries around to the case. Setting the ladder in place, he climbs up until eye-level with a set of brown and gold *Chambers Encyclopaedia*, and pulls out volume seventeen from its pressing neighbours. He blows off a fine layer of dust and rests it on the ladder's flat rung. The front cover creaks open like a gate. Flicking through to the page on the Kingdom of Serbia, he's reminded of the smell of fallen leaves in the Edinburgh Gardens. Here and there small sketches break up the dense print. He reads the first few lines. Mr Harridence is right: the language is old-fashioned and hard to understand. But the book's perfect for his plan.

Vlad's still breathing deeply and staring at the triangle when Nick places the book on the table.

'Are you ready?' Nick says.

'Ready for what?' Vlad asks, a note of apprehension in his voice.

'To bring your Serbian ancestors back to life.'

The usual nervous energy having dissipated from his features, Vlad gazes at the book with a concentration Nick's never seen before. He instructs him to feel the book's weight, smell its age, take in the rustle of its pages whispering like the souls of the dead.

'Now close your eyes, Vlad, but keep your hands on the book.'

Nick reads about a Serbian prince Rastko who left the palace to become a monk on Mount Athos, where he changed his name to Savvas. When his father, King Stephen, discovered what his son had done, he gave up the crown and joined him, changing his name to Simeon. But in reading, Nick adds to the text things he knows will make an impression on Vlad. He puts in that the prince was a wild boy, more interested in hunting than reading, and that he stole a Bible from church and set it alight in dry grass to flush out some game.

'Can you feel the magic power, Vlad?'

'Yeah, Nick, I can,' he says, a tremor in his voice.

'Can you feel the spirit of your ancestors?'

'Yeah, Nick, I can.'

'They're rising from their graves and coming toward you?'

'Yeah, I can see Savvas,' he says, eyes shut tight. 'Read some more, Nick. What made him become a monk?'

Nick rustles the page and continues pretending to read, making up whatever comes to mind, remembering his mother saying that tears bring forth tears. Rastko became a monk because the Virgin of the Sorrowful Face appeared and told him how the burnt Bible's smoke had risen to Heaven and made all the angels weep. Feeling the thorns of his terrible sin, fearing the fire of Hell, the prince broke down and cried bitter tears for three days and nights. He then went out to the burnt forest, tore off his royal robes, and covered himself in ash, vowing to wear black for the rest of his life.

'I've also killed birds and cats,' Vlad says in a faltering voice, 'and I've also stolen books.'

'Don't open your eyes yet,' Nick says.

His plan's working like a charm: Vlad's sniffling, looking frightened, a tear squeezing from his shut left eye.

'I'm like Rastko,' he says.

'He's your ancestor, Vlad.'

'What if I go to Hell?'

Nick reads on about how Savvas and Simeon built a great monastery called Hilandari on Mount Athos, and how Savvas went back to Serbia and became archbishop and called on young men to give up their cruel and thieving ways for a monk's life in Hilandari, and how father and son were buried together under the monastery's church, dedicated to the Presentation of the Holy Virgin, where their bones lie to this very day. Looking up, Nick's taken aback by Vlad's tears dripping on the table.

'Savvas is calling me,' he sobs.

Nick's suddenly afraid he's taken things too far.

'What's he saying, Vlad?'

'He's crying for me – me, a worthless nobody – telling me to stop stealing and start living for God.'

'The book says he's a saint, Vlad, so he must be close to God.'

'A saint? Crying for me?'

Vlad wipes his face with both hands and scrapes back the chair.

'Where are you going?' Nick asks, concerned.

'Savvas is calling me,' he says as if in a trance.

'Vlad, it's only …'

But he's already walking toward the front counter, hands deep in his pockets. Ghostly Mr Harridence straightens up from his work and watches him, tapping the date-stamp on his palm. Vlad opens his jacket and raises his jumper to show he's not making off with anything.

'Sorry,' he says to the librarian.

Mr Harridence studies him a moment.

'I'll bring them back,' says Vlad, wiping his eyes.

'By the due date,' says the librarian.

'All of them, you'll see, I swear to God.'

He places the first three fingers of his right hand on his heart, bows to the librarian, and leaves looking down at the floor.

Nick returns the volume to the shelf, concerned by Vlad's state of mind. What if his charade unhinges him permanently? Anything's possible with a fiery nature like his. What if guilt gets the better of him and he turns all that energy and aggression on himself? He considers walking home with him, telling him he mustn't identify too much with Rastko who lived in another time and place. But standing on the ladder and looking around, Nick suddenly feels again the library's pull: the charm of these old encyclopaedias lettered in gold, heavier than the bricks that crumbled from the Macedonian Club; the numbered order on the shelves that will stand as long as there's arithmetic; the power of words over the little woman now reading the back cover of a book – a magic that brings a sweet smile to a not-so-attractive face, that raises her from poor Fitzroy to a place richer than Toorak, that turns her flesh and bones to the stuff of timeless thought. Yes, there's a permanence here he likes. He's thirteen, growing fast, his upper lip darkening with a moustache that will soon need shaving. This change is not only in his appearance: he's become quieter when with the boys, more thoughtful, wondering about where he'll be in five, ten, fifty years from now. Death's been on his mind, too, from when *Dedo* Risto died a few months ago. He's been in Australia eight years and doesn't remember much of the village – outdoor steps leading up to a bedroom, oleanders in tin pots around the courtyard, a neighbour's tree heavy with yellow quince, children running around a band playing in the village square. So when news of his death came he wasn't sad at first because it was like they were talking about a stranger, but then, seeing how his parents took it, their tears, especially his father's, who'd never cried before, how they dressed in black, the wheat his mother boiled and decorated with a cross made of sugared almonds for his six-week memorial service – all this got to him and he began to question the meaning of his own life. Maybe it's this growing-up that's brought about his feeling for the library. Yes, it's not only Vlad who's seen the light, his eyes have also been opened by this place. Suddenly, he wants to become a member of the library, borrow books on Alexander, spend cold afternoons exploring encyclopaedias, learning, sharpening his mind, who knows, maybe even losing himself in a novel the way the little woman does, and Steven Cornwell at school.

'The book was perfect, Mr Harridence.'

'Those old *Chambers* are worth their weight in gold.'

'Some of the words were hard, but I got around them.'

'Are you Serbian?' he asks, turning away.

'I'm Macedonian.'

As he shuffles about for something on the table behind him, Nick notices his white hair's fluffy over his collar, in need of a trim, and the shine on the elbows of his black coat.

'You Macedonians must like reading,' he says, returning with a sheet of paper. 'There's a girl from around here who borrows five or six books every week. Maybe you know her.'

His fingers run through the borrowers' slips and pull out a small stack of cards.

'Helen Stoikos, she lives in Gore Street.'

Nick knows the name – she's also a student at Fitzroy High School, a few years above him. Excited by the connection, he asks about becoming a member. The librarian explains he'll need to come in with either parent, making sure to bring their driver's licence or notice of council rates. Things weren't so strict years ago, but people have been giving false names and addresses and making off with valuable books. He's about to turn away again when curiosity gets the better of Nick.

'Mr Harridence,' he begins, and stumbles, 'how … old are you?'

'Older than old Eratosthenes,' he chuckles.

'Who was he?'Nick asks, pleased the librarian has a moment for him.

'He was in charge of the great library in ancient Alexandria, which was unfortunately burnt to the ground.'

'What happened to …?'

'Eratosthenes? Oh, he died long before that terrible fire, and just as well, for I'm sure he would have thrown himself in it. What better end for any librarian than a funeral pyre of books? No, old Eratosthenes refused food and just faded away when he realised he was going blind and would no longer be able to read.'

'You mean he starved himself to death?'

'Books were his bread.'

'But couldn't he get someone to read for him?'

'He lived through his eyes, not his ears.'

'Does it matter if a word's read or heard? Isn't its meaning the same?'

'You're a bright boy,' he says, a smile dimpling his cheeks. 'No, a word read and the same word heard have different meanings. The reader recreates the world through the act of reading. He raises the word from its shadow and restores it to light. The hearer's more passive, taking in what someone else has raised, and so it's once removed from the true meaning of the word. Eratosthenes lived for the word the way others live for the world.'

Yesterday all this would have gone over Nick's head and he might have considered old Eratosthenes a lunatic, but an hour in the library, and Mr Harridence's words, have given him a new feeling for books, so he's now almost able to understand how a man might starve himself to death when staring at a life without reading. Eratosthenes flickers in Mr Harridence's eyes: an old man finding more meaning and pleasure in reading the word rose by candlelight than seeing the flower on a summer's day. Nick thanks the librarian for his help and promises to return with his father.

'I'll be here to stamp your books,' he smiles, and wipes a trickle of silver from the corner of his mouth.

For an instant – maybe because somewhere a white cloud has lifted and the bare trees on Napier Street suddenly stand out in afternoon light – the old librarian's hair appears finer than an infant's just washed with Velvet soap, his eyes glow with knowing drawn from every gold-lettered volume he's ever shelved, every word he's read, every nightmare of Alexandria's library going up in flames. His pale hands are spotted with the full-stops of ninety summers, veined with strange characters, like those drawn with blue ink in moments of absent-mindedness. The skin of his lined forehead is tissue-thin, thoughts almost visible, swirling like the galaxies in Nick's science textbook. The moment will stay with him forever, real and yet unreal, with Mr Harridence no longer flesh and blood and bone, but the ghost of Eratosthenes, a spirit charged by contact with the printed word.

Several weeks later Nick asks Zlatko why Vlad hasn't been seen in the park or at the corner shop. Zlatko shakes his head, saying his brother's decided to change his ways by becoming an altar-boy in the Serbian Orthodox Church. Each Sunday, dressed in a blue robe their mother made, he helps the priest during the service, following him with a candle or holding his censer. Zlatko can't explain what's come over him. Where he would've been out all weekend roaming the streets looking for adventure, he now remains inside, alone in his room.

'Why?' Nick asks, feeling responsible.

'He's learning to read Serbian.'

'He should be improving his English.'

'Says he wants to read the Bible in Serbian.'

Not only this, Vlad's confided to Zlatko, and then on a three-fingered oath of secrecy, that on turning fifteen, old enough to leave Collingwood Tech, he'll stowaway on a ship bound for Greece. Once there he plans to make his way on foot to some place called Mount Athos, to Hilandari, a Serbian monastery there, where he wants to spend the rest of his life as a monk, in the spiritual company of Saint Savvas and Saint Simeon.

Holding back a smile, Nick nods, thinking of his fortuitous meeting with Vlad and the strange effect the library's had on both of them.

24

A year marked by unrest and change, adolescence burgeoning from boyhood's bud, Nick's awareness of his growing self and a tumultuous world beyond Fitzroy, his first shave with his father's razor, unmasking a stranger with manly nose and jaw, those flesh-dissolving dreams, pleasant but messy, embarrassing on washing day when his mother scrubs yellow stains from white underpants, his forehead blazing with conscious pimples as youths world-wide protest and riot in city squares, his voice sounding strange even to himself against the rumble of tanks through the streets of Prague, heated arguments with his father above Dylan wailing *The Times They Are a-Changin'*, the sudden appetite for reading fiction, especially Hemingway, as two assassinations blacken newspapers just after Easter, his winning jump at the All High Sports inspired by Bob Beamon's gravity-defying leap at the Mexico Olympics, fear of conscription a few years away fuelled by nightly images of the Tet offensive, taking heart from Fitzroy's win against Collingwood as the tinder of revolution spices the air, his mind expanding with *2001: A Space Odyssey* as Apollo 8 blasts off just after Christmas to tinsel the full moon.

Yes, 1968, and Fitzroy High School is struggling to accommodate its students, even with the new two-storey wing attached to the original red-brick building: over a thousand bodies, four thousand limbs, ten thousand fingers, all restless in a couple of acres, and still arriving mainly from Europe. With a shortage of proper classrooms, teachers use sheds and kitchens and laundries with makeshift blackboards and too few chairs. At recess and lunch time a torrent of students fills a quadrangle meant for a few hundred. Apart from flying balls, rough soccer games, sprinting contests, frequent fights, there's the dreaded Syndicate: boys in form 4 who terrorise the place with sudden outbursts and rampages that cause mayhem. When nothing else is doing they fall on one of their own, pummelling him with fists and feet, which the victim accepts without complaint. One time they surrounded little Jimmy Wu, the only Chinese at the school, whose ancestors went back to the Gold Rush days, and whose parents run the Chinese restaurant on Brunswick Street. Laughing about how high they could throw and catch him, the bigger members of the Syndicate picked him up by the arms and legs, stretched him in four directions, and prepared to hurl him upward, when one of them said Jimmy might have a black belt in karate, at which they placed him gently on the ground and backed away.

Officials and politicians are often at the school, having their pictures taken with the tall, major-general-looking Principal on one side and the short, corporal-looking Deputy-Principal on the other. Newspapers reporting their visits say the crowded conditions are responsible for fights and feral behaviour. An article in *The Age* pointed out that most of the students were from peaceful villages with few people and no fences, and they were finding the school's overcrowded conditions unsettling, which made effective teaching and learning impossible. From time to time stories circulate that Falconer Street might be sealed off to passing traffic and used as playing space at lunch time, but nothing's ever come of this, and the Principal and Deputy do their best to keep the place running.

Nick doesn't see too much of the Principal, with the exception of Monday mornings, when he marches out in a black gown for the National Anthem at the weekly assembly in the quadrangle. The little Deputy's more visible, especially in the mornings, handling discipline and the timetable. His lizard-like look terrifies boys sent to his office for misbehaving. It's not so much the sting of his strap, rather the lash of his tongue which silences even the toughest of boys. But the Deputy's a mean-looking lizard only in the morning, for something happens after lunch that turns him into a sleepy frog. Nick's heard it's something to do with his tongue and the way he's constantly licking his lips. One of the senior boys observed that he licked his lips ten times a minute during morning assembly, while in his British History class just before lunch the count went to up to thirty. Rumour has it he's a drinker, the taste of whisky always on his lips, strong in the morning, weaker before lunch. Nick thinks this might be true. Living close to the school and going home for lunch, he's often seen the Deputy walking along Delbridge Street. He appears a harmless figure: hat low over his eyes, trousers hitched high by suspenders, socks showing, black shoes scraping the footpath, pointing almost in opposite directions. Nick's sure the slight sway in his body is from visiting the pub on the corner of Queens Parade and Wellington Street. Maybe it's the few shots of whisky with his counter lunch that slows his lip-licking, bulges his eyes with sleepiness, and takes the sting off his strap.

It's a wet Sunday afternoon, no weather to be out kicking the ball, so Nick's about to start Hemingway's *The First Forty-Nine*, when the school photo catches his attention. The photographer was late this year, coming in bleak winter instead of bright summer, so the shot was taken indoors, the art room cleared and set up with benches for the occasion. A moment snatched from the back pocket of time, Nick thinks, running a finger over the black and white image. Form 3A, thirty-nine in the photo, twenty-four girls, fifteen boys, all in dark blazers with the winged-horse Pegasus on the breast pocket, above the Latin words *Nil Sine Labore*, nothing without work, which is very apt because most of their parents are labourers in factories. Nick muses: looking at this photo in time to come, will he remember the blazers were dark-blue and Pegasus shone like the sun and the slanting lines on the ties were brown and gold? There he is, standing third from the left in the second row, baring a grin at what the photographer said. He's one of the taller boys, having shot up the past year, but he hasn't grown in recent months, and probably won't grow any more as he's already half-a-head taller than his father.

Thirty-nine, with three absent – though present in the minds of classmates wondering why they're away – and a teacher on either side, male and female, as though to keep them in line. The female teacher's young, attractive, wearing a mini-skirt and black stockings with a lacy pattern on the sides. This is her first year at the school, she takes French, and sometimes sit cross-legged on a chair set away from her table. She's a favourite with the boys and has a way of bringing out the best in them. Even those with no interest in study, who came to school because they aren't old enough to leave, race to sit at the front, saying they like the way she says those French letters.

Nick smiles at Santo Giavanucci, chest out, full-faced, his beaming smile going one way, thin tie the other. He's been in Australia a year or two and speaks English with an accent stronger than his breath after a mortadella sandwich. But this doesn't bother him in the least, and the fact that he's certain to fail every subject. When the Maths teacher asked him for the sum of positive one and negative one, he thought for a moment, and took the answer whispered by the boy sitting next to him.

'Positive eleven,' he replied.

'No, Santo,' said the teacher, 'not positive eleven.'

'*Managia*, is not fair, sir,' he replied.

'What's not fair?' said the teacher.

'Why, sir, you give me always the hardest question?'

A burst of laughter filled the room. Santo looked around and laughed louder, while the teacher tried to settle things, despite a smile tugging at his lips. The class joker and clown, Santo is, always singing and laughing and talking about girls. And when the talk of girls becomes really exciting he hums *Americano,* swaying his hips like Sophia Loren in the film. Yes, he likes music and singing, which got him in trouble at the weekly assembly. The nervy Accounting teacher reported him to the Deputy for making fun of the National Anthem. It was afternoon by the time he was called to the office. A few others waiting outside the open door heard the exchange.

'Son, were you making fun of the Anthem?' asked the Deputy.

'No, sir, I like very much the National Hanthem.'

'You were humming the tune in a disrespectful manner.'

'I no understand the words, sir, so I sing like this.'

He puckered his lips and hummed the tune.

Looking drowsy sitting behind his desk, the Deputy told him not to hum at assembly and sent him off with a warning to behave himself or else. Santo straightened up in attention and saluted him.

'On your way, son, and no more of your Mussolini cheek.'

'Sir, *per favore*, please, can you tell me why the Hanthem say for the Queen to rain over us for long time? If it rain everybody get wet and we not have the assembly.'

'Are you being smart with me, son?'

'No, sir, I'm *stupido*. I fail everything.'

One lunch time Santo invited Nick and several others to his place to sample his father's homemade wine. Daring each other, they finished off a jug and returned to school unable to walk the lines in the quadrangle. In Geography they couldn't stop laughing. The teacher threatened them with the Deputy, detention, a thrashing, but they just laughed and snorted in his face until he gave up in frustration and ignored them for the rest of the lesson.

Santo, the Neapolitan crooner, has no interest in the Vietnam War, in protests and demonstrations, in Jimmie Hendrix or Bob Dylan – no, the world's all right as long as his pockets are full of salty pumpkin seeds. He's ever ready to offer a handful for a front-row seat in French. Nick can still hear his excited whisper, 'I saw black, I saw black', though it was nothing more than wishful thinking because no-one else saw a thing. Another time he came out with, 'I saw red, I saw red', which Nick didn't understand until others explained. And then there was the time the French teacher asked him to stand up and read. He blushed and said he couldn't because of a sore stomach. But when she insisted, with an arch of her eyebrows, he stood up slowly, holding the textbook in one hand, a large loose-leaf folder in the other in front of his groin.

And there, towering above all, solemn-faced Anton Vekovic. He arrived on a summer's day not knowing a word of English, wearing a brown leather jacket lined with wool meant for the Yugoslav winter. But he left the school only six months later, just after the photo was taken. A shy boy, he never looked anyone in the eye, his prematurely bushy eyebrows covering his downward gaze from unwanted looks. He sat through each class, eight periods a day, scribbling in a blue exercise book. How intently he hunched over that book, as though working on some secret to be kept not only from prying eyes but from the sunlight cribbing over his shoulder. He didn't say a word in all the time he was here. Whenever the roll monitor called his name he'd reply by raising his index finger shaped like a question mark. Not a word of self-assertiveness, even on the day of the House athletics sports, when the captain, impressed by his lean, long legs, entered him in the long-distance race. Not a word in his own defence as he stood waiting for the starter's gun. Not a word of complaint to cheering classmates as his breathing faltered after the first lap. Not a word to the officials as he spluttered to the halfway mark. Not a word to the captain urging him on as he gasped and staggered and collapsed over the finishing line. Not a syllable to save himself from death's asphyxiating grip as a few teachers ran out with a first-aid kit and revived his speechless lungs with asthma-spray. Ah, Anton Vekovic, Nick thinks, you should be smiling in this photo like the rest of us, not staring at the future with a squint, your line of sight avoiding the confronting camera. Ah, Anton Vekovic, Nick laments, if only I'd reached out and given you a friendly tap on the shoulder. If only I'd sat next to you once, even for a few minutes, and glanced at the secrets in that exercise book. But by mid-year you were gone as silently as you'd come, probably to work in a factory that didn't require speech but your Yugoslav height.

Nick focuses next on Rhonda McAllister. Strange, she's been in 3A since the beginning of the year yet it's like he's seeing her for the first time. Suddenly she isn't the plain-looking, pimple-faced sheila who walks pigeon-toed in shoes crushed at the heel, but a girl with feelings, who hurts when boys laugh behind her back. She looks much older than the others, almost woman-like, with the dark rings under her eyes visible even in the photo. It seems to Nick she's missed adolescence, going from childhood straight to unhappiness. As with Anton, Nick hasn't said a word to her, or accorded her more than a passing glance, but then she's hardly at school, and when she does attend she's shunned even by the girls, sitting alone mostly, staring at the bare desk top. She's from a poor family with a dozen younger brothers and sisters. When the rumour first spread that one of them is hers, Nick was appalled, recalling the girl in The Haven and the terrible things she said. As roll monitor last term, he placed a few peaks beside her name at the beginning, then a string of circles soon followed, two each day. She's present in the photo by chance, just happening to be at school, sitting a little hunched in the front row, hands folded on her lap, stringy haired, looking as though ashamed before the camera. And as with Anton, Nick now regrets saying nothing to her on the day. You've done well to be here for the photo, he should've said. May the years fall lightly on your shoulders, he should've said, as his mother says in Macedonian. Yes, there's so much he should've said, but he's a popular boy in the presence of bullish boys, and it's unbecoming to be friendly with an unhappy girl. She hasn't been to school the past month and some are saying she won't come back at all.

'Rhonda McAllister,' Nick says, as though calling her name in taking the roll. 'I hope the future brings you happiness, even though nothing will ever make up for what you went through this year.'

What's Harry Tatoulas staring at with that defiant look? There in the middle of the second row, head cocked to one side, in a blazer buttoned tightly, borrowed for the occasion. What does he see beyond the photographer, beyond the wire fence surrounding the school, beyond this suburb of factories and pubs? He was one of the first to test the Principal's threat of expulsion for boys having long hair and sideburns. He came to the science room – the first time Nick had ever seen him in a classroom – made Harry stand and demanded he cut his hair. The class froze as anger suffused the Principal's face. But Harry just stood there, his right hand jingling coins in his pocket, eyes steeled. What was he thinking at that moment? Maybe Bob Dylan was on his mind and that in this time of change neither the Principal with his major-general manner nor the lizard-tongued Deputy could keep the truth blowing in the wind from sweeping through the school. When the Principal finished ranting and turned to leave the room, Harry spoke up, surprising everyone by overcoming his slight stammer.

'Sir,' he said, jingling the coins louder. 'I was born in Sparta.'

'What of it, Tatoulas?'

'The ancient Spartans had long hair.'

'Tatoulas, you've been warned.'

'And they combed it before going to battle.'

Harry wasn't expelled, or even suspended, and soon other boys stopped visiting the local barber and grew their hair long, while girls sneaked off with needle and thread and, away from their mothers, took up the hems of their dresses.

Yes, Harry, the wheeler and dealer, whose pockets are always full of money and eyes alert to any opportunity. Where others are excited by sport or girls or study, his heart's set on doing business. His locker's for storing goods, not books, and boys crowd around at lunchtime, wide-eyed at its contents: Levis jeans and jackets, records, cigarettes, *Playboy* magazines, tickets to the footy finals.

One Saturday morning at the Victoria Market Nick saw Harry making the most of a situation that presented itself. He was minding his father's purchases beside a Christmas-tree vendor who'd just put up a sign: back in five minutes. Unaware of the sign, or maybe unable to read it, a man approached, selected a tree and handed Harry the money. In an instant Harry overcame his surprise and seized the opportunity. Disposing of the sign, he stood in front of the trees and hawked them at a price cheaper than the advertised. People flocked to them, like cockatoos to a gum tree, and in a few minutes he sold them all, pocketed the money, and waited for his father around the corner.

Focusing next on Anna Sawicki, Nick wonders why she's looking aside. Did something catch her attention just as the camera clicked? Someone walking down the corridor whose identity will never be known? A siren of some sort in the distance? Or was it nothing more than a fleeting thought, the type that flashes past at the speed of light, resulting in a sidelong glance. She has developed early, already with the breasts of a woman, though her fair hair still springs with natural curls. Where a vain girl would flaunt those God-given gifts, Anna's self-conscious, embarrassed, and wears her blazer buttoned. She came from Poland a few years ago and picked up English almost at once, using sophisticated words in her essays. The English teacher reads them aloud to the class as examples of good writing. He says she might become another Joseph Conrad. The Polish-born author wrote some of the greatest novels of the century, even though he learnt English at the age of twenty. Nick's good at mathematics, thanks to his father's drilling as a kid, but she outscores him in tests. She wants to be a scientist but her parents have other plans. The week after the photo was taken Anna went missing and hasn't been to school since. Nick recalls her tears and other girls comforting her, but he didn't know why, thinking girls are emotional by nature, crying over trifles, especially at that time of the month. He's since learned that, as she was approaching sixteen, her parents wanted her to leave school and start working. They showed her a photo of a stranger, a man ten years older than her, who'd soon be arriving from Poland to be her husband. Terrible arguments followed, she threatened to throw herself in front of the train at Rushall Station, around the corner from where they live. She begged the English teacher to speak to her parents, and he did, but this was a family matter, they said, a village custom going back generations. And then she wasn't at school one day, two, and on the third Nick saw her parents, together with the police, leaving the Principal's office. A few days later he heard she'd run away to Sydney where, maybe to spite her parents and drive a nail through their hearts, she sent them a five-page letter, addressed from Kings Cross, written in a mixture of Polish and English.

What will become of you, Peter Apostolou, Nick thinks. The Art teacher's comments in his report book capture his spirit in two words written bold and in capitals, followed by three exclamations marks: the beast. As his parents speak little English he translated this as: the best. An honest kid, with a fierce sense of right and wrong, he justified the lie by saying it made his mother happy, and he wanted nothing more than to see his hardworking parents happy, especially his mother, who was having trouble adjusting to life in Australia. She clapped her sad hands in joy, while his chain-smoking father nodded through a cloud of smoke. His mother's only brother was an icon-painter in Athens, and suddenly she saw her son following in his footsteps, practising the ancient tradition in Australia. Yes, inch-for-inch, pound-for-pound, he is the best – the strongest in form 3, with the quickest hands, whether at table tennis, handball against the wall, or swinging punches at some injustice. There he is, at the end of the second row, hands on hips, square-shouldered in a blazer about to burst, tie crooked. Short and stocky, he's a tight fist of energy, and, having a dark complexion, could easily pass as an Aboriginal kid. A couple of years ago, when Lionel Rose became the bantamweight champion of the world, people would often comment on the resemblance.

In many ways he's a natural phenomenon, like lightning or thunder, startling all with unexpected outbursts of energy. One moment he's telling friends about his father's bravery fighting for the communists in the Greek Civil War, the next he's off like a shot, tearing through the quadrangle, tumbling in somersaults, walking on hands, hurtling onto a group of unsuspecting boys and bringing them down like ten-pins. He was born for action, not thought, for reckless daring, not caution and self-regard. Nick will never forget the time Peter climbed on the roof for the soccer ball. He kicked it down and shouted he intended to jump – a height of at least ten feet. They tried to dissuade him, saying he'd break his legs, but this only served to draw him closer to the edge. And then, shouting *eleftheria i thanatos*, which someone translated as freedom or death, he took a flying leap, smiling at them barely able to watch. They all grimaced in pain at that bone-crunching thump, but he leapt up like a cat, dusted his trousers from the roll, and insisted they continue the game.

What will become of him, Nick ponders, unruly Peter Apostolou? His undisciplined energy can't be contained by a classroom, just as his left-handed scrawl refuses to stay between the lines of a page. Nick sees him as a character from an earlier age, a time with fewer rules and restrictions, when mythical heroes still walked the earth and challenged the gods. And he was quick to challenge Eddie Brookes, who walked around the school like a god, his voice opening a path through crowded corridors, his fist extracting money from younger kids. At lunch time hundreds crowded into the lane behind Paul's milk bar on the corner of Woodside and Michael Street. Nick and a few others tried to keep Peter from going through with it, saying Eddie was older, a seasoned fighter, from a family of crims in Collingwood, but he shrugged off their grip along with their concern and strolled to the lane picking at a bunch of black grapes. As Eddie shaped up, working himself into a frenzy by swearing and calling him a black wog, Peter sprang at him like a panther, caught him in a headlock, let fly with five or six lightning lefts, and dropped him to his knees. Most had come expecting a long fight, like the one a few weeks earlier between Eddie and Sammy Azzopardi, which went up and down the long lane and exhausted both fighters, until Eddie took advantage of Sammy catching his breath and booted him in the balls, laying him out flat. But this was over in seconds, leaving many disappointed. As Eddie struggled to his feet, wobbling his bleeding nose from side to side, saying to those around him the black wog jumped him like a mad dog, swearing to fix him next time, Peter walked off to the woodwork room, for a hit of table tennis.

For weeks after, talk of a return match filled the quadrangle, with boys saying Eddie's older brothers were training him hard. But when their paths crossed in the yard Eddie would scowl, rubbing his nose with a fist. Shortly after Eddie was gone, expelled to Collingwood Tech, though some said he couldn't face the humiliating defeat and wanted to leave, abusing the timid English teacher with that intention.

What does the future hold for Peter Apostolou? He'll never wear collar and tie working nine-to-five in a bank or the Public Service. Yes, he has the potential to be a champion table tennis player, or a wrestler who might represent Australia in the Olympics, but he'll never realise his talent because his temper kicks at discipline and training. He could become a professional boxer, maybe another Lionel Rose, but his hands are too restless to be laced in gloves and the ring too restrictive for a spirit like his. Daring and fearless, he could run Melbourne's underworld, striking hard at his enemies, were it not for his uncompromising sense of right and wrong. Who knows, he may be drawn back to his beloved Greece. Nick's heard him cursing the recent dictatorship there, raging at being stuck in Australia while Greece is bound in the Junta's chains, promising to be back there once he turns eighteen. Yes, he was born to be a revolutionary, maybe another Ché Guevara. His spirit burns like an acetylene torch, blazing not for wealth or material possessions or fame, but freedom and justice. Yes, he's a natural phenomenon, and spirits like his don't live to old age, they die in battle, leading the charge, shouting *eleftheria i thanatos*.

Nick sighs looking at lovely Jennifer Williams. Taking out the photo in years to come, will he remember her eyes were the green of his mother's mint leaves in the vegetable patch, her hair gold as the loose wheat in the train carriages under the footbridge? She glowed wearing the summer uniform at the beginning of the year: yellow-checked dress up past her knees, white socks around slender ankles, and her even tan from the Christmas holidays. She isn't as pretty as Sandra Rosario, or as made-up as Angela Hatsis, and he barely noticed her most of last year, but then he took little interest in any girl. Footy was his life and girls had no place in a man's game. And then around the middle of September, during the excitement of finals time, when the apricot tree sprinkled his backyard pink with confetti, something about her caught his attention – maybe the spring in her walk, the musical quality of her voice, the openness of her smile – and suddenly he was hooked, but too shy to breathe a word to anyone. How his heart kicked when she'd hand him a sheet of paper, or call out his name in taking the roll, even at the fragrance she'd leave behind walking past. If only he was more like George Temos or Frank Zanetti – they're at ease with girls, laughing and teasing and whispering jokes that make them blush. Yes, he's fallen for girls before, but always at a distance, and the feeling would pass, leaving barely a ripple. It was different with Jennifer Williams. Was it infatuation or love? He can't say, though it felt more like an illness, especially on weekends, when he couldn't get her out of his mind. He hardly spoke to his parents, didn't want to see the boys, and moped around the house thinking only of her. Yes, he must have been out of sorts, maybe depressed, because not even the excitement of the grand final, the roar of a hundred thousand people, could shift his thoughts. Looking back on it now, he can't believe it. There he was, sitting high up in the Northern Stand, Carlton playing Essendon in a cliff-hanger, Alex Jesaulenko, the hero of all migrant kids, cutting up the opposition, and all he could think of was Jennifer Williams. His heart should've been tumbling like the shining red leather, yet it felt heavier than a sack full of mute lead.

No Mondayitis for him, no, he couldn't wait for school. His spirit rose on seeing the morning light playing with her curls as she stood there, on the girls' side, at the Principal's assembly. And once in the classroom he soared like Jezza at the sound of her voice. What was it, Jennifer Williams, love or infatuation? Are they different? He doesn't know, but by mid-October the feeling passed as suddenly as it had come, along with the blossom swept away by the wind. Yes, maybe it was an illness, a spring virus, because his head cleared, his heart felt light again, and, with footy season over, he began training at the Collingwood Harriers, long-jumping three feet further than his previous year's best.

25

Nick's heart sinks when his father mentions the possibility of a summer job. He's sold newspapers on street corners in winter, helped at the Macedonian Club, collected bottles at the footy, sold wheat to pigeon breeders, scavenged lead and sold it to scrap-metal merchants, but this was all part of being a boy, nothing more than child's play. A summer job's different: it's real work, seven to four, five days a week. It's like being snatched from boyhood and thrown into the world of men. Noticing his unhappiness, Menka intercedes, saying he's too young for work, especially in *that* place. Taking heart from her support, Nick speaks up, saying he isn't ready to take on a man's job.

'A man's job,' his father scowls. 'I was your age when war broke out and your *Dedo* went off to fight on the Albanian Front. I grew up very quickly when your *Baba* held out our last handful of flour.'

'But those times were different,' Nick says.

'I can still see that flour,' he says, with that remembering look. 'Mixed with husks and what looked like ash.'

'We came here to get away from war and starvation,' Menka says.

'So he can spend all summer loafing on the beach.'

'No,' Nick protests, feeling more confident now that he's taller than his father. 'To read – books on Alexander and the Macedonians.'

This appears to allay him, but only for a moment, and then he's stern again, saying books have their place in the world, but it's also important to read people and situations, for which there's no better school than the factory floor.

After stewing on things for a few days, Nick accepts a balance is needed between words and the world. Strange, only a few months ago he'd mock Steven Cornwell for wasting his time reading novels, now it's come back to bite him, just as his mother warns about making fun of people. In some ways it's like the revenge of the books: they lie open like a trap, especially those hard-backed ones, catch him by the nose, and lead him from one to another. Yes, if the reading-bug goes unchecked it might make a hermit of him, as happened to Tassos up the street. He was a regular at the Busy Bee until books caught him by the eyes, and now he never comes out. Some say he's suffered a nervous breakdown because of his obsession with books. When Nick meets his parents, they beg him to come around and call their son out to play. Nick's been a few times and it's always the same: Tassos comes to the front door with a bleary look from reading and says he's working on this or that theory, even trying to improve Einstein's Theory of Relativity. And so, not wanting to end up like glassy-eyed Tassos, Nick reconciles himself to the necessity of summer work. This aside, though, he's always been mindful of his parents' sacrifice and struggle settling in Australia. At times, reading in the comfort of his room, he feels a pang of guilt at the thought of them labouring at work. Is it right for him to be relaxing over a book while his mother toils in the shoe factory? He eventually accepts work over summer as a two-fold blessing: it will ease his parents' concern about him becoming like Tassos and lessen his guilt at deriving pleasure from a book.

Nick leaves school at the end of November, right after the exams, and starts work at the Richmond abattoirs. His father arranged it with a cousin whose blue FJ Holden sounds three sharp honks at quarter-past six in the morning. In summer they start and finish early, so the animals out in the holding pens don't suffer too long in the heat. The honks send a shiver down Nick's spine, but he says nothing to his mother, who gets up earlier than usual to make his lunch and wave good-bye.

On the first morning he's directed by the red-headed foreman to the clothing room. It's run by Basher, a grey-haired man with arms covered in faded tattoos. He walks with a limp and is constantly mumbling. As Nick stands at the counter, wondering what he's doing here, Basher comes from the back of the storeroom, cursing and swearing.

'Well, what are you fucken after?' he says.

Taken aback by his aggressive manner, Nick struggles for words.

'It's my first day.'

'And by the fucken look of you,' he chuckled, 'it'll be your last.'

'Neil told me to come here.'

'Tell that bastard to get stuffed.'

'He said I need overalls and …'

'Look, cobber, I've been here long enough to know what you fucken need.'

He leans over the counter, looks Nick up and down, and, swearing and grumbling, limps off to the shelves at the back, returning with a pair of white overalls, black gumboots and a green cap. He flicks open an exercise book tied to the counter by a string and asks for a name. He then studies Nick a moment and says he doesn't look like a wog. But his curiosity lasts an instant, when he growls again for Nick's name and bows over the book.

'Man-bloody-goes-what?' he says. 'Why don't you wogs have proper fucken names like Sims or Cain? No, they're either a fucken country mile long or they don't make any fucken sense. Now out with it again, cobber, and slow this time, letter by letter, so I can bloody well write it in the book.'

Nick changes, stores his things in a locker, and climbs the metal stairs leading to the offices and the mutton chain. The raw smell at the front gate turned his stomach. His father's cousin laughed, saying it's always worst on the first day. But the stench on these metal stairs is almost unbearable. He holds his breath on the walkway overlooking the holding pens restless with livestock. The thought of spending six weeks in this place fills him with revulsion. He's at the point of turning back when Neil, the foreman, barges out of the office, gives Nick a knife, and sweeps him along in his rush. Nick's boots thump the metal landing in keeping up with him, though Basher somehow got the size right. Another flight of stairs and Neil opens the door to the noise of the mutton chain. The look on Nick's face is telling: Neil slaps him on the back and laughs, saying lamb chops would taste better than ever after today. Sheep are rising on a squealing chain from a room down below, hanging from a hook through their hind legs. Blood drips from throats almost completely cut, heads hanging by a sinew, nodding as though to some happy tune. Small white teeth show through what to Nick appears a faint smile. Bulging eyes hold him in their stare and pull him into the horror of what's happening down below. Nick's not squeamish, having watched a relative kill and skin and gut a lamb in their backyard last Easter, but the extent of the slaughter here is overwhelming.

Neil draws him along, telling him to think of the golden pay packet at the end of the week. The line of sheep snakes slowly through the cacophonous room, moving past workers cutting off the heads and tossing them down a chute, peeling off fleece like a shirt and exposing pink skin, slitting open the stomach, pulling out the insides and placing them on moving trays, washing the bodies with a pressure hose, weighing them, stamping them, pushing them into the cool room six at a time. As they work, men shout and sing and tease each other from across the room. A man with a thin moustache winks as Nick goes past and, at the top of his voice, asked how many times a day he pulls himself. Those nearby burst out laughing. A teenager flicks a few drops of blood on the leg of Nick's overalls and welcomes him to the club. Shocked, Nick hurries after the foreman to the end of line, where he's left with an older worker who speaks little English. Lazlo, or Lazy, as everyone calls him, shows Nick how to find the kidneys in the mass of warm fat, cut their cords, and throw them in a tub.

The cry 'all dead' coming from the far end of the room is greeted with whistles and cheers from the labourers. Nick feels like cheering more than the others because he's managed to see out his first day. The slaughtermen leave shortly after the cry goes up, but the labourers work on for another half hour, until the last body is in the cool room and there isn't a spot of blood on the benches, trays and floor. Nick's proud looking Basher in the eyes when handing him the stained overalls. He scratches a naked woman on his forearm, swears at the men behind Nick, and pushes across the counter a fresh pair for tomorrow.

And that's what Nick does for six weeks – cut out kidneys on the mutton chain. Each day about one thousand five-hundred sheep come up from the sticking-room and wind their way to him at the end of the line. Three thousand kidneys a day, fifteen thousand a week, almost a hundred thousand in six weeks. A mountain of kidneys, enough to feed a nation, all passing through his hands. Dark kidneys, fist-sized, hidden deep in layers of impenetrable fat, lighter ones snuggled in more yielding fat, down to small ones just hanging there and removed with a slight tug. As a break from the monotony, he sometimes swaps places with a few of the permanent younger labourers – boys only a few years older than him – who operate the scales, attach weight-tags to the hind leg, or push the stamped bodies along the overhead rails into the foggy cool room.

At home no amount of showering and scrubbing can cleanse the fatty smell from his hands and arms. Food doesn't taste the same, especially chops, and he runs from the kitchen when his mother fries kidneys, which his father enjoys with pickled cabbage and a glass of *rakija*. This aside, the work's hard, and by the end of the day he's too tired to go out with the boys. As for reading, his eyes close after a page. Noticing his fatigue and loss of appetite, Menka pleads with Vangel at dinner, saying the job's too demanding and will ruin the boy's health. But he silences her with that squinting glare, reminding her, and Nick, of what he went through in the village in his youth.

'It will make a man of him', he says, cutting into a steak, knife grinding the plate. 'He'll thank me for it,' he says, fork prodding pieces of kidney.

Encouraged by his mother's support, angry at how he dismisses her, Nick comes close to telling him he's had enough. But he holds back. Why? To help with the mortgage? No, the house is almost paid off. The twenty-seven dollar weekly wage? No, he's not interested in fashionable clothes or racing bikes or record collections. The wage means little as most of it goes straight into his bank book where it's nothing more than a growing sum. So why doesn't he just come out and tell him the job's unbearable and he wants to quit? Not to embarrass him in the eyes of his cousin who arranged the job? Or is it because deep down he wants to earn his praise? Hear him telling friends how his son held down a man's job at the abattoirs for six weeks? Or is it something else? A need to experience the hardships they're going through working as labourers? Yes, maybe his silence stems from a need to feel close to them by suffering at the abattoirs. In the end maybe it's really this, together with a kind of stubborn pride that keeps him going. In his mind he makes things bearable by seeing work not as a means to an end but as challenge, a test of whether he has the strength of character to endure the ordeal for six weeks. Viewed this way, the tedious work takes on a mythical dimension. His labour resembles those of Hercules. Just as he was set twelve labours – one even cleaning out a stinking stable – whose completion would reward him with a place among the gods, so Nick's perseverance in the bloody abattoirs would earn him a place in his parents' hearts, especially his father's.

Returning to the mutton chain after lunch, dragging his shadow clinging to his gumboots, he stops for a moment on the metal landing overlooking the pens bustling with sheep, cattle and pigs. Leaning on the railing hot from the sun, he's struck by the fact that not one animal will be alive by the end of the afternoon. The food triangle comes to mind. Animals are bred and slaughtered for humans to live and build cities and create works of art and make discoveries in science. But are humans the top of the triangle? What if some higher intelligence is subtly herding humans into cities for its existence? What if angel-like beings harvest humans not for their flesh but their thought? Is this why religions preach purity of mind?

A bull lows mournfully, causing a stir among the cattle, uneasiness before the wooden ramp leading up to the killing-bay. A man who introduced himself to Nick in the canteen works in there, using a gun that shoots a bolt between the animal's eyes. He showed Nick around one lunch time and offered him the gun, saying it was easy, as long as it was held firm against the recoil. They were standing in front of a black steer sandwiched tight between metal grills. Saliva dribbled from its mouth, while its big eyes shone with the chain waiting to lift it upstairs to the processing room.

‘Thanks, but I can’t,’ Nick said.

‘Do you eat steak?’

‘Yeah, Mum cooks it at home.’

‘This is where it starts,’ he said, putting the gun in Nick’s hand.

It was warm from his grip and heavy.

‘I can’t do it.’

‘The steer won’t feel a thing,’ he said, patting it on the head. ‘It’s much quicker and cleaner than the knife.’

Nick tried returning the gun but he wouldn’t take it.

‘How come you can cut up steak with a knife?’

‘That’s different,’ Nick said. ‘This is …’

‘This is cruel, hey? And I’m a killer?’

‘No, it’s just that …’

He took Nick’s hand and put the gun to the steer’s head.

‘Now pull the trigger.’

Nick didn’t know what to do: walk away and offend him, or go through with it and offend himself. But why was he so determined to have him shoot the steer? There was an excited look about him as he tightened his grip and Nick could feel his breath on the side of his face. Was this some kind of game for him? Testing to see how far he could push? Maybe wanting to make an accomplice of Nick, draw him into his circle of death?

‘Nice and easy,’ he said.

Nick’s arm was now fully extended and his finger on the trigger.

‘You can do it,’ he said, leaning over Nick.

Suddenly Nick was alarmed with him gripping his hand and breathing down his neck. To get away from him he had to pull the trigger. The steer moved its head up to down, as though annoyed by the barrel. Nick closed his eyes and squeezed. A loud thud pushed him back against the man, who kept him from falling. The head dropped to one side, though the steer was still standing, kept up by the grills. Nick stepped away from him, releasing the gun in his hand, shaking, sickened by blood oozing from what looked like a third eye.

‘Nothing to it, was there?’ he said.

He took a cloth and wiped blood from the bolt protruding from the barrel.

'Bet you enjoyed it,' he grinned.

Shocked, Nick watched as he wrapped the chain around the steer's back ankle and pressed a button, freeing it from the grills, raising it effortlessly, as though it were pure spirit.

A man jumps into the pig pen and begins whacking the herd with a rubber hose. Grunting and snorting, they scuttle up a ramp in single file, to a room where they're silenced by electric current to the head. Nick's startled by the actions of a large pig at the back of the herd. As though sensing its fate at the top of the ramp, it suddenly mounts another and begins quivering all over. The man swears and lands several whacks on its back. The pig lets out a squeal and, still mounted, thrusts back and forth, back and forth, though without entering the pig below. More whacks follow, but instead of subduing the pig, they make its thrusting more convulsive. The next instant jets of golden sperm arc through the air, as though from a fountain of life. When the spurting stops, the pig dismounts and grunts up the ramp.

Trying to make sense of what he's just witnessed – in minutes a burst of current will give the pig an ultimate convulsion, and in thirty minutes it will be hanging upside down in the cool room – the village suddenly comes to mind. At the beginning of the year *Dedo* buys a suckling pig and calls it Saint Nicholas. He, along with his mother and *Baba,* feed and fatten it until it outgrows the sty. Then, just before Christmas, helped by neighbours, *Dedo* ties the pig's snout with rope and pulls it out of the sty. Two fires turn and twist in the yard: a large cauldron of water boils above one, cooking pots surround the other. Women help his mother and *Baba* scrub the wooden boards set on trestles. He runs around the yard with his friends, all red-faced from the cold, until the men hold the pig still by whatever they can grab. When *Dedo* picks up the *tesla* he and the others stop and gather around. *Dedo* calls the pig's name several times, as if this will somehow soften the blow, and then clubs it between the eyes with the hammer end of the *tesla*. The animal falls with a shudder and is dragged to a hole in the ground. *Dedo* steps on its head and slits its throat. In what seems an instant the hole became a pool of blood. The men lift it onto the boards and the women scald it with boiling water. Everyone then joins in scraping its skin with knives and removing all trace of hair. *Dedo* cuts it open and pulls out the steaming insides. He and the other children draw closer, excited, having seen elsewhere what would follow. *Dedo* squeezes the piss from the bladder, washes it in a bucket of warm water, inflates it by blowing into a reed, and ties both ends with a bit of string. Whatever sorrow he felt for poor Saint Nicholas vanishes the instant *Dedo* hands him the pink ball. This is a Christmas present beyond belief. He runs off hugging the gift, chased by the neighbourhood children.

Another siren sounds five minutes before the chain's set in motion again. Nick observes the sheep pressing into each other, a single white body clattering up to the sticking-room, the slaughtermen already in there, sharpening their knives on steel. What is it about their manner that moves him more than either the cattle or pigs? Is it the innocence of their downward look? Or the trusting way they climb the ramp, as though smelling the green pastures of paradise?

The last week of 1968 and Nick's in the canteen with a hundred other workers in white uniform, some eating lunch, others playing cards, a few reading newspapers in their own language. After their initial curiosity, the men have stopped asking him questions and now either ignore him completely or give him a passing wink. This suits him fine because it means he can sit at a table with several others and, instead of making small talk, which he finds difficult, read the book he's brought from home. Books are great for privacy when with people, he thinks. The men at his table even lower their voices, respecting his intensity. But right now Nick's not reading but looking at the school photo he slipped into the book last night, thinking about the year in form 3 and how it flew past. Maybe it's being in this place, among all these strangers, away from all that's familiar, but he can't help looking back on the school year with a certain fondness he didn't feel at the time. Here it is, the whole year caught in an instant, clear in the light slanting through meshed window behind him. When he's older and much of the year has faded from memory, just like the years he spent in the village, this black and white photo will remain, unless it also fades, like a newspaper left out in the sun.

26

Having survived the abattoirs, Nick's pleased to be back at school. But from the first weeks in form 4 he senses a difference in himself and his attitude to those around him. He entered the abattoirs a high-spirited boy and came out introspective, more questioning, with a sombre view of the coming year.

His mother hasn't been well the last few years, mainly with back problems from standing at the bench in the shoe factory, but she continues pushing herself, because, as she says, that's what a woman must do. Nick goes with her to doctors as an interpreter, but they can't do much, and when one suggests an operation she resigns herself to the pain.

The first intimation of his mother's other condition is in early March, just before the start of the football season. Hearing of his waning interest in the game, the club's coach and president visit one evening and urge him to continue playing, telling his parents how much potential he has, pointing to the collection of trophies on the mantelpiece. Last year Nick would polish them every week, buffing with a soft cloth until his reflection shone. But having neglected them in recent months, he's now embarrassed they're brown with tarnish. His father shrugs his shoulders, telling the visitors it's the boy's decision. Nick struggles to explain why his feeling for the game has changed. They persist, saying talent scouts from the League attend matches at this level. Nick says he's stopped growing and doesn't have the height needed to play for Fitzroy. They bring up Bob Skilton: he won a third Brownlow Medal last year and is no more than five-foot eight. In the end, Nick feels sorry they've come all the way from Preston, sorry the president has a hare-lip, and agrees to play on.

A week later, returning from training, Nick's surprised to find his parents sitting in the living room, something they don't often do. His mother's usually at her sewing machine when the housework is done, saying nothing useful ever came from watching television. His father's taking no interest in his favourite show, *Homicide*.

'What's wrong?' Nick asks.

His first thought is something's happened to one of his grandmothers back in the village. They look at each other, making him even more concerned.

'Your mother,' his father says, 'she's got a lump.'

A knot tightens in Nick's stomach at the word lump. It was only last year that Charlie's father died from a lump at the back of his neck.

'Where?' Nick asks, unable to look at his mother.

His father indicates the right armpit.

'Mum, how big is it?'

'It's nothing,' she says, biting her lower lip the way she does when worried. 'It's nothing – a swollen muscle from all that work at the factory.'

This makes Nick feel a little better, though his thoughts are still on Charlie's father and how the lump finished him off in a few months.

'How long have you had it?' he asks.

'I first felt it last Easter.'

'Last Easter? That's almost a year ago. Why didn't say something?'

'It's nothing,' she says, reaching out for Nick's hand. 'It doesn't hurt.'

'You should've said something,' Vangel says in a dull voice.

The following day the doctor examines Menka behind a screen as Nick answers the questions he puts to her. Nick doesn't like the sound of his voice, especially the note of surprise at the size of the lump. He arranges an x-ray the same day and refers them to a specialist. A cloud of uncertainty gathers over the house. Vangel tries to dissuade her from going to work, but she insists the lump will subside and go away. Her confidence raises Nick's spirit. Surely, he thinks, she knows her body better than any doctor.

A few days later the specialist places the negatives on the screen and, with the rubber end of a yellow pencil, points to a dark area near Menka's right armpit – the very place where, as a child, Nick was told babies came from. It's the size of an egg, and for some reason he thinks of Easter and the eggs his mother dyes dark red. The darkness of the area frightens and confuses him. At first it looks like a foetus, but only for an instant, and then it becomes a cloud that seems to be growing, threatening to swallow the family.

'What is it?' Menka asks Nick.

Nick puts the question to the specialist, who replies it might be a swollen lymph gland, or something else, adding that a small operation is needed to determine exactly. The words 'something else' alarm Nick, but he tries to contain his feelings. Not knowing lymph gland in Macedonian, he uses her words, saying the lump could be a swollen muscle. When he tells her about the operation, she says the *bossitsa* doesn't like women taking time off work, even if they are on their death-bed.

In the week following the biopsy, the specialist's 'something else' echoes in Nick's head day and night. He takes in nothing at school, neither what friends are saying nor the teachers' instructions. The darkness of the x-ray shadows his mind, appearing wherever he looks: the blackboard, the patched bitumen on the road, the spread of Vegemite on his toast.

The day before their appointment for the results, Menka insists on going to work, fearing the *bossitsa*'s reaction to another day off. Vangel swears the *bossitsa* can go to hell and unpacks her work-bag. Unable to face school knowing she'll be alone all day, Nick stays home to keep her company, pretending he has a stomach ache. They don't say much to each other, but just being together seems to lift the x-ray's darkness.

Just after breakfast Nick happens to enter the living room as his mother takes down the icon lamp in the kitchen, her back turned to him. She fills the glass with oil, lights the wick, and places it back in front of the icon. She then bows and crosses herself, but much slower than usual, finally placing her outspread fingers on her right breast. He watches with a sinking feeling. Last year, in the flush of his passion for sport, he turned away from all this religious make-believe, embracing instead the truth of Marx and Guevara and communism. The cross was a crutch for the weak, he reasoned, the hammer and sickle were for the strong. Paradise wouldn't be brought about by candles and prayer, but through rifles and revolution. But suddenly, at the sight of his mother's pale hands, those ideas become distant. Feeling vulnerable, he summons the face of Marx he's seen in books, hoping to draw some strength, but he's stern, harsh in his grey beard and eyebrows, his eyes calculating, as though dismissing the individual in his drive for the collective good. As his mother remains bowed, praying, Nick glances at Christ in the icon case. The flame's glow plays over his bearded face, brings it to life, as though about to say something. He holds a book in his left hand and his right is raised, making a sign with his fingers, the thumb and the fourth forming a circle. His mother looks up from her prayer.

'*Zlaten Ristos*,' she whispered in Macedonian, crossing herself again.

Nick feels a swell of emotion at the words 'precious Christ'. He crosses himself three times and leaves the living room before she turns around.

If Nick was half-hearted about playing football a month ago, the events of the past week have completely deflated him. This afternoon he goes to the corner phone box and calls the coach. He isn't home so he leaves a message with his wife, saying his mother isn't well and he'll be away from the club until she's better. Hearing the emotion in his voice, she says he must love her very much to be giving up footy. She wishes her a quick recovery because he's a valued member of the team. Nick wants to thank her, but chokes and hangs up the black phone.

Later the same afternoon, Nick's with his mother at the sink, helping wash and peel potatoes. He hopes his father won't do overtime or stop off at the pub. He feels better when they're all together at the end of the day. He offers to rub the red dirt from the potatoes, but she says her hands are already dirty. Something in the red dirt must have recalled the village, because she goes on to say how they worked in the fields, breaking clods after the plough. She urges Nick to study hard so he doesn't end up working in a factory.

'Six weeks at the abattoirs was enough,' Nick says.

'It opened your eyes to lots of things.'

'Don't worry, Mum, I won't end up in a factory.'

'Promise me you'll have a clean job?'

'I promise,' he says, glancing up at the icon.

'A job with a tie.'

'A tie and white shirt,' he says, gripping her hand.

Some of Nick's friends are talking about leaving school at the end of the year to work in banks or in the Public Service. He's good with numbers and the idea of a bank appeals to him, though he's said nothing to his parents.

'I'm thinking of working in a bank,' he says.

She passes him a potato to wash and slice in quarters.

'I'd like to see you in a bank.'

'Of course you will,' Nick says. 'And you'll even see me as a manager.'

She smiles and rubs the dirt from her hands.

'But your Greek will have to improve,' she says.

'My Greek? Why?'

'Knowing English, Macedonian and Greek, you'll be worth three people, and become a manager in no-time.'

'Don't worry, Mum, everything will be alright.'

'Why shouldn't I be alright?' she says, rubbing another potato vigorously. 'I suffered a whole month of seasickness. Remember? I didn't leave that cabin at all, couldn't lift my head from the pillow. My throat was dry from my soul struggling to get out. You'd run off to the tap in the passageway and bring me a glass of cool water. Remember? I survived that and I'll survive this devil of a lump.'

Nick's eyes blur with tears at the memory of the voyage.

'I'll take out the peels,' he says, just managing to keep from falling apart.

Last night's dream was unusual, if that's what it was. Nick's hovering above a red desert, like somewhere in the Australian outback, enjoying a feeling of lightness, when something, a force, pulls him away at a great speed. When he comes to his senses he finds himself in outer space, Earth a small sphere in the distance. Suddenly he's terrified at the thought of being alone in the universe. As Earth becomes smaller, his terror grows, until a voice announces he's now an idea and in no need of a body. Panicking, he shouts for his mother, who gave him a body, and Earth, which has sustained it. And then he's conscious of a struggle to reclaim his own body, to re-enter it, feel again its heaviness. He wakes, but only to find himself hovering over the desert again, crying for his body lying on the red dust, curled like an embryo. The next instant he's back in his body and trying to open his eyes. He wakes a second time, though not in his bed, but in their backyard. He's happy to see his mother hoeing the vegetable patch. She waves with a hand covered in dirt. He picks up a red brick, the one his father uses to keep the laundry door open, and places it on his head, thinking it will serve to anchor him to the ground. But when the brick became painfully heavy, he realises this is also a dream and struggles again to wake. He does. The room's dark, the clock's green hands are at quarter-past three, and his body feels like lead.

That morning, as the specialist explains the results, a void opens in Nick's being, and the dream comes back in a flash. He rotates the stethoscope around his neck, catching their reflections in the silver disc. Menka turns from the specialist to Nick, not understanding, helpless in the silence between two languages. The fingers of her right hand twist the gold cross hanging from a fine chain. Nick doesn't know what to say. He wants to be out of that bare consulting room, wants to be running in the park, running home after a game of footy, home to his parents and dinner waiting on the table. He pulls himself together, just enough to say she needs another operation, slightly bigger this time, after which everything will be alright. Menka bites her lips and lowers her eyes.

'Is cancer in here, Doctor?' she asks.

'I'm afraid so, Mrs Mangos.'

'You cut this off?' she says, indicating her right breast.

'It's your best chance to get better.'

'When, Doctor?'

'I'll arrange it as soon as possible.'

'Please, Doctor, soon.'

At home, with Vangel still at work, they sit in the living room for some time, mostly silent, frozen in the mirror above the mantelpiece.

'You mustn't worry,' she says.

He nods, unable to say a word,

'Let them take the breast,' she says, with an edge to her voice. 'And the other one, too, for all I care. The Amazon women cut off their own breasts to pull the bow-string as far as possible. And in the old days women would blacken their breasts weaning children. Don't worry. Let them take it. You'll be closer to my heart when we embrace.'

Nick breaks down and cries in her arms. She presses him to her breast, wiping his tears, caressing his cheeks, encouraging him with stories of how she survived the horror of the war years.

'People in the village lost arms and legs from mines,' she says, 'and you're crying because of a useless breast.'

They both feel a little better after his tears.

'As long as they don't take these,' she says, raising her hands.

She hugs him again.

'You should be at school.'

'I'm not missing much.'

'You've missed so many days because of me.'

'I'll catch up.'

'I'm sorry,' she says. 'I'll make it up, you'll see.'

'No, Mum, there's nothing to make up.'

Feeling another swell of emotion, he turns away and says he needs to go to the park for a while. As he leaves the house she's at the sewing machine, cutting and hemming his father's new overalls.

The park looks peaceful and inviting at this time of day. With everyone either at school or at work there's nobody at the Busy Bee corner. Swaying on the bin outside the shop, a big, shiny crow pecks at the rubbish, littering the footpath. The changes in the past year have also extended to this meeting place. The once lively gathering of more than twenty boys has shrunk. Some of the boys have shifted, their parents selling up at a good price for more spacious homes in the outer suburbs. Others are working long hours in trades and too tired for talk at the end of the day. And the few with cars have discovered the joys of life beyond North Fitzroy. At the ping of the doorbell, Nick half expected to see one of the boys tearing open an ice cream, but an old woman in black comes out instead, a loaf of bread tucked under her arm. She waves at Nick, scaring off the crow, which flies off heavily with a loud cry. Nick looks around, sees no-one about, and waves back.

He hasn't been in the park for weeks – only an illness would've kept him away for so long in the past. He's less miserable walking across the footy oval, kicking aside tufts of grass from recent mowing. The smell of green is still fresh and strong. The cricket pitch has been buried in soil. Chalk powder clings to his shoes from the newly-marked boundary line and goal square. A year ago these white lines would have quickened his heart, now they barely stir him. He can't get the specialist out of his head, and the look in his mother's eyes when she said the word cancer. At the time he was struck by having seen that look before, though unable to recall when or where. Now it comes to him: the passport photo, in which she has the same anxious look, as though staring into the distance, beyond the horizon, to see what Australia would be like and whether they'd be happy there. Yes, at that instant, as she found the courage to say that word, she was staring into the distance again, straining to see what lay ahead for her, maybe fearing that dark continent, where everyone's an immigrant, and whose language and customs nobody knows. Cancer – why her? She's never smoked and the only alcohol she has is the Communion wine. Before today's results Nick feared the word and tried to block it from his mind. He doesn't know the Macedonian word for it, or whether such a word exists, apart from calling it 'the bad one'. Yes, at that instant, his mother must've been terrified, but somehow found the courage to say it aloud, and, through saying it, maybe lessening its hold on her.

‘Cancer,’ he says aloud. ‘Cancer,’ he repeats, determined to rise above the fear it instils. ‘Cancer,’ he shouts, as though calling it to appear from behind a tree, ready to take it on, to rid it from the world and from his mother’s breast.

He takes a path between rows of over-arching elms. The shade’s still thick, the sky barely visible through the leaves. A familiar-looking gardener is working in one of the circular flowerbeds. He’s unhurried, at ease with everything around him, the dark soil, the flowers and trees. Nick wonders if anyone in his family has come down with cancer. And then the trees catch his attention, their steadfast, crusty trunks, their strong limbs, all that silent sap pushing up against gravity. How old are these massive trees? At least a hundred years. They’ve seen boys like him come and go, they’ve sprouted generations of leaves and watched them scatter off in autumn winds, they’ve endured, these great fountains of life. They give of themselves, and when the time comes they let go. Yes, these powerful fountains of life might help his mother, impart their strength and wellbeing, enable her to overcome the life-defeating force in her body. The idea takes hold and he snaps off a leafy branch growing from the base of a tree. Yes, he’ll sneak it inside and slip it under his mother’s bed as a source of strength and wellbeing.

Menka has the operation in April and is home for Orthodox Easter. They try getting her to rest, avoid using her right arm, but she won’t hear of it, saying there’s baking to be done and eggs to dye. As for the shoe factory, Nick went there to give the *bossitsa* a letter from the specialist. He held his breath against the smell of glue. Some of the women shook their heads and whispered his mother’s name. When the *bossitsa* read that Menka couldn’t attend work for a month she folded the letter in a huff and turned sharply to the women. That was all – no well-wishes for his mother who’s been there six years, no encouragement of any sort. Menka was keen to know her reaction, and when Nick told her, she gestured with her hand and called her *magaritsa* – she-ass.

On the morning of Good Friday Nick accompanies his mother to the Greek Church on Victoria Parade. She's wanted to make an offering to *Bogoroditsa* since coming home from the hospital. The offering caused some tension the previous night. Nick heard it from the living room. When Menka told Vangel she wanted to offer the Turkish gold coin she wore around her neck on special occasions, he wouldn't allow it, though restraining his objection, reminding her the coin was a wedding gift from his parents. Nick couldn't understand his objection, having seen offerings hanging from icons in church: gold crosses, chains, rings, even watches.

'*Bogoroditsa* appeared to me in hospital,' Menka said. 'She stood at the foot of the bed with an outstretched hand.'

'And did she ask for the coin?'

'She didn't ask for anything.'

'Then why the coin, woman? Make a donation if you must, ten dollars, twenty, but not the coin, it's …'

'Valuable?'

'Yes, valuable. My *dedo* made ten of them working as a *hamal* unloading ships in Istanbul. He bought land with nine, and gave the tenth to my father, who gave it to you. And when our boy comes of age, it will go to him, as it should be.'

'Australia will be good to our boy, he won't miss the coin.'

'And will it go to *Bogoroditsa*?'

Menka remained silent.

'No, it will end up in the pocket of some Greek priest, who'll probably lose it at a card game. My *dedo*'s hard work, our boy's inheritance – thrown away to a Greek priest. It's not right, woman.'

Nick didn't know whose side to take. His father had a point: God and *Bogoroditsa* didn't need a gold coin. And the fact that it was intended for him suddenly made him possessive of it. But he also felt for his mother, who lived and practised her faith, unlike his father. She lit the icon every week, baked and exchanged food hampers with other women on All Souls Day, fasted not for a week but forty days at Easter. Now, in the shadow of cancer, that faith was even more important to her. Yes, the coin had a family history and it was valuable, but did that outweigh his mother's heart-felt belief? If making an offering helped her face the future with a little more strength, then she had every right to donate the coin. As for what would eventually become of it – whether the priest lost it in a card game or it was used to pay for some work in the church – that didn't matter.

The church is busy with women adding the finishing touches to what his mother calls the *epitaphio* – the flower-covered bier men will carry in the procession around the block this evening. His mother places a coin in a tray, takes two thin orange candles from the front counter and extends one to Nick. He follows her lead: lighting his, planting it in sand, crossing himself and bowing to kiss the icons at the entrance. He watches from near the side door as his mother speaks to the priest. They stand to the right of the central gates leading into the altar, in front of a glass-covered icon of *Bogoroditsa* hung with silver and gold. His mother bows, receives the priest's blessing, then takes the chain and coin from around her neck and hangs it with the other offerings. She returns to Nick with a sure step – the step he knows so well – firm, brisk, shaped by years of working in fields, carrying water from the village tap, setting off in the morning for the factory. The colour has returned to her cheeks after the operation. She's wearing a light-blue dress with dark swirls and a sash around the waist that outlines her breasts. There's nothing to indicate what's happened and Nick wonders what she places in the right cup.

'I promised *Bogoroditsa* the coin,' she says.

'You'll be alright, Mum.'

'Your father said I should've kept it for you.'

'Men don't wear gold coins,' Nick says.

She gazes a moment at a woman tying purple ribbons to the columns of the *epitaphio*. A large cross with the image of the crucified Christ stands upright in the centre of the bier.

'Kolche,' she whispers.

A shadow gathers on her face.

'Promise me something.'

'What is it, Mum?'

'When my time comes, promise me you'll ...'

'Mum, please, you'll be alright.'

'Promise me, Kolche.'

Her sharp tone checks his rising emotion.

'My funeral service – I want it in this church, not ...'

'*Bogoroditsa,* Mum,' he says. 'She'll look after you.'

'Yes, she will, but your father's set in his ways.'

Fighting back tears, Nick promises, calling on the image of Christ in the bier to be his witness. This seems to set her mind at ease: the shadow slips from her face and there's even a faint smile as they leave from the side door.

In mid-July the chilly air crackles with preparations for the moon landing. It's an historic event, but Nick may as well be on another planet: his mother's suffering from a terrible cough. At first they take it as nothing more than a cold, but when various mixtures fail to silence it, the specialist arranges for more x-rays. He points to another dark region – either bronchial infection or something else – and again it proves to be something else: the cancer has spread to her lung. An operation is out of the question, he says, and she's now in God's hands.

A cloud has swallowed them again. *Bogoroditsa* hasn't helped. Nick's first reaction is to take back the gold coin, but the look in his mother's eyes restrains him. He now realises she made the offering knowing what was happening in her body. He doesn't go to school, staying home to care for her while his father works. The cough persists day and night, shaking her body, weakening her, diminishing her appetite, dimming the shine in her eyes. Vangel endures the cough without complaint: he could sleep in one of the upstairs rooms but remains with her, feeling every burst, still managing to get up early for work the following morning. Each cough's like a blow to Nick's stomach. On the occasions it eases he feels a stirring of hope, but it's short-lived: the cough starts again, stronger, hacking, pounding them all.

In the end the cough becomes so debilitating Menka's hospitalised and sedated. Weak and worn-out she deteriorates quickly. Pneumonia sets in and an oxygen mask is strapped over her face. For three days, slipping in and out of consciousness, she gasps and struggles for each breath. Vangel doesn't leave her bedside, sitting on a chair, head resting on a pillow. This evening Nick's there, too, sleeping in an armchair in the waiting room. In the morning an elderly relative advises they call a priest. Pale and unshaven Vangel looks at her as though in a daze.

'Yes, please, Mara, call the priest from St George.'

Nick knows this to mean a Macedonian priest. He accompanies the woman downstairs, telling her he'll phone the priest and arrange for him to come. He looks up the Greek Church in the phone book. Despite the priest's poor English, Nick manages to explain the urgency of the situation. In the reception area people are gathered around the television set, watching the coverage of the Apollo 11 moon landing. The astronauts are making preparations for the descent.

'This day will be remembered in a thousand years,' says a woman.

'I hope the moon doesn't fall down on us,' remarks an older woman.

'The Greeks, you see, we are first to the moon,' says a big-chested man.

'Mate, they're Americans in there,' says a young man.

'Americani, yes, but Apollo is Greek god, and he first on moon.'

'It's all bullshit,' says a man with an arm in a sling. 'Don't believe everything you see in the idiot box. It's all American propaganda, shot in some Hollywood studio, to make out they're better and smarter than the Soviets.'

Nick's taken little interest in the lead-up to this historic event, but suddenly his indifference turns to anger. He wants the mission to fail. His mother's dying while the entire world is goggle-eyed with curiosity. If all that money were spent on finding a cure for cancer his mother wouldn't be dying and they wouldn't be suffering.

He returns upstairs, not knowing how to tell his father, who's now caressing her hand, something Nick's never seen before. He holds back the tears. Menka's eyes are closed, chest rising and falling, the oxygen in the mask whistling between gasps.

'I phoned the priest.' Nick says. 'He'll be here soon.'

Vangel nods without taking his gaze from Menka's hand with the plastic identification tag loose around her thin wrist. Greek, Macedonian, Australian – it doesn't matter anymore, Nick thinks. How can such things possibly matter in the face of death? There's now only his mother, a woman, breathing hard, thin in a white starched gown. There's only the promise he made in church. He takes her other hand.

'Dad,' he says, feeling her weak pulse, 'I called the priest from *Evangelismos.*'

He looks up, eyes heavy, empty, as though not understanding.

'*Evangelismos*?' he finally says. 'A Greek priest?'

'It's what Mum's wants, Dad. She made me promise.'

'Greeks, they've got her gold coin, isn't that enough? Must've they have her soul, too?'

'No, Dad,' Nick says, all choked up, 'her soul's ours – it will always be ours.'

Perhaps too worn out to argue, Vangel slumps down in the armchair in a defeated kind of way.

The priest arrives carrying a black bag. After shaking their hands, he leans over Menka and speaks to her in a gentle way. She opens her eyes, tries to say something through the mask, but the priest places his hand on her head and her body becomes limp. He places a gold-embroidered cloth over his neck and lights a small censer which releases a thread of fragrant smoke. He then says a prayer and touches her forehead with a small brush dipped in oil. During this Menka's eyes open and close. When he finishes, he leans over her again and says something Nick doesn't understand. Menka opens her eyes and, summoning her last reserve of strength, pulls aside the mask.

'*Efharisto*,' she whispers, over the sound of the oxygen.

Vangel replaces the mask and eases her back onto the pillows. He also thanks the priest and shakes his hand, slipping a ten-dollar note into his grip.

Menka stares at the ceiling as though seeing something beyond, her chest labouring, oxygen whistling between tortured gasps. It seems to Nick her soul's struggling to free itself and enter eternity. And then she slumps back on the pillow, breathless, still, oxygen wheezing from the mask. She's left without saying goodbye, Nick thinks, breaking down, without so much as a final look, left for a journey over an endless ocean, left them holding her lifeless hands.

A middle-aged nurse comes in, feels her wrist and closes her eyes. She turns off the oxygen, removes the mask and asks them to stand outside for a few minutes. Releasing his mother's hand, Nick notices the plastic tag around her wrist: her name, hospital number, date of birth.

As they wipe their tears in the corridor, too numb to say anything, Nick hears cheering and clapping from the waiting room at the far end. A nurse coming from that direction, black shoes squeaking on the floor, smiles and says Neil Armstrong has set foot on the moon. Nick glances at the smooth-flowing clock on the wall: a few minutes to four.

The following days pass in the shadow of grief and preparations for the funeral. Nick stays home from school to help his father with visitors coming to pay their respects. He wants to be alone, to think only of his mother, but customs have to be observed. When visitors say *Bog da'a prosti* he feels a pang of anger. Why are they calling on God to forgive her? She did nothing wrong, never spoke badly of anyone, never harmed a soul. If anything God should ask his mother's soul for forgiveness. He struck her down with cancer and a cruel death. Nick tries to put on a brave front pouring *rakija* for the men and lemonade for the women. They stay a short while, mostly in silence, some saying a few things about Menka: what a fine housekeeper she was, how hard working, how she made the best pastries. A few relatives advise Vangel on what needs to be done on these occasions. An elderly woman keeps telling him to stop drinking and think of the boy, but he dismisses her with scowl.

'Which church is it to be?' she asks.

He glances at her, eyes heavy with *rakija*. Nick's heart contracts.

'St George,' he says, pouring another glass.

'But your wife, *Bog da'a prosti*, went to *Evangelismos*.'

'St George,' he repeats, tapping the glass on the table, spilling a little *rakija*.

The woman shakes her head and continues clearing glasses from the table. Nick takes the extra chairs back to the kitchen.

'St George,' he says, 'that's where the funeral will be. She's in the freezer, *Bog da'a prosti*, so it doesn't matter to her anymore. But it matters to me and the boy – it matters, doesn't it, Kolche? It matters because we spoke to her in Macedonian, our mother-tongue. We said everything in Macedonian – our joys and sorrows. We shared our life, our hopes and nightmares, in Macedonian. And I'm going to see her off in the Macedonian Church. Yes, she went to the Greek Church, and we went with her – for years we went with her, Kolche and me, and that was all right – but she's in a freezer now, all alone in a dark freezer, and we're going to send her off in the Macedonian Church. Joy and sorrow, they're in the blood, and just as Macedonian songs lighten the heart, so Macedonian hymns will lighten our grief.'

Nick's caught between the promise to his mother and his father's drunken, heart-felt words. He has to take a stand. In life it was important to his mother to go to the Greek Church and his father agreed. In this time of death and sorrow it was equally important to his father for the funeral to be in the Macedonian Church – it would ease his sorrow and help him come to terms with these dark days. Yes, he promised his mother, and he'd have to live with that broken promise the rest of his life, but in the depths of his heart he knew she wouldn't hold it against him. Yes, she'd understand he was just trying to help the living to live.

The day before the funeral Nick's preparing his clothes last ironed by his mother. The shoe box at the bottom of the cupboard catches his attention. He places it on the bed and opens the lid: his stamp album, ribbons and medallions from athletics, the dark-blue passport with which they came to Australia, the Bible with the blood-stained blade of grass from the Council Yard, and the *dekara*, which he wore around his neck when younger. He holds it up to the window and looks through the hole: he sees the village and Mimi the dwarf and the little girl in the coffin. But the recollection is vague – part memory, part dream, and maybe partly his mind filling in blanks. He slips the coin in his pocket and replaces the box in the cupboard.

Women are bustling about downstairs, arranging food for the funeral. Nick resents them being in his mother's kitchen, rattling cutlery and utensils that hardly made a noise in her careful hands. Avoiding the kitchen, he leaves from the front door and goes to the park and keeps walking to the Brunswick Street Oval. He sits in the Members' stand for some time, not thinking, not feeling, just staring at the long-disused black-backed scoreboard. Two small boys in Fitzroy jumpers run onto the oval, happily kicking the red ball to each other. Nick wonders about their mother and if he'll ever be happy again.

The coffin is carried into the Macedonian Church by relatives, the white towels on their shoulders cushioning the weight. The dark, shining wood catches Nick's reflection as it floats down the aisle. It's set on a chrome trolley before the altar gates. The funeral director turns several fasteners, removes the lid, and places it upright against the wall. Standing at the front next to his father, Nick can see his mother inside. She's wearing her new light-blue dress and matching jacket. She bought it last summer for a relative's wedding. His eyes fill with tears as others sniffle and sob. Her face has a yellowish tinge and her profile is sharper. The priest emerges from the gates. Nick wonders whether his mother's still alive. He jingles the censer in walking around the coffin. Puffs of fragrant smoke rise with his words. Nick glances at his father, hoping to draw some strength, but his face is rigid, his gaze fixed on the coffin. Again the thought of their journey to Australia comes to mind and he swallows back a swell of emotion. The shape of the coffin reminds him of a boat. She's about to set off on another long journey, over an ocean of tears, to a place without suffering and pain. The priest's gown glitters from the candles planted in sand-filled trays. He begins reading from the Gospels bound in a silver jacket. A sparrow darts in from the front door, flutters about, and perches on the coffin's lid. An assistant opens the door at the back, at which the bird swoops past the coffin and flies out. The priest finishes with the hymn Eternal Memory. Leading the mourners past the coffin, Nick follows his father, crossing himself three times and kissing his mother's cold, waxen forehead. He stands there, tears dripping into the coffin, onto the icon resting on her breast, he just wants to stand there and look at her forever. A relative whispers for him to move on and stand next to his father and accept people's condolences filing past. He feels the *dekara* in his pocket, thinking to places it on the icon – not an icon of *Bogoroditsa*, as he expected, but Christ resurrected, with keys, bones, nails, hammer, hook all scattered about his bare feet – but something holds him back.

From the church in Fitzroy they drive to the cemetery in Fawkner. The grave's been cleanly excavated, the mound of earth covered in green tarpaulin. Mourners and white clouds are reflected in yellow puddles on the gravel path. Candles are sheltered from a fresh breeze in a cut-out petrol drum. After another short service, men in dark suits from the funeral service lower the coffin to its resting place. When the priest finishes chanting Eternal Memory again, an elderly woman hands him a small bottle of red wine, kissing the back of his hand. He pours a little into the grave on three occasions and casually drops the bottle, which shatters on the silver statuette of Christ fixed to the lid, sending a shudder through Nick. The thought of stains and scratches on his mother's shining coffin cuts him to the quick. The woman then passes the priest a bowl of boiled wheat. He sprinkles three tablespoons over the coffin and this, too, he tosses inside. The hollow thud is a blow to Nick's chest.

After a few words with the priest, Vangel stands on a nearby grave belonging to a Greek man and invites everyone to stay back for a serving of food and drink in memory of his wife. Looking around, he spots little Pavle and signals for him to come to the front. A murmur rises from the mourners. What's Vangel doing? Is he out of his mind? Has he no respect for the poor woman? Knowing his father, Nick isn't surprised. Pavle flicks open his case and takes out the cornet. He turns his back to the gathering, practises a few shaky notes, and then stands next to Vangel still on the Greek's gravestone.

'For the departed wife, mother and friend,' he says. '*Bog da'a prosti* and may the earth rest lightly on her.'

Pavle relaxes his fingers, presses a few silent keys, and begins, nervously at first, screeching out several off-key notes. People wince and call on him to get down, to show respect for the solemn occasion, but he closes his eyes and fumbles his way, finally finding the melody – the one he played at the Fitzroy Town Hall the night of the brawl, the one Nick's mother would hum bowing over the sewing machine. His notes become surer, stronger, more resonant. And just as on that night, the murmuring stops, people turn to each other, nodding sadly, but with warmth, eyes shining with tears. Nick looks around at all these familiar faces – faces he's grown up with, faces without names, faces he's never spoken to – and suddenly he's grateful they're here, sharing his sorrow, lightening his grief. And then, from the back of the gathering, a man starts singing. Another murmur rises but quickly subsides as the singer steps forward and stands beside Pavle. Nick recognises him, the man in the Town Hall that night, the dancer with the white sombrero, the *Zaiko* character. He sings in a moving voice, bare head thrown back, gold teeth catching the afternoon light. *Kokoshkaro* cries out *Ah, maiko mila* – maybe because his mother died recently back in the village – and joins *Zaiko.* Pavle's playing merges with the voices, the notes becoming mellower, more moving, until several women sigh *Ah, pusta Afstralia* – cursed be Australia – and take up the song. And then everyone's singing, Macedonian rising from the cemetery, tears flowing from all eyes, from Nick's, too, strange tears, bittersweet, light as drizzle.

Singing through his sorrow, Vangel throws out his arms to the side and starts dancing. People turn to him, not in disapproval, but with heartfelt sympathy. They draw back to make space for him to dance in the face of death. *Kokoshkaro* joins on Vangel's left and *Zaiko* follows. They lift one leg, pause, set it down lightly, then raise the other, moving slowly around Menka's grave, eyes closed, taking in each note, measuring each step. Nick was too young to feel this melody the night in the Town Hall – maybe a person must experience suffering to appreciate these old tunes – but he feels it now, the melody's mysterious life-force, moving from generation to generation, taking from one and giving to another, sustaining and being sustained. He joins in next to his father, arm on each other's arm. Vangel nods, maybe as his father nodded, and holds Nick firmly by the shoulder while reaching for the sun with his right hand. Nick follows his lead, awkwardly to start with, but unconcerned because he's dancing for his mother and little brother who never made it into the world and *Dedo* Petro who died coming to Australia and the girl in the coffin whose *dekara* he took. As his steps fall in with his father's, his mother comes to mind, not as she was in hospital, pale and worn out, but glowing with life kneading dough for her pastries. He glances into the grave, at the coffin stained by wine, sprinkled with wheat, scattered with bits of broken glass, and he's not afraid. Tomorrow, yes, tomorrow, grief will descend again and he'll feel empty and lost, but for now the melody and singing and dancing raise him above that. Yes, while Pavle plays his silver cornet, those long, quivering notes turn Nick to spirit, they join the living and the dead, take him back to the village, where he and his mother are preparing to set out for Australia.

Walking back to the car park, where food's being passed around on paper plates in memory of his mother, Nick looks back over his shoulder: a few grey pigeons are pecking happily at the foot of her grave.

Having finished, the removalists are standing in the shadow of their van. Vangel and Nick go back into the empty house for the last time to make sure they've left nothing behind, yet knowing they're leaving everything behind. Too big for the two of them, the house was sold a few months after the funeral. They don't say much going from room to room, and when they do speak, their words echo in the emptiness. They look around, seeing what isn't there: the outline of a wedding photo that hung on the wall, impressions in the carpet where a bed stood, the stillness above the mantelpiece where an oval mirror moved with their coming and going. Vangel's hands are deep in his pockets, hat's brim low over his eyes, toothpick in his mouth. From time to time Nick sneaks a glance at him, hoping to find some warmth, a little tenderness maybe, a spark of encouragement to make what lies ahead easier. But all he sees is the grimness of a bluestone pitcher. There's no sorrow in his face, only bitterness and anger. Australia hasn't been the Lucky Country for him and he's now drowning those dreams in drink.

They're leaving behind the crimson curtains Menka made to cover several fireplaces. In the living room the sunflowers on the linoleum have lost their waxy glow. After complaining for years she finally got her new white stove, but it's staying, even though the sticker's still on the glass door. They're leaving behind the apricot tree covered in fragrant blossom. It pains Nick to think of the new owners having all those golden apricots in a couple of months. They're leaving behind his initials in the patch of concrete in front of the laundry shed. In the hallway Nick points to a crack along the ceiling. May the whole house crumble and fall, Vangel says, not bothering to look up. The black cross from his mother's candle last Easter is still visible on the lintel of the front door. They stand there a moment, Vangel looking down at the worn doorstep, Nick at his mother's roses in need of pruning, the stillness outside the Busy Bee in afternoon light, McKean Street already a world away. They're prodded by a sharp whistle from one of the removalists, while the other, wearing a sleeveless Fitzroy jumper, slams the van's back doors shut.

www.ingramcontent.com/pod-product-compliance
Ingram Content Group Australia Pty Ltd
76 Discovery Rd, Dandenong South VIC 3175, AU
AUHW020138130726
429791AU00003B/74

9 781925 984828